PLYWOOD PLANBOOK

American Plywood Association

CONTENTS

Publisher: Jonathan Latimer; Editorial Assistance: Patricia Bowlin; Art Director: Don Burton
Book Design & Assembly: Lloyd O'Dell; Typography: Cindy Coatsworth, Joanne Porter, Kris Spitler

Published by HPBooks; P.O. Box 5367, Tucson, AZ 85703 602/888-2150
ISBN: 0-89586-034-1
Library of Congress Catalog Number: 80-80173 © 1980 Fisher Publishing, Inc.
Printed in USA

PLYWOOD HANDBOOK

Plywood is produced from thin sheets of wood veneer, called *plies*, which are laminated together under heat and pressure with special adhesives. This produces a bond between plies that is as strong or stronger than the wood itself.

Plywood always has an *odd* number of *layers* consisting of one or more plies. Plies within a layer are arranged with their grains parallel to each other. Layers then are assembled with their grains perpendicular to each other. This cross-lamination of layers distributes the wood's inherent strength along the grain in both directions. This creates a panel that is split-proof, puncture-proof and, pound for pound, one of the strongest building materials available.

Plywood offers other advantages, too. It comes dry from the mill, so it is never *green*. The cross-laminated construction restricts expansion and contraction within individual plies, so panel swelling and warping is almost eliminated. Plywood can be worked easily by anyone with ordinary skills and common carpentry tools. It holds fasteners well and does not split when nails are driven near panel edges. It is easily glued. It accepts and holds stains and paints exceptionally well. And it is available in every area of the country in a wide variety of grades, textures and thicknesses.

PLYWOOD'S USES

Probably no building material is as versatile as plywood. Its applications are limited only by the user's imagination. Builders and contractors use plywood in homes, apartments, mobile homes, office buildings, churches and schools for a broad range of structural and aesthetic applications. Industry uses plywood for cargo containers, crates, pallets and bins, truck and boxcar linings, concrete forms, boat hulls, highway signs, furniture and other products. In and around your home, plywood can be used for paneling, partitions, doors, furniture, cabinets and built-ins, shelving, fences, patio decking, outdoor storage units and hundreds of other home workshop projects such as those in this book.

HOW TO BUY

To qualify for grademark identification, such as the APA grademarks shown and recommended in this book, softwood plywood must be produced in conformance with the provisions of *U.S. Product Standard PS 1 for Construction and Industrial Plywood*. This manufacturing specification was developed cooperatively by the softwood plywood industry and the U.S. Department of Commerce. The American Plywood Association (APA) is a nonprofit trade association whose member mills manufacture approximately 75 percent of the construction and industrial plywood produced in the United States. APA grademarks on plywood panels signify that the manufacturer of that plywood is committed to APA's rigorous program of quality inspection and testing. The quality control

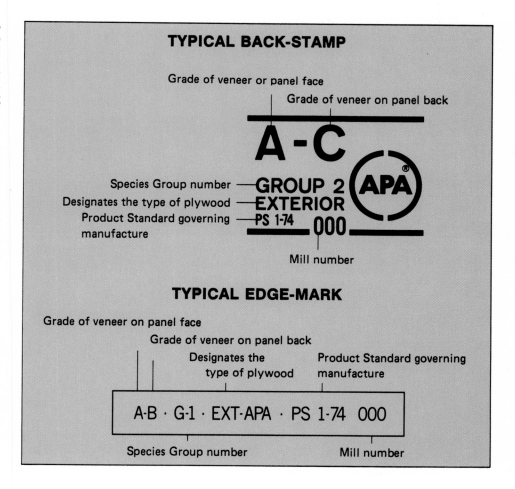

TYPICAL BACK-STAMP

Grade of veneer or panel face

Grade of veneer on panel back

A - C

Species Group number — **GROUP 2** (APA)
Designates the type of plywood — **EXTERIOR**
Product Standard governing — **PS 1-74**
manufacture **000**

Mill number

TYPICAL EDGE-MARK

Grade of veneer on panel face

Grade of veneer on panel back

Designates the type of plywood

Product Standard governing manufacture

A-B · G-1 · EXT-APA · PS 1-74 000

Species Group number   Mill number

PLYWOOD GRADES FOR EXTERIOR USES

Grade (Exterior)	Face	Back	Inner Plies	Uses
A-A	A	A	C	Outdoor, where appearance of both sides is important.
A-B	A	B	C	Alternate for A-A, where appearance of one side is less important. Face is finish grade.
A-C	A	C	C	Soffits, fences, base for coatings.
B-C	B	C	C	For utility uses such as farm buildings, some kinds of fences, etc., base for coatings.
303® Siding	C (or better)	C	C	Panels with variety of surface texture and grooving patterns. For siding, fences, paneling, screens, etc.
T1-11®	C	C	C	Special 303 panel with grooves 1/4" deep, 3/8" wide. Available unsanded, textured, or MDO surface.
C-C (Plugged)	C (Plugged)	C	C	Excellent base for tile and linoleum, backing for wall coverings, high-performance coatings.
C-C	C	C	C	Unsanded, for backing and rough construction exposed to weather.
B-B Plyform	B	B	C	Concrete forms. Re-use until wood literally wears out.
MDO	B	B or C	C	Medium Density Overlay. Ideal base for paint; for siding, built-ins, signs, displays.
HDO	A or B	A or B	C-Plugged or C	High Density Overlay. Hard surface; no paint needed. For concrete forms, cabinets, counter tops, tanks.

PLYWOOD GRADES FOR INTERIOR USES

Grade (Interior)	Face	Back	Inner Plies	Uses
A-A	A	A	D	Cabinet doors, built-ins, furniture where both sides will show.
A-B	A	B	D	Alternate of A-A. Face is finish grade, back is solid and smooth.
A-D	A	D	D	Finish grade face for paneling, built-ins, backing.
B-D	B	D	D	Utility grade. For backing, cabinet sides, etc.
C-D	C	D	D	Sheathing and structural uses such as temporary enclosures, subfloor. Unsanded.
Underlayment	C-Plugged	D	C and D	For underlayment or combination subfloor-underlayment under tile, carpeting.

VENEER GRADES

A
Smooth, paintable. Not more than 18 neatly made repairs, parallel to grain, permitted. May be used for natural finish in less demanding applications.

B
Solid surface. Shims, circular repair plugs and tight knots to 1 inch across grain permitted. Some minor splits permitted.

C plugged
Improved C veneer with splits limited to 1/8 inch width and knotholes and borer holes limited to 1/4 x 1/2 inch. Permits some broken grain. Synthetic repairs permitted.

C
Tight knots to 1-1/2 inch. Knotholes to 1 inch across grain and some to 1-1/2 inch if total width of knots and knotholes is within specified limits. Synthetic or wood repairs. Discoloration and sanding defects that do not impair strength permitted. Limited splits allowed. Stitching permitted.

D
Knots and knotholes to 2-1/2 inch width across grain and 1/2 inch larger within specified limits. Limited splits allowed. Stitching permitted. Limited to Interior grades of plywood.

of the member mill is subject to verification through an APA audit—a procedure designed to help the manufacturer conform to the quality standards prescribed by PS 1, and APA's own performance-engineered proprietary specifications. Panels with a mark reading "Shop Cutting Panel—Other Marks Void" identify panels that do not conform to PS 1 or APA grade requirements.

Type—Plywood is manufactured in two types: Exterior type with 100 percent waterproof glue, and Interior type with highly moisture-resistant glue. Interior type plywood may be bonded with either interior or exterior glue, although today most is made with exterior glue. Specify Exterior type plywood for all permanent outdoor projects, and whenever the project will be exposed to continuous moisture or high humidity. For other applications, Interior type may be used.

Species Group—Wood from more than 70 species is used in manufacturing plywood. Species are divided on the basis of strength and stiffness into Groups 1 through 5. The stiffest and strongest woods are in Group 1, the next stiffest and strongest in Group 2, and so on. The Group number in the American Plywood Association grademark generally refers to the weakest species used for face and back plies. Group 1 and 2 species are most commonly used in plywood manufacture.

Grade—Each type of plywood includes a variety of plywood grades. These are generally identified by the veneer grade used on the face and back of the panel, such as C-D or A-B. The veneer grade for the *face* is given first. Veneer grades define the appearance of the panel in terms of the number and size of repairs allowed during manufacture, and natural unrepaired growth characteristics, such as knotholes. The best looking veneer grades are A and B. C-Plugged is an improved C-grade veneer. The minimum grade of veneer permitted in Exterior type plywood is C-grade. D-grade veneer is used only for backs and inner plies of Interior type plywood.

Appearance Grades—Plywood grades are also divided according to their use into *appearance* and *engineered* grades. Appearance grades are designed for use where appearance is an important consideration. These include APA 303 Sidings, sanded panels such as A-A, A-B and B-D, and Medium Density OverLay, known as MDO. MDO plywood has a special resin-treated wood-fiber surface permanently bonded to one or both sides of the panel. The overlaid surface is an excellent base for paint. Appearance grades with both sides of appearance quality such as A-A, A-B and MDO with both sides overlaid, are grademarked on the panel edge. All other panels are grademarked on the back.

Engineered Grades — Engineered grades are designed for demanding construction applications where properties such as bending strength and stiffness are more important than appearance. Among the Engineered Grades are the sheathing

CLASSIFICATION OF SPECIES

Group 1	Group 2		Group 3	Group 4	Group 5
Apitong (a), (b)	Cedar, Port Orford	Maple, Black	Alder, Red	Aspen	Basswood
Beech,	Cypress	Mengkulang (a)	Birch, Paper	Bigtooth	Fir, Balsam
American	Douglas Fir 2 (c)	Meranti, Red (a)	Cedar, Alaska	Quaking	Poplar, Balsam
Birch	Fir	Mersawa (a)	Fir, Subalpine	Cativo	
Sweet	California Red	Pine	Hemlock, Eastern	Cedar	
Yellow	Grand	Pond	Maple, Bigleaf	Incense	
Douglas Fir 1 (c)	Noble	Red	Pine	Western Red	
Kapur (a)	Pacific Silver	Virginia	Jack	Cottonwood	
Keruing (a), (b)	White	Western White	Lodgepole	Eastern	
Larch, Western	Hemlock, Western	Spruce	Ponderosa	Black (Western	
Maple, Sugar	Lauan	Red	Spruce	Poplar)	
Pine	Almon	Sitka	Redwood	Pine	
Caribbean	Bagtikan	Sweetgum	Spruce	Eastern White	
Ocote	Mayapis	Tamarack	Black	Sugar	
Pine, Southern	Red Lauan	Yellow-poplar	Engelmann		
Loblolly	Tangile		White		
Longleaf	White Lauan				
Shortleaf					
Slash					
Tanoak					

(a) Each of these names represents a trade group of woods consisting of a number of closely related species.

(b) Species from the genus Dipterocarpus are marketed collectively: Apitong if originating in the Philippines; Keruing if originating in Malaysia or Indonesia.

(c) Douglas fir from trees grown in the States of Washington, Oregon, California, Idaho, Montana, Wyoming, and the Canadian Provinces of Alberta and British Columbia are classed as Douglas Fir No. 1. Douglas Fir from trees grown in the states of Nevada, Utah, Colorado, Arizona and New Mexico are classed as Douglas Fir No. 2.

APA Texture 1-11
303 Siding

Special 303 Siding panel with shiplapped edges and parallel grooves 1/4 inch deep by 3/8 inch wide. Grooves 4 or 8 inches apart o.c. are standard. Other spacings are sometimes available. T 1-11 is generally available in thicknesses of 19/32 and 5/8 inch. Also available with scratch-sanded, overlaid, rough-sawn, brushed and other surfaces. Available in Douglas fir, cedar, redwood, southern pine and other species. At left, unsanded T 1-11; at right the more commonly available rough-sawn surface.

Rough-Sawn
303 Siding

Manufactured with a slight rough-sawn texture running across the panel. Available without grooves or with grooves of various styles; in lap sidings, and panels. Generally available in thicknesses of 11/32, 3/8, 1/2, 19/32 and 5/8 inch. Rough-sawn is also available in Texture 1-11, reverse board-and-batten (5/8 inch thick), channel groove (3/8 inch thick), and V-groove (1/2 or 5/8 inch thick). Available in Douglas fir, redwood, cedar, southern pine and other species.

Kerfed Rough-Sawn
303 Siding

This rough-sawn surface with narrow grooves provides a distinctive effect. Long edges are shiplapped for a continuous pattern. Grooves are typically 4 inches apart o.c. Also available with grooves in multiples of 2 inches apart o.c. Generally available in thicknesses of 11/32, 3/8, 1/2, 19/32 and 5/8 inch. Depth of kerf-groove varies with panel thickness.

GUIDE TO IDENTIFICATION INDEX ON ENGINEERED GRADES			
Thickness (inch)	**(C-D INT—APA/C-C EXT—APA)**		
	Group 1 & Structural I	**Group 2* or 3 & Structural II***	**Group 4****
5/16	20/0	16/0	12/0
3/8	24/0	20/0	16/0
1/2	32/16	24/0	24/0
5/8	42/20	32/16	30/12†
3/4	48/24	42/20	36/16†
7/8		48/24	42/20

NOTES:
* Panels with Group 2 outer plies, and special thickness and construction requirements, or STRUCTURAL II panels with Group 1 faces, may carry the Identification Index numbers shown for Group 1 panels.

** Panels made with Group 4 outer plies may carry the Identification Index numbers shown for Group 3 panels when they conform to special thickness requirements.

Brushed
303 Siding

Brushed or relief-grain surfaces accent the natural grain pattern to create striking textured surfaces. Generally available in 11/32, 3/8, 1/2, 19/32 and 5/8 inch. Available in redwood, Douglas fir, cedar and other species.

Channel Groove
303 Siding

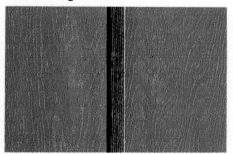

Shallow grooves, typically 1/16 inch deep by 3/8 inch wide, are cut into the face of 3/8 inch thick panels spaced 4 or 8 inches o.c. Other groove spacings available. Shiplapped for continuous pattern. Generally available in surface patterns and textures similar to Texture 1-11 and in thicknesses of 11/32, 3/8 and 1/2 inch. Available in redwood, Douglas fir, cedar, southern pine and other species.

Reverse Board-And-Batten
303 Siding

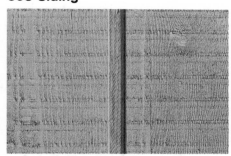

Deep, wide grooves cut into brushed, rough-sawn, coarse sanded or other textured surfaces. Grooves about 1/4 inch deep by 1 to 1-1/2 inches wide are spaced 8, 12 or 16 inches apart o.c. Panel thickness are 19/32 and 5/8 inch. Provides deep, sharp shadow lines. Long edges shiplapped for continuous pattern. Available in redwood, cedar, Douglas fir, southern pine and other species.

Medium Density Overlaid
303 Siding (MDO)

Available without grooving, with V-grooves spaced 6 or 8 inches apart o.c. or in T 1-11 or reverse board-and-batten grooving shown on the left. MDO panel siding is available in thicknesses of 11/32, 3/8, 1/2, 19/32 and 5/8 inch. Also available in precut horizontal-lap siding with 12 or 16 inch widths, 3/8 inch thickness and lengths to 16 feet. MDO is available factory-primed. MDO siding is overlaid on one side and available with embossed texture or smooth surface.

panels—C-D Interior, C-C Exterior and Structural I and II C-D and C-C. C-D Interior with exterior glue, commonly called CDX, is by far and away the most commonly available sheathing grade. It will withstand considerable exposure to weather and moisture during construction, but must not be mistaken for fully waterproof C-C Exterior plywood. Structural I and II panels are designed for especially demanding structural applications.

Sheathing grades of plywood carry an Identification Index of two numbers in the American Plywood Association grademark, for example, 24/0 or 32/16. The number on the left indicates the maximum recommended spacing in inches for roof framing when the panel is used as roof sheathing. The number on the right indicates the maximum spacing for floor framing when the panel is used for subflooring.

APA 303 Siding Patterns and Grades—APA 303 Sidings include a wide variety of surface textures and patterns, most developed for optimum performance with stain finishes. Typical surface patterns are illustrated on this page. Groove spacing, width and depth may vary with the manufacturer. Where the characteristics of a particular wood species are desired, specify by grade and species preference.

303 plywood siding products are manufactured in four basic classes:

Special Series 303, 303-6, 303-18 and 303-30. Each class, as shown in the table on page 8, is further divided into grades according to categories of repair and appearance characteristics. Grade designations appear with the APA grademark, thus making it easy to select and specify the siding appropriate for any particular project. Depending on species, repairs and finish, fine products can be found in all grades.

303 Siding panels with the identification 16 o.c. Span in the grademark may be applied directly to vertical studs 16 inches apart *on center*. Panels marked 24 o.c. Span may be applied directly to vertical studs spaced 24 inches apart *on center*.

303 SIDING FACE GRADES

Class	Grade	Patches	
		Wood	Synthetic
Special Series 303	303-0C	Not permitted	Not permitted
	303-0L	Not applicable for overlays	
	303-NR	Not permitted	Not permitted
	303-SR	Not permitted	Permitted as natural-defect shape only
303-6	303-6-W	Limit 6	Not permitted
	303-6-S	Not permitted	Limit 6
	303-6-S/W	Limit 6 — any combination	
303-18	303-18-W	Limit 18	Not permitted
	303-18-S	Not permitted	Limit 18
	303-18-S/W	Limit 18 — any combination	
303-30	303-30-W	Limit 30	Not permitted
	303-30-S	Not permitted	Limit 30
	303-30-S/W	Limit — any combination	

LAYING OUT & CUTTING

Lay out the dimensions and cut your plywood with care to avoid waste and simplify your work. When many pieces are to be cut from one large full-size panel, you'll find it easiest to sketch the arrangement on a piece of paper before marking the plywood for cutting. Be sure to allow for the width of the saw kerf between adjacent pieces.

Try to work it out so your first cuts reduce the panel to pieces small enough for easy handling. Be sure to plan your sequence of operations so all mating or matching parts will

LAYING OUT & CUTTING

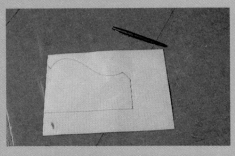

The layout method shown here is designed to reduce error. First carefully lay out each part with a pencil on a piece of paper. Use a straight edge and compass to insure accuracy. Graph paper or cardboard can make your drawings even more accurate, particularly on curved pieces. After you have made all your drawings, cut out each drawing and lay it on the plywood. Arrange the drawings to minimize the number of cuts you have to make. Plan to make long, straight cuts first. This allows you to take advantage of the speed offered by a circular power saw or large hand saw. The resulting smaller pieces will also be easier to handle when you have to make more intricate cuts.

If you have several similar cuts to make, using a guide can help you be more accurate. Measure carefully to avoid mistakes.

You can reduce splitting by sawing at a low angle. This keeps more teeth in contact with the wood and makes a smoother cut. If you are right-handed, watch the cutting line from the left side of the blade. If you are left-handed, watch it from the right side.

When cutting with a table saw, make sure the good face of the plywood is up. With a portable power saw, the good face should be down.

have the same saw setting. Note the direction of the face grain. Except where otherwise indicated in the plan, you'll want this to run the *long way* on the piece you are cutting. Mark the better face unless you are going to cut with a portable power saw; in that case, mark. the back.

When Hand Sawing, place plywood with the good face *up.* Use a saw with 10 to 15 points per inch. Support the panel firmly so it won't sag. You can reduce splitting on the underside by putting a piece of scrap lumber under the panel and sawing the scrap along with the plywood. It also helps to hold the saw at a low angle. The most important thing you can do, however, is to *use a sharp saw.*

Power Sawing on a radial or table saw should be done with the good face of the plywood *up.* Use a sharp combination or fine-tooth blade without much set. Let the blade protrude above the plywood just the height of the teeth. You'll find handling large panels easier for one man if you build an extension support with a roller. It can have a base of its own or may be clamped to a saw horse.

A Portable Power Saw should be used with the good face of the plywood *down.* Tack a strip of scrap lumber to the top of each saw horse and you can saw right through it without damaging the horse. Your best choice of blade is either a *Fine Tooth Plywood* or *Fine Tooth Cut Off.* Keep blades sharp.

A Saber Saw lets you cut irregular curves and shapes. If you place the front of the saber saw platform

against the face of the panel and tilt the blade downward to scratch the panel surface, you can work the saw into the panel for interior cuts without having to drill a pilot hole. This technique is usually called a *plunge cut.* Pay special attention to selection of saber saw blades: Use the finest tooth possible to get a smooth, even cut for the best finish, A 4-inch blade with 6 to 10 teeth per inch will work well.

Clamping a board to the piece you are cutting will provide a guide for making long straight cuts.

Making a plunge cut is simple with a saber saw. This technique is especially useful for making doors or other pieces that need to fit tightly in place.

MAKING INSIDE CUTS

Inside cuts look more difficult than they are. With a saber saw, you can use a plunge cut as shown on page 9. Or you can use the method shown here.

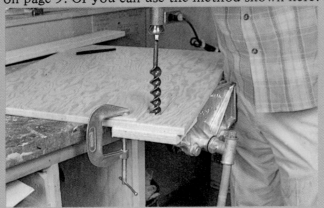

First, drill a pilot hole into the wood that will be waste when the cut is finished. If you can, try to work the drill hole into the design of the cut. Clamping a piece of scrap wood behind the area being drilled will reduce splintering.

Use a small hand drill for small diameter holes or where the tolerances are tight. Make sure the hole is large enough for the saw blade to move freely.

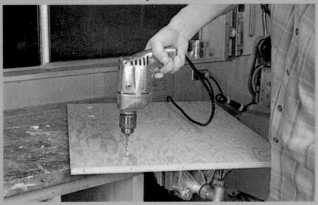

A power drill is quick and accurate.

To cut with a coping saw, remove the blade from the frame, insert it through the pilot hole, and re-attach the frame. Make sure the frame has enough depth to let you cut smoothly. Allow some edge margin for final smoothing.

A compass saw can also be used for inside cuts if the angles of the curves are not too tight for the blade to move around. A compass saw will make a rougher cut than a coping saw.

A saber saw blade is easy to insert. Use a file and sandpaper for final shaping.

Planing Plywood Edges with plane or jointer won't be necessary if you make your cuts with a sharp saw blade. For very smooth edges that won't even require sanding use a *hollow-ground blade*. If you do any planing, work from both ends of the edge toward the center to avoid tearing out plies at the end of the cut. Use a plane with a sharp blade and take very shallow cuts.

Sanding before applying a sealer or prime coat should be confined to edges. Most appearance grade plywood is sanded smooth during manufacture—one of the big timesavers in its use. Further sanding of the surfaces will merely remove soft grain. After sealing, sand with the direction of grain only. A sanding block, one type which is shown here, will prevent gouging.

SANDING

For best results in sanding, wrap the sand paper around a piece of scrap wood. This will help keep edges sharp and square.

Sand with the grain of the wood. With most plywood, only a light sanding will be needed. When possible, sand before putting the project together.

It is best to plane from either end toward the center. Set the plane blade for a shallow cut to minimize splintering. Check the edge for squareness with a tri-square.

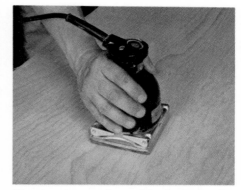

Move power sanders with the grain also. Be careful to avoid damaging surface veneers.

Edges can be sanded with a power sander, especially if you want to chamfer or bevel the edge. Be careful not to splinter corners. Fill any gaps in the edges before you sand.

Overlaid Plywood is Exterior type plywood permanently protected with a resin-treated facing of either Medium Density Overlay (MDO) or High Density Overlay (HDO). Both types can be worked in the same manner as regular plywood with these exceptions:

• Sawing and drilling of overlaid plywood should always be done with the cutting edge of the tool entering the good face of the panel, rather than the back.

• Tools should always be sharp and fed slowly into the wood. Do not force tools.

• Chipping where the tool exits can be minimized by using a piece of scrap wood as a backup, or, in the case of sawing, by laying tape along the line of the cut on the good face of the panel.

• Before surface-gluing HDO plywood, it is important to roughen the surface by light sanding. This will ensure a stronger bond.

CHAMFERS & BEVELS

To cut away a part of an edge, mark the angle of the edge you want with a rule. A chamfer is a partial cut. A bevel goes from face to face. Then mark the edges of the angle along the face and back of the plywood as shown in the two top photos. Make shallow cuts with the plane held at about 30° to the edge of the wood. For a curved edge, it is usually easier to make several cuts and sand them.

Chamfer   Bevel

Chamfer   Curved Edge

PUTTING PLYWOOD TOGETHER

Butt Joints are simplest to make, suitable for 3/4-inch plywood. For thinner panels, use a reinforcing block or nailing strip to make a stronger joint. In both cases, glue will make the joint many times stronger than if it were made with nails or screws alone.

Lap Joints are used whenever two boards cross. An *overlap* is simply one board laid across another and fastened. A *full lap* requires cutting a U-shape notch in one board to accommodate another board. A *half lap* requires cutting notches in both boards so they fit together and form a flat surface. The easiest way to lay out the notch is to lay

A butt joint is made by placing the end of one piece of wood against the face of another. Glue and nails or screws hold the pieces together.

The half lap or end lap shown here is made by cutting both boards to accommodate the other. This joint has more strength than a butt joint.

one board over the other and mark its outline with a knife or pencil. Then you can set the depth of the cut according to the thickness of the board. Use a fine tooth saw to make the cut. Lap joints can be supported with glue and either nails or screws.

Rabbet Joints are neat and strong, and easy to make with power tools. This is an ideal joint for drawers, buffets, chests or cupboards.

Miter Joints are the least noticeable and are easily finished. They require precision machining and careful fastening.

Dado Joints, quickly made with a power saw, produce neat shelves. Use a *dado head* with blades shimmed out to produce these grooves in a single cut.

A rabbet joint is made by cutting a notch, the rabbet, out of the end of one piece of wood, and fitting the end of another piece into it.

FRAME CONSTRUCTION

Frame construction makes it possible to reduce weight by using thinner plywood. The frame can be constructed with rough grades of wood, if it will be concealed. The plywood sheathing not only conceals the frame, its strength makes the project more rigid. Use glue and screws or nails as recommended in plans.

A miter joint is made by cutting 45° angles in the ends of both pieces and joining them to form a 90° corner. If you are using a hand saw, use a miter box.

Cut the dado out using a power saw with a dado blade or a hand saw and a chisel. The end of the first board should fit perfectly in the dado.

Dado joints are widely used for shelves and furniture. Use one piece of wood to mark the shoulders of the dado on the other.

SELECTING NAILS

Plywood Thickness In Inches	Nails used in Construction
1/4	3d or 4d Finishing Nails; 1/4- or 1-inch Brads; or 1-inch Blue Lath Nails where heads are allowed to show.
3/8	3d or 4d Finishing Nails.
1/2	4d or 6d Finishing Nails.
5/8	6d or 8d Finishing Nails.
3/4	6d Casing Nails; or 8d Finishing Nails.

Drilling a pilot hole for nails can help avoid splitting near edges.

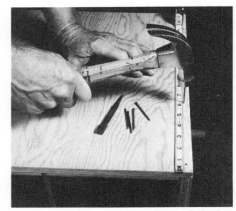

Nails should be spaced about 6 inches apart for most projects. Use a nail set to conceal nail heads beneath the surface of the wood. Holes can be filled with putty or wood dough.

NAILS

Nail size is determined primarily by the thickness of the plywood you're using, as shown in the chart on this page. Used with glue, all nails shown here will produce strong joints. Substitute *casting nails* or *finish nails* wherever you want a heavier nail.

Pre-drilling is occasionally called for in precision work or where nails must be very close to an edge. The drill bit should be slightly smaller in diameter than the nail to be used.

Space nails about 6 inches apart for most work. Closer spacing is necessary only with thin plywood where there may be slight buckling between nails. Nails and glue work together to produce a strong, durable joint.

SCREWS

Flat-heat wood screws are useful where nails will not provide adequate holding power. Glue should also be used if possible. Sizes shown in the chart on this page are minimums; use longer screws when the work permits. Rubbing soap on the screws will make them easier to drive.

Screws can be concealed by *countersinking* the holes and filling them with wood dough or surfacing putty. Apply filler so it is slightly higher than the plywood, then sand it level when dry. This also works well with nails driven below the surface of the wood.

SELECTING SCREWS

If splitting is a problem, as in edges, make hole for threaded portion 1/64" larger than shown here

Plywood Thickness In Inches	Screw Length In Inches	Screw Size	Drill Size For Shank In Inches	Drill Size For Thread In Inches
3/4 5/8	1-1/2 1-1/4	#8	11/64	1/8
1/2 3/8	1-1/4 1	#6	9/64	3/32
1/4	1	#4	7/64	1/16

Placing screws for maximum holding power requires drilling three holes. A pilot hole, slightly smaller than the diameter of the threads, is drilled equal to the length of the screw. A second hole, equal in diameter and depth to the screw shank, is drilled in the pilot hole. Finally, a countersink is used to make a shallow depression to hold the screw head. When the screw is in place, it is concealed with putty or wood dough.

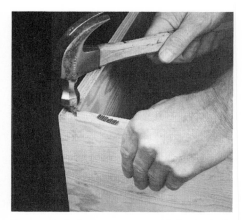
Corrugated fasteners are quick, but do not have much holding power.

OTHER FASTENERS

Corrugated fasteners can be used to reinforce miter joints in 3/4-inch plywood or to hold joints together while glue sets.

For some jobs, sheet metal screws are valuable; they have more holding power than wood screws, but come only in short lengths and do not have flat heads. Sheet metal screws can be concealed by *counterboring* the hole to make room for the head below the surface of the wood. Then cover it with wood dough or surface putty.

Bolts and washers are good for fastening sectional units together and for installing legs, hinges or other hardware when great strength is required.

SELECTING GLUE				
Type of Glue	Description	Recommended Use	Precautions	How To Use
UREA RESIN GLUE	Comes as powder to be mixed with water and used within 4 hours. Light colored. Very strong if joint fits well.	Good for general wood gluing. First choice for work that must stand some exposure to dampness, since it is moisture resistant.	Needs well-fitted joints, tight clamping, and room temperature 70° F or warmer.	Make sure joint fits tightly. Mix glue and apply thin coat. Allow 16 hours drying time.
LIQUID RESIN (WHITE) GLUE	Comes ready to use at any temperature. Clean-working, quick-setting. Strong enough for most work, though not quite as tough as urea resin glue.	Good for indoor furniture and cabinetwork. First choice for small jobs where tight clamping or good fit may be difficult.	Not sufficiently resistant to moisture for outdoor furniture or outdoor storage units. Thoroughly clean up squeezed out glue in areas to receive stain finish.	Use at any temperature but preferably above 60°F. Spread on both surfaces, clamp at once. Sets in 1-1/2 hours.
RESORCINOL (WATER-PROOF) GLUE	Comes as powder plus liquid, must be mixed each time used. Dark colored, very strong, completely waterproof.	This is the glue to use with Exterior type plywood for work to be exposed to extreme dampness.	Expense, trouble to mix and dark color make it unsuited to jobs where waterproof glue is not required. Needs good fit, tight clamping.	Use within 8 hours after mixing. Work at temperatures above 70° F. Apply thin coat to both surfaces; allow 16 hours drying time.

GLUE

Choose your glue from the chart on this page based on the work you are doing. Before applying the glue, make sure you'll end up with a strong joint by checking that both pieces make contact at all points.

Apply glue with a brush or stick. End grain absorbs glue so quickly that it is best to apply a preliminary coat. Allow it to soak in for a few minutes, then apply another coat before joining the parts. Wipe off all excess glue when project is to be finished with stain or varnish.

Clamp the joints tightly with clamps or with nails, screws or other fasteners. Place blocks of wood under the jaws of the clamps to avoid damaging the plywood. Some glues will stain or seal wood and

Check the fit of your joint before applying glue. Apply the glue you choose according to the manufacturer's instructions. Clamp, using scrap wood to protect the surface, and let dry. Bar clamps like those shown here, are very useful.

make it difficult to achieve a good finish. Quickly wipe away any excess. Test for squareness, then allow glue to set. Sand the area after drying.

Clamps are like extra hands. This type applies even pressure over a large area.

OTHER ADHESIVES

Hot Melt Glues are sometimes used with plywood. They work best with relatively small parts. Remember, they cool and set very quickly.

Epoxy Glues have only limited use with wood because they are expensive and most are not ideally formulated for use with wood. Some epoxies may prove successful for some applications.

Contact Cements are useful for applying laminates and edge stripping to plywood. They are not recommended for structural joints.

Wall-Panel Adhesives are handy for applying decorative paneling or facing. You'll probably need to use a few nails per panel to prevent panels from pulling away from wall due to warping.

Casein Glues are slow-setting and useful for complex or difficult assemblies.

ASSEMBLING

Planning ahead pays off in assembly steps, just as in cutting parts. Frequently, your easiest solution is to break down complicated projects into sub-assemblies. They are simpler to handle and joints are usually more accessible. Apply clamps with full jaw length in contact with the work. If the jaws are not parallel, pressure is applied to only part of the joint and it may be weak.

A handy trick for clamping miter joints in cabinets is to glue triangular blocks to the ends of each mitered piece. Place paper between the blocks and the work for easy removal. Let glue set. Apply glue to mitered ends and pull together in alignment with clamps. Remove clamps after glue has set, pry blocks away and sand off paper.

Special clamps can frequently save work and help you do a better job. Various types of *edge-clamps* are used to glue wood or plastic edging to plywood. *Bar clamps* or quick *C-clamps* grip the panel which is protected by scrap wood. Then edge clamping fixtures are inserted to bear against the edge-banding material while glue sets.

C-clamps have many uses. Here triangular blocks have been added for holding a miter joint. The technique is described at the right.

These clamps are specially designed for holding molding or edging in place.

INSTALLING

Frame walls allow you to hang cabinets by using long wood screws through the cabinet backs. Screws must be driven into wall studs for secure holding power. Locate the first two studs by tapping the wall, then measure off intervals equal to the distance between those studs to find the other studs. Tap for each stud to make sure it is really there.

Hollow masonry walls require the use of *toggle bolts* or *Molly bolts*. First, drill a hole with a star drill or carbide-tipped bit. Then insert the bolt and tighten. After that you can loosen the bolt and use it to hang the cabinet. For gypsum board walls, Molly bolts can be used where stud fastening is not possible, provided loads are relatively light.

Concrete, stone or other solid masonry walls require *anchor bolts*. Fasten the base to the wall with black mastic, letting it squeeze through the holes. Hang the plywood unit after the mastic has set, using washers. Toggle bolts in expansion shields may also be used.

The type of wall determines how you should hang your cabinets. You can drive long wood screws through the cabinet back into the studs in frame walls.

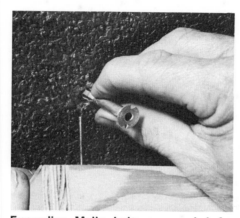

Expanding Molly bolts are needed for hollow masonry walls.

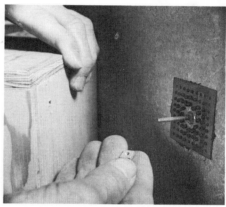

Anchor bolts are attached to a concrete wall with black mastic. Holes are drilled through the cabinet back and the back is held on the bolts with nuts.

DRAWERS

Drawers can be easily made with a saw and hammer. Simple butt joints are glued and nailed. The bottom should be 3/8-inch or 1/2-inch plywood for rigidity. On the style shown here, the drawer front extends down to cover the front edge of the bottom.

Another method, shown at the far right, employs an additional strip of wood glued and nailed to the front panel. This reinforces the bottom and lets you to use 1/4-inch plywood for drawer bottoms.

Power tools make sturdy drawers easy to build. The picture shows one side, dadoed on outer face for the drawer guide, being put into place. Cut rabbets in the drawer front to fit the sides. Dado the sides to fit drawer back. All four

It will speed construction if you place the nails on the drawer bottom before you put it in place. Note how the drawer front overlaps to conceal the bottom.

A strip of wood glued and nailed along the front of the drawer adds strength.

This style of drawer requires power tools to make the dado for the drawer guide and rabbets to fit the drawer back.

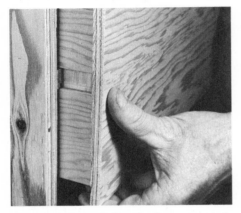

This guide is made by plowing a groove in the drawer side to fit over a strip of wood glued to the inside of the cabinet.

Another type of glide is made by plowing the groove in the cabinet inside and gluing the matching strips to the drawer.

parts are grooved to take a 1/4-inch plywood bottom.

Two types of drawer guides are easy to make with power tools. In the first, a groove is plowed in the side of the drawer before assembly. It fits over a strip glued to the side of the cabinet. This procedure is reversed for the second version. Here the cabinet side is dadoed before assembly. A matching strip is glued to the side of the drawer. Even heavy drawers slide easily on guides like these if waxed or lubricated with paraffin after finishing.

You can also design drawers where the bottom forms the guide. Only hand tools are needed to make this drawer. A 3/8-inch or 1/2-inch plywood bottom extends 3/8 inch beyond the sides of the drawer, forming a lip along each side. This lip fits into slots formed with 3/8-inch plywood pieces glued to the inner surface of each side of the cabinet. A gap just wide enough to take the lip is left between the pieces.

With power tools you can make a simpler and lighter version of the same drawer. The bottom is 1/4-inch plywood cut 3/8 inch wider than the drawer on each side. This drawer slides in slots dadoed into the cabinet's 3/4-inch plywood sides.

Here the bottom of the drawer overlaps both sides to form glides.

The bottom forms the glide, and the oversize front conceals the grooves in the cabinet sides.

SLIDING DOORS

Close-fitting plywood sliding doors are made by rabbeting the top and bottom edges of each door. Rabbet the back of the front door, and the front of the back door. This lets the doors almost touch and increases the effective depth of the cabinet. For 3/8-inch plywood doors rabbeted half their thickness, plow two grooves in top and bottom of cabinet 1/2 inch apart. With all plywood doors, seal all edges and give backs same paint treatment as front to prevent warping or weathering.

For removable doors, plow bottom grooves 3/16 inch deep and top grooves 3/8 inch deep. After finishing, insert door by pushing up into excess space in top groove, then drop the door into bottom. Plowing can be eliminated by using a fiber track made for sliding doors available at your hardware store.

You only need hand tools when the version of the sliding door shown here is used. Front and back strips are stock 1/4-inch quarter-round molding. The strip between is 1/4 inch square. Use glue and brads or finish nails to fasten strips securely. Sliding door cabinet track also may be used.

HANGING SHELVES

The neatest and strongest way to hang a shelf is by making a dado joint or using metal shelf supports. A dado requires power tools and does not allow you to change shelf height. Inexpensive shelf supports that plug into blind holes drilled 3/8 inch deep in the plywood sides of the cabinet are available. Drill additional holes to permit moving shelves when desired. Another support device is a slotted metal shelf strip into which shelf supports may be plugged at any height. For a better fit, set shelf strips flush in a dado cut or cut out shelves around shelf strips.

This sliding door is made by rabbetting grooves in the top and bottom edges.

Another type of sliding door is made with square and quarter-round molding.

Simple shelf hangers are available at most hardware stores.

Fit the top of the door into the top groove and let it drop into the bottom groove.

CABINET BACKS

Cabinet backs are usually made of 3/8-inch plywood, although some designs may call for thicker wood. The standard method of attaching backs to cabinets and other storage units calls for rabbeting the cabinet sides just deep enough to take a plywood back. For large units that must fit against walls that may not be perfectly smooth or plumb, the version in the top left photograph is better. A rabbet is made 1/2 or even 3/4 inch deep. The lip that remains after the back has been inserted may be easily trimmed wherever necessary to get a good fit between plywood unit and house wall.

Nail the cabinet back into the rabbet by driving nails at a slight angle. Use 1-inch brads or 4d finishing nails. When the back will not be seen, 1-inch blue lath nails can be used.

Two-hand or air-powered staplers are excellent for nailing cabinet backs. They drive long staples, setting them below the surface if desired, and greatly speed up the work. They are sometimes available on loan or rental.

When hand tools are used, attach strips of 1/4-inch molding for the back to rest against. Glue and nail back to molding.

You can also apply cabinet backs without rabbets or moldings. One way is to nail the back flush with the outside edge. A second way is to set the back 1/2 to 7/8 inch away from edges. The back becomes inconspicuous when cabinet is against a wall. The back will be even less conspicuous if you bevel it. Install a 3/8-inch plywood back flush with the edges of the cabinet, then bevel with light strokes of a block plane or power saw.

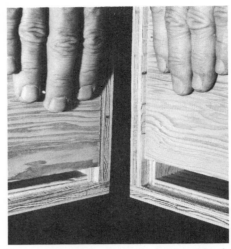

For most cabinets, use the style of back on the left. If your cabinet must fit flush against an irregular surface, the edges on the style at the right can be trimmed for a perfect fit without marring the back.

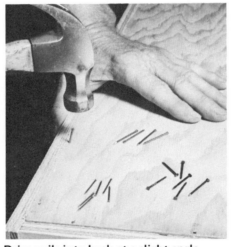

Drive nails into back at a slight angle.

Molding can be used to hold a cabinet back. Attach with glue and nails.

Here are two ways to attach backs without rabbets or molding. The back at the left is nailed flush to the cabinet. The back at the right is inset to make it less visible.

You can also bevel cabinet backs to make them less noticeable.

A two-handed stapler requires a hammer to drive the staples.

FINISHING EDGES

There are many ways to finish plywood edges. You can achieve handsome, solid results by cutting a V groove and inserting a matching wood strip, but this method is comparatively difficult. A simpler way is to use thin strips of real wood edge-banding. They are already coated with pressure sensitive adhesive. You simply peel off the backing paper and apply to plywood edges according to the manufacturer's recommendations. Some brands require a solvent or heat to activate the glue.

Laminated Plastic surfacing materials may be applied to table edges with the same contact cement used in applying table tops. Apply to edges first, then to counter or table top. A thicker, more massive effect can be created by nailing a 1- or 1-1/4-inch strip all around the edge.

To fill end grain on plywood edges that are to be painted, several varieties of wood putty are available. They are either powdered, to be mixed with water, or ready for use. Plastic spackle also works well. Sand smooth when thoroughly dry. You may want to respackle and sand to insure a fine, smooth surface. Then paint.

Rounded edges can be made with half-round molding or by sanding edges to the shape you want.

If you plan to paint your project, shape and sand the edges, then paint. If you want the grain to show, some edge covering should be used.

When adjacent edges of a plywood panel are to be covered, the framing strips should be mitered or butted at the corners.

If you do not have clamps available, masking tape can be used to hold edges until the glue dries.

If you plan to use a heavy bar clamp, it is sometimes easier to lay it on a surface and set the work in the clamp. Use smooth strips of scrap wood to protect the surfaces from clamp marks.

CHOOSING HARDWARE

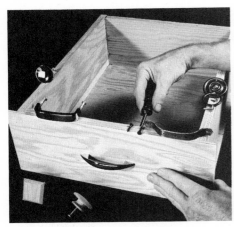

Pulls and handles are available in many styles.

Finger cups are used for sliding or rolling doors.

This simple pull is easy to make.

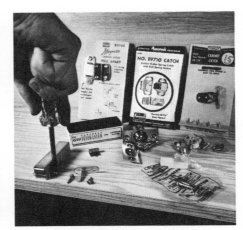

Many types of catches are available.

Door hinges can become part of the decoration in your design, or they can be concealed as shown on the following page.

PULLS, HANDLES & CATCHES

Drawer pulls and door handles are widely available. Use metal or wooden ones to add style to your project. They come in a variety of traditional and ranch styles as well as in many modern designs.

Sliding and rolling doors are easily equipped with finger cups that you simply force into round holes. For large doors, use rectangular cups or large round ones fastened with screws. Round pulls at top are suitable where clearance is adequate, or you can make simple rectangular grips from wood.

The simplest drawer pull is a notch cut into the top of a drawer front. It may be rectangular, V-shaped or half-round. You can omit the notch from every other drawer, opening the unnotched drawer by means of a notch in the drawer below. Or you can slope the drawer fronts so the drawer may be pulled out by grasping the projecting bottom edge.

Catches come in many varieties. The conventional *friction type* is shown at extreme right in the lower righthand picture. The *touch type*, being installed, lets the door open at a touch. A *magnetic catch* has no moving parts to break. *Roller catches* made of polyethelyne are smoother and more durable than steel friction catches.

HINGES

Surface hinges are quickly mounted. They require no mortising, add an ornamental touch and come in many styles. A pair of H or H-L hinges will do for most doors. For larger doors, or to add rigidity to smaller ones, use a pair of H-L plus one H, or use three of the H type. Tee or strap hinges help prevent sag in large doors. On tall doors, one or two added hinges between those at top and bottom will help minimize warping.

Doors that overlap their frames,

as shown in the top left photo at right, are neatly hung with semi-concealed hinges. They are excellent for plywood because screws go into flat grain. These have a 1/2-inch inset and are made for doors of 3/4-inch plywood rabbeted to leave a 1/4-inch lip. Such hinges are made in many styles and finishes, semi-concealed or full-surface.

Concealed pin hinges give a neat modern appearance to flush doors. They mount directly onto the cabinet side. Construction is simplified because no face frame is necessary. Only the pivot is visible from the front when the door is closed. Use a pair for small doors, three, called *a pair and one-half,* for larger doors.

Semi-concealed hinges.

Concealed pin hinges.

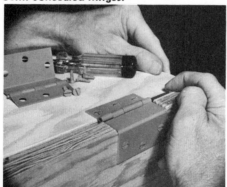
Semi-concealed, loose pin hinges.

Nylon wheel for rolling doors.

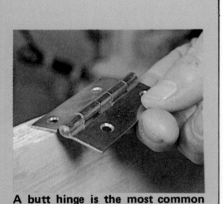

A butt hinge is the most common type. They are usually recessed beneath the surface of the work in a mortise. Cutting the mortise to hold hinges must be done accurately. If the hinge is improperly aligned, the connecting parts may fit unevenly.

A variation of the butt hinge is the lapping cabinet hinge. It attaches to the surface, rather than the edge of the panels.

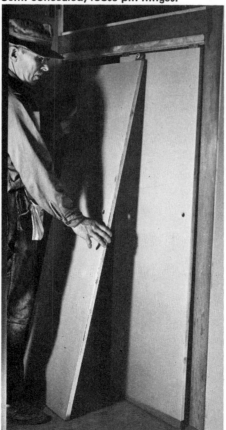

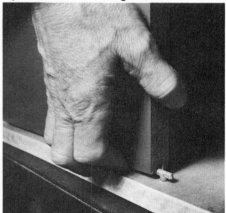
Bottom T guide for sliding or rolling doors.

Install sliding doors by snapping wheels onto their track, then placing the bottom over the T guide.

Doors are easier to hang if at least one side of the hinge mounts from the front, so you can see what you are doing.

Semi-concealed, loose-pin hinges offer the same appearance when door is closed as ordinary butt hinges. Only the barrel shows. They're much better for flush plywood doors, though, because screws go into flat plywood grain. A variation called a *chest hinge* may be used in the same way.

Rolling doors for closets and large storage units may have rollers at either top or bottom. Top-mount hardware is usually smoother in operation, particularly when the door is tall and narrow.

Two metal brackets fasten to the top of each door with a pair of screws. Nylon wheels with ball bearings roll in a double-lipped track that is fastened to the door frame with screws. Single-lipped track is also available for single doors. Installation is simple, with no mortising required.

The door bottom is kept in line by a simple T guide for each door. Two strips of 1/4-inch quarter-round molding, with 1/4 inch space between, can be used to form the slot if power tools are not available for making the slot.

PLYWOOD PANELING

Textured plywood's large size and inherent structural properties make it an ideal siding material. In the APA Sturd-I-Wall System, one layer of Exterior APA Plywood performs both as sheathing for strength, and siding for appearance and weatherability. Plywood siding is easily applied over sheathing too.

For New Walls—Plywood paneling may be applied directly to the studs. All vertical edges will naturally fall over framing. The standard eight-foot panel will usually run from floor to ceiling and attach at top and bottom plates. Otherwise, install cross blocking at horizontal joints to provide a solid

nailing base. This can be 2x4s toenailed into place where horizontal joints will fall. With 1/4-inch plywood, horizontal blocking with 2x4s at mid-wall height is recommended, or use gypsumboard or 5/16-inch plywood sheathing for backing. Also, fire stops may be required by your local building codes. Check with your local officials.

For Old Walls—You can nail new plywood paneling directly over existing plaster and gypsumboard walls, but you must plan so panel edges occur over existing studs behind the plaster. If this is impossible, installing 1x2 furring strips, horizontal and vertical, is recommended. When installing paneling over masonry or concrete walls, such as in a basement, furring strips are mandatory. An added advantage is that furring strips allow you to install insulation between the wall and the paneling.

Adhesives—It's often faster and easier to apply paneling with adhesives. If the existing wall is unsuitable, plywood sheathing will make a good base. When using adhesives on an old wall, remove wallpaper and loose paint where the adhesive will be applied. You can use special panel adhesive with a caulking gun or regular contact cement. In either case, follow the manufacturer's directions.

Support Spacing and Nailing—When plywood paneling is fastened with nails, support spacing depends on panel thickness. Most textured plywood paneling is at least 3/8 inch thick. Supports may be spaced up to 24 inches on center (o.c.). However, when 3/8-inch thick panels are grooved, you will get better results if you use supports no more than 16 inches o.c.

Space nails 6 inches o.c. at panel edges and 12 inches o.c. at intermediate supports. Use casing or finishing nails, 6d for plywood from 5/16 to 1/2 inch thick and 8d for 5/8 inch or Texture 1-11. When using grooved panels, you can nail through the grooves to the stud.

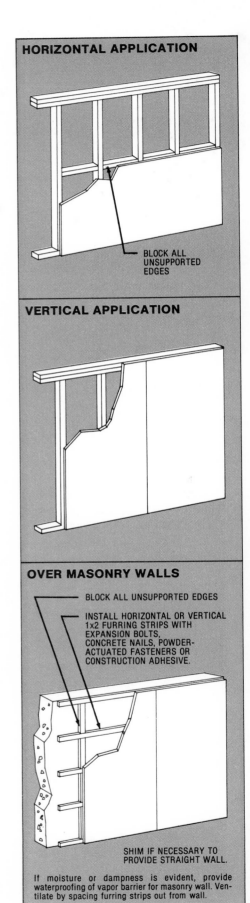

HORIZONTAL APPLICATION

BLOCK ALL UNSUPPORTED EDGES

VERTICAL APPLICATION

OVER MASONRY WALLS

BLOCK ALL UNSUPPORTED EDGES

INSTALL HORIZONTAL OR VERTICAL 1x2 FURRING STRIPS WITH EXPANSION BOLTS, CONCRETE NAILS, POWDER-ACTUATED FASTENERS OR CONSTRUCTION ADHESIVE.

SHIM IF NECESSARY TO PROVIDE STRAIGHT WALL.

If moisture or dampness is evident, provide waterproofing of vapor barrier for masonry wall. Ventilate by spacing furring strips out from wall.

INTERIOR FINISHING

INTERIOR FINISHING		
Type of Finish **Use only lead-free finishes**	**Recommended For**	**Applications**
PAINT — Oil—flat paint, semi-gloss or gloss enamel	Medium Density Overlay, regular plywood, striated, embossed.	Apply over stain-resistant primer recommended by manufacturer of topcoat.
PAINT — Latex emulsion	Regular and textured plywood, Medium Density Overlay.	Apply over stain-resistant primer recommended by manufacturer of topcoat.
PAINT — Textured paints	Regular plywood, Medium Density Overlay, Texture 1-11.	Use stain-resistant primer recommended by manufacturer of topcoat.
STAINS, SEALERS	Regular plywood, textured.	Apply stains with companion sealer or over sealer separately applied. Follow with satin varnish or lacquer for increased durability. Where sealer alone is desired, use two coats.

PREPARING PANELS

Plywood for interior paneling may be of sanded grade, overlaid or any of the several textures. MDO plywood needs no preparation and can be finished with conventional paints or enamels for an exceptionally smooth and durable surface. Textured panels may be finished directly with clear sealer, stains or latex paints. Sanded plywood may be finished with paints, enamels or stains. The only sanding required is to smooth filler or spackle applied to any openings in the panel face, or to remove blemishes.

To touch-sand, always sand *with* the grain, using fine sandpaper. Do not paint over dust or spots of oil or glue. All knots, pitch streaks or sap spots in sanded or textured plywood should be touched up with sealer or shellac before the panels are painted. No other panel preparation is needed.

USING PAINTS

The chart on this page should help you decide the correct paint, stain, or sealer for a particular job. Note that finishes vary greatly depending upon the grade of plywood you are using. Products too, vary from manufacturer to manufacturer; read the label instructions carefully before beginning any work.

Water-Base Paints are emulsions of resin (usually polyvinyl acetate), acrylic, or styrene-butadiene latex and water. They are often called *latex paints* and are easily applied with a brush, roller or spray. Color retention is good and they dry quickly, but they are not completely washable. When using these paints, prime the plywood surface with a primer recommended by the topcoat manufacturer. This will prevent grain raise and minimize staining.

Gloss and Semi-Gloss Enamels— These are extremely durable, washable finishes, usually with an alkyd-resin base. They are also available in acrylic-latex water-base type. Their use is primarily in kitchens and bathrooms for trim or cabinets.

NATURAL FINISHES

Smooth or smooth-textured plywood for natural finishes should be carefully selected for pattern and appearance. For the most natural effect, use two coats of clear sealer as a finish to maintain a clean panel surface and avoid soiling.

Plywood's repairs and grain irregularities can be pleasantly subdued with light stain finishes applied in either of two ways. The stain should be tested on a sample containing color differences or patches in the panel to demonstrate the finished appearance.

Color Toning—Color toning requires *companion stains* and *non-penetrating sealers*. These have the advantage of requiring only one step for application of stain and sealer. It is necessary to tint a small amount of sealer with stain until the desired tone is obtained on a sample. Then, mix enough stain and sealer in the same proportion to do the entire job and apply it by brush or spray. After drying and light sanding, a coat of clear finish is added to give the desired luster and durability.

The sealer is a heavy-bodied non-penetrating type with non-hiding

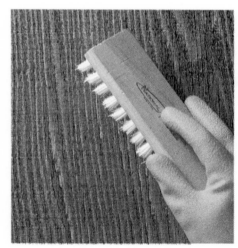

Before you apply a finish, brush the surface of the plywood to remove dust and splinters.

pigments, which preserve natural wood appearance. Tones of light gray, brown or tan go well with wood colors and provide the best grain masking.

Light Stain—This method of applying a natural finish mellows plywood's grain pattern and requires more steps than color toning, but does not require special companion stains and sealers. The panel is first whitened with pigmented resin sealer or interior white undercoat cut *one to one* with thinner. Before it becomes tacky, the sealer is wiped off to permit the grain to show. Then, clear resin sealer is applied, allowed to dry and sandpapered lightly. The color is added with a thin application of tinted undercoat, thin enamel, pigmented resin sealer or light stain. This is wiped to the proper color depth. After drying and light sanding, a coat of satin varnish or brushing lacquer is applied to provide luster and durability.

SPECIAL EFFECTS

Stippled or Textured Finish—This finish may be used along with tape to hide joints in plywood paneling. Stipple texture paints are usually latex and the plywood must be sized or sealed with an oil-base or stain-resistant primer. The stipple is then applied as recommended.

Wall Coverings—Fabric-backed films such as vinyl are available in unlimited patterns and textures. Joints between panels and openings in the panel surface should be filled with a joint compound and the entire surface sized or sealed with a product such as shellac. A latex adhesive is applied to the back of the wall covering and the covering pressed firmly to the plywood wall.

Multicolor Spatter Finish—Spatter finish is usually a lacquer with a blend of two or more colors of uniform fleck size. When applied with spray equipment, the colors remain separate and distinct, creating an unusual decorative effect. This finish requires an undercoat. It can be applied lightly over a colored

background, or fully over primer. It works well with V joints between plywood panels, which are discussed on this page.

TEXTURED PLYWOOD

Textured plywood, such as rough sawn, patterned surfaces or Texture 1-11, may be finished for attractive natural appearance. They should be protected against soiling with two coats of a clear sealer, or, where color is wanted, with pigmented stains. If desired, the few repairs and grain irregularities in the panel can be concealed by using color toning or the light stains as previously described.

PREFINISHED PLYWOOD

A number of producers make prefinished plywood for paneling. This may be select *softwood, hardwood faced* or *grain printed* plywood. These panels are normally available with washable light stain or natural finishes which are resistant to dirt and fingerprints.

JOINT TREATMENTS

The tendency in recent years has been to accentuate the joints in plywood wall and ceiling panels. This simplifies construction and, when panels are located according to a plan, it can be quite attractive. Most often seen are *V joints* between panels. These are made by shaving the edge of each panel with a 45-degree bevel, about 1/8 inch deep. The bevels can be overlapped to conceal the joint, or set point to point to accentuate it. Joints are commonly accentuated in natural finish panels and frequently in painted panels. *Butted joints*, covered with simple moldings or battens, are also used.

Where paint finishes are to be used, smooth joints can be prepared by conventional dry wall taping. This is most satisfactory when textured or multicolor spatter finish is applied.

EXTERIOR FINISHING

Whether you are finishing a new house or refinishing an older home, a quality stain or paint can keep the plywood looking good. And care in applying the proper finish can make considerable difference in the length of its life.

WHY USE A FINISH?

The primary functions of a finish are to protect the siding from the weathering process and to help maintain its appearance. Weathering erodes and roughens unfinished wood. Different finishes give varying degrees of protection, so the type of finish, its quality, quantity and the application method must be considered in selecting and planning the finish or refinish job. The finish is the final touch on any building, so it's important to do it right the first time.

Water repellent preservatives help reduce the effects of weathering if reapplied often enough, but they offer only minimum protection. Semi-transparent stains are next in effectiveness, then solid-color stains. The most effective finish is a two-coat paint system consisting of primer and top coat, which gives the greatest protection against weathering and erosion of the wood's surface.

CARE AND PREPARATION

Plywood should be stored and handled with care to avoid exposure to water or weather before it is finished. Storage in a cool, dry place out of the sunlight and weather is best. If left outdoors, any straps on the plywood bundles should be loosened or cut and the stacks covered. The covering should allow good air circulation between the plywood and the cover itself to prevent condensation and the growth of mold.

The first finishing coat should be applied as soon as possible because there is a definite relationship between the finish's performance and the length of time the raw wood has been left unprotected, especially to sunlight, wetting and drying. Do not apply finishes to a hot surface.

SEALING EDGES

End grain picks up and loses moisture much faster than side grain. All panel edges should be sealed to help minimize possible damage. Horizontal edges, especially lower edges where drips may occur, should be treated with special care because of the greater exposure to wetting from rain and water. Sealing both blind and exposed edges increases the life of the siding and the final finish. Edges cut during construction should be sealed too.

A liberal application of a good water-repellent preservative compatible with the final finish should be used for edge sealing if a stain is to be used on the siding's face. If the siding will be painted, use the same exterior house paint primer that will be used on the face. Edge sealing is easiest when the panels are in a stack. Use a brush to apply the primer.

STAIN FINISHES

High-quality stains best meet the architectural intent of textured plywood sidings. They add color and penetrate the surface for a durable, breathing finish. Stains add to the beauty of plywood siding, showing off its rustic, rough texture.

Stains are manufactured in two categories: semi-transparent and solid color. Properly applied, both will weather to a surface that is easily refinished without much preparation.

Semi-Transparent Stains—Available in a variety of hues, semi-transparent stains give maximum grain show-through. Only oil base semi-transparent stains are recommended. Other types do not provide adequate protection.

Semi-transparent stains are normally used to emphasize the wood's natural characteristics. This type of stain will show color differences in the wood itself, or between the wood and any repairs.

One or two coats of stain should be applied in accordance with the manufacturer's directions. Two coats will give greater depth of color and a longer life for the finish.

Semi-transparent stains are recommended for 303 series plywood siding with face grades of 303-0C (clear, no patches), 303-NR (natural rustic, no patches but permits open knotholes), and 303-6-W (up to six wood patches per sheet). Semi-transparent stains may be used on other grades if it is desirable to show color contrast. The stain should be tested on a sample containing color differences between the wood and any patches or within the wood itself to demonstrate the finished appearance.

Brushed plywood surfaces should be finished according to the plywood manufacturer's recommendations; otherwise use an oil base semi-transparent stain.

Semi-transparent stains are *not* recommended for 303-0L plywood or any overlaid panel such as MDO.

Solid-Color Stains—These highly pigmented, opaque stains cover the wood's natural color but allow its

It is easier to seal edges of plywood while it is stacked before use.

texture to show. Either oil base or latex emulsion solid-color stains may be used.

These stains give a solid, uniform color and work well to mask the wood's own color differences. They also tend to obscure panel characteristics such as knots and repairs. Correctly applied, quality opaque stains provide good bonding to the panel.

Opaque finishes are particularly recommended for grades 303-6-S and 303-6-S/W, as well as 303-18 and 303-30 with any type of patch. Where a solid color is desired, they may be used on any siding grade.

EXTERIOR FINISHING			
303 Series Plywood Siding Grades	Semi-Transparent Stains (oil base)	Solid Color Stains (oil or latex base)	Paints Minimum 1 primer plus 1 top coat (acrylic latex)
303-0C	X	X	X
303-0L	Not Recommended	Consult Manufacturer	X
303-NR	X	X	X
303-SR	If Contrast is Acceptable	X	X
303-6-W	X	X	X
303-6-S	If Contrast is Acceptable	X	X
303-6-S/W	If Contrast is Acceptable	X	X
303-18-W	If Contrast is Acceptable	X	X
303-18-S	If Contrast is Acceptable	X	X
303-18-S/W	If Contrast is Acceptable	X	X
303-30-W	If Contrast is Acceptable	X	X
303-30-S	If Contrast is Acceptable	X	X
303-30-S/W	If Contrast is Acceptable	X	X

Both stain and paint should be applied smoothly and evenly. Be sure to avoid lap marks.

If a solid-color stain in a light hue is to be used on wood where extractive staining is anticipated, use an oil base, not a latex (water-thinned) stain.

For overlaid panels, 303-0L, some siding manufacturers recommend an acrylic latex solid-color stain or a two-coat paint system. Oil based stains are not recommended for this grade.

PAINT FINISHES

Never use typical shake and shingle stains or paints on plywood. They form a weak film on the surface and do not penetrate well. Usually they become brittle within a short time and, when cracks appear, water gets underneath to flake away the finish. Such a surface is very difficult to prepare for refinishing.

Acrylic Latex—A top-quality acrylic-latex exterior house paint and companion primer formulated for wood are recommended if paint is used on textured plywood. It is the *only* finish recommended for sanded plywood.

Primer and Top Coat—A minimum two-coat paint system, consisting of one coat of primer and one top coat, is essential. And the primer is always the more important of the two coats.

Primers are formulated specifically for controlled penetration, optimum bonding to the substrate, and minimal extractive staining.

Some latex systems use an oil or alkyd primer followed by the latex top coat for extractive staining woods. Other systems use up to two coats of a specially formulated stain-blocking latex primer, sometimes with emulsified oil included. In any case, select companion products designed to be used together and preferably from the same manufacturer. A stain-resistant primer with compatible acrylic-latex top coat will help avoid difficulties. Two top coats will give significant improvement in the finish's life and performance.

Top-quality acrylic latex painting systems may be used on any of the 303 series face grades.

Both smooth and textured Medium Density Overlay (MDO) plywood, 303-0L, may be finished with any top-quality exterior house paint system formulated for wood.

APPLICATION METHODS

The application method is as important as the finish material itself. It is poor economy to buy a quality stain or paint and then cause it to fail prematurely because of improper application.

Apply finishes only to clean and reasonably dry surfaces under good weather conditions. If siding is very dry, application and performance of a latex finish is improved if the surface is dampened with a wet cloth or brush first. Remove dirt

and loose wood fibers with a stiff-bristle brush. Final brushing should be along the grain to erase any marks.

A clean surface is the first step in achieving satisfactory performance from the finish. Do not paint or stain in the rain, when temperatures are low, or in direct sunlight when the panel is hot. Minimum temperatures are 50°F (10°C) for latex and 40°F (5°C) for oil systems.

Staining—For best performance, stains should be brushed on. The brush works the stain into the surface and gives a more uniform appearance. Application with a long-napped roller is next in order of preference. It tends to work the stain into the surface, although not as well as brushing. When using latex solid-color stains in hot weather, the siding may be dampened first with a wet cloth or brush to prevent too rapid drying and improve performance.

Spraying is the least desirable method and usually gives the poorest results. If used, the spray must be applied liberally and then back-brushed. Back-brushing or similar methods work the stain into the surface and under loose particles, particularly on rough surfaces. This also helps to even out spray patterns, giving a more uniform appearance.

If spray is fogged onto the siding, too little is applied and it adheres only to the outer surface of loose dust and fibers. These easily erode in the natural weathering process.

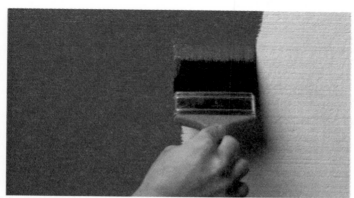

Apply a primer and allow it to dry before applying a top coat.

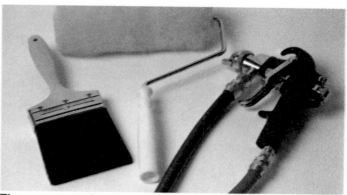

There are several ways to apply paint. Choose whichever one is best suited to your project, and follow the paint manufacturer's instructions.

Factory finishing uses machines to brush in the stain to achieve a good finish. Stain is applied under controlled conditions to assure optimum spread rate and uniformity. Finished panels are protected from the weather before delivery to the jobsite.

Regardless of the method of application, follow the coverage rate recommended by the stain manufacturer. Use the quantity specified for rough surfaces or double the amount listed for smooth work when finishing textured plywood.

On windy or dry days, take care to avoid lap marks.

Painting—Primer should be applied with a brush to form a continuous film with good penetration into the surface and to provide a good base for top coats. The top coats, preferably brushed on, may also be applied by roller or spray gun.

If a latex primer is being used, it helps to dampen the siding first with a wet cloth or brush. This prevents too rapid drying and improves the spreadability of water-base primers.

WEATHERING

The finish on almost any siding will begin to show its age after prolonged exposure to sun and weather. The weathering process gradually erodes the finish and causes it to become brittle and crack, lose its adhesion, fade or mildew.

Where no finish protection is applied or where the finish has weathered away, sunlight and moisture will erode the wood surface. For continuing performance, it is important to maintain the finish.

Sewing & Hobby Center

CONSTRUCTION NOTES

Lay out pieces on plywood according to panel layout. Allow for saw kerf width when laying out. Be especially careful when laying out curved corners. Label each piece for easy identification.

Cut out pieces. A saber saw will make this task much easier.

Begin assembly by glue-nailing the back of the center section to the sides.

Glue-nail shelves in place in center section. Note that shelf for sewing machine is 3/4-inch plywood.

Cut a 1/2-inch wide shim from scrap plywood and glue it to the back of the pegboard. This will make the space necessary for using pegboard hangers.

Glue-nail pegboard to center section.

Glue-nail storage bins into position.

Attach shelf supports and fold-down counter with piano hinges.

Assemble side sections according to plans. Attach ironing board door to side with piano hinge.

Attach side sections to center section with piano hinges.

Fill and smooth any exposed edges.

Finish as desired.

Attach magnetic door catches as desired.

MATERIALS LIST

Quantity	Description
6	4 ft. x 8 ft. plywood panels of 1/2 in. APA grademarked A-A or A-B Interior, A-C Exterior, or Medium Density Overlay (MDO)
1	4 ft. x 8 ft. plywood panel of 3/4 in. of the same grade
	Continuous piano hinges:
2	77 in. long for front doors
2	14 in. long for shelf supports
1	56 in. long for ironing board door
1	37 in. long for work shelf
1	32 in. x 17-1/2 in. panel of 1/4 in. pegboard
4	Magnetic catches and plates
Optional	1/8 in. x 1 in. aluminum bar stock to measure of machine base perimeter
Optional	#6 flathead screws for attaching bar stock to box
As required	6d finishing nails for glue-nail assembly of cabinet
As required	White or urea-resin glue for glue-nail assembly of cabinet
As required	Wood dough or surfacing putty for filling any small gaps in exposed plywood edges
As required	Fine sandpaper for smoothing
As required	Paint, stain, or antiquing for finish

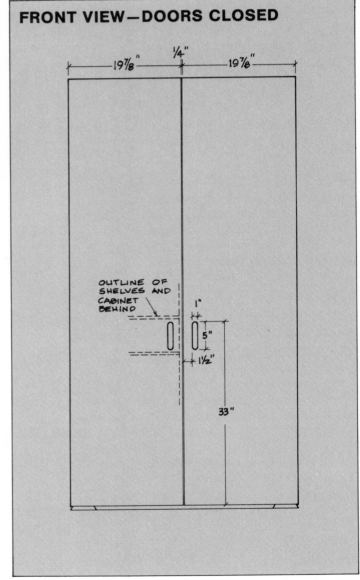

FRONT VIEW—DOORS CLOSED

19 7/8"   1/4"   19 7/8"

OUTLINE OF SHELVES AND CABINET BEHIND

1"
5"
1 1/2"

33"

EXPLODED VIEW

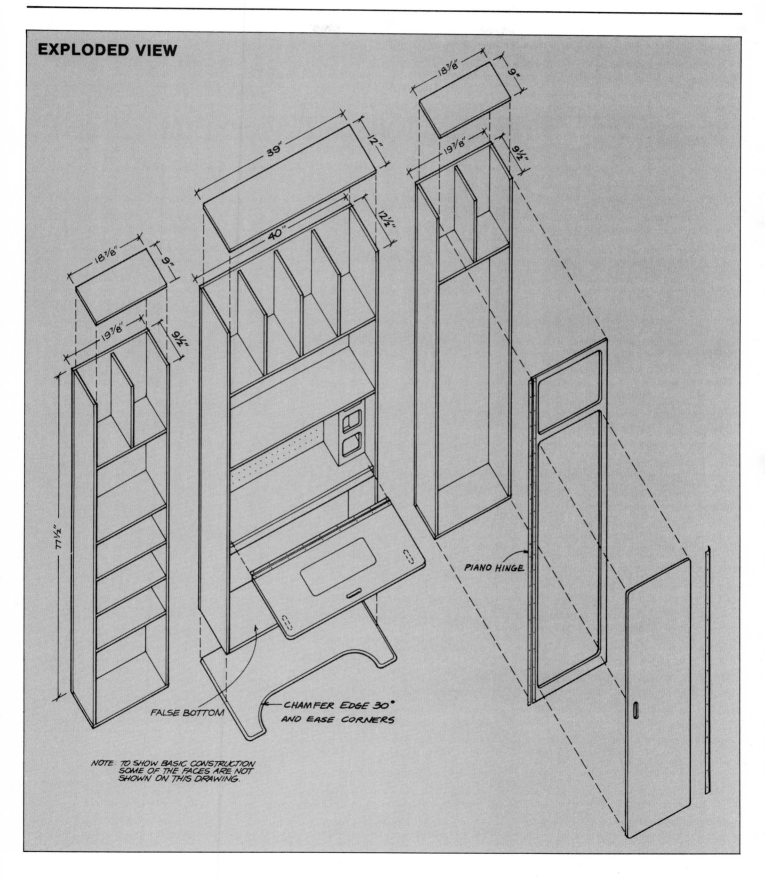

FALSE BOTTOM

CHAMFER EDGE 30°
AND EASE CORNERS

PIANO HINGE.

NOTE: TO SHOW BASIC CONSTRUCTION
SOME OF THE FACES ARE NOT
SHOWN ON THIS DRAWING.

PANEL LAYOUT

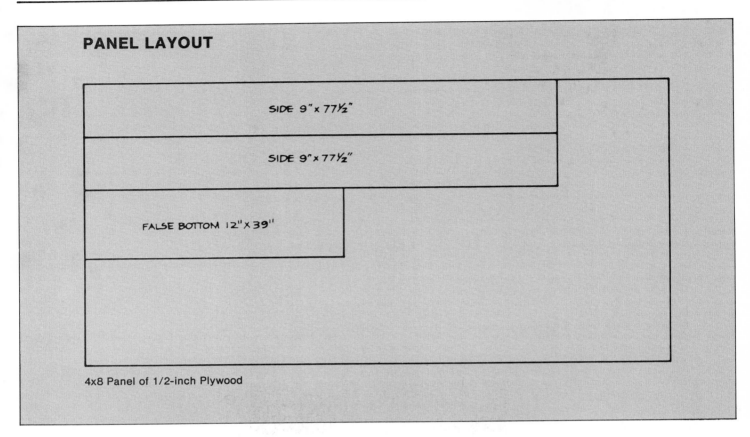

4x8 Panel of 1/2-inch Plywood

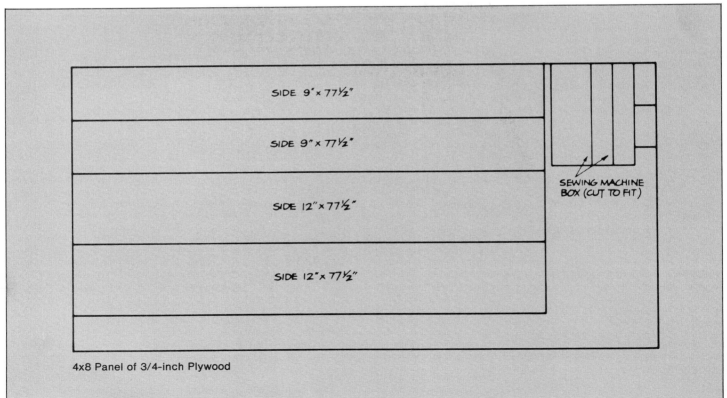

4x8 Panel of 3/4-inch Plywood

PANEL LAYOUT

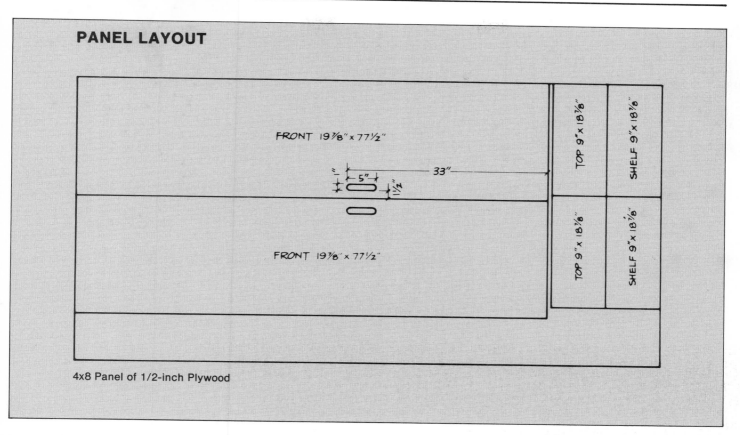

4x8 Panel of 1/2-inch Plywood

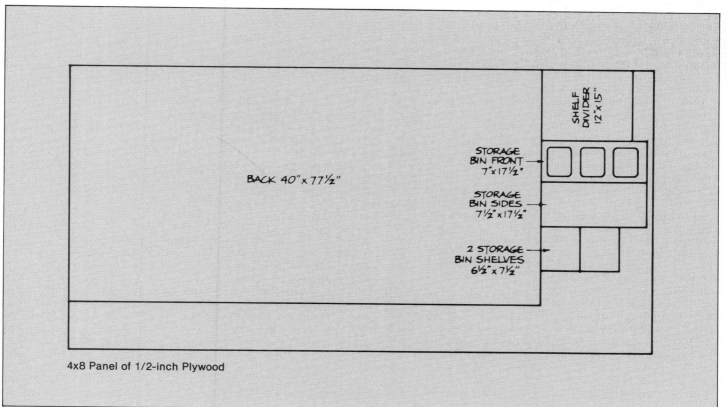

4x8 Panel of 1/2-inch Plywood

PANEL LAYOUT

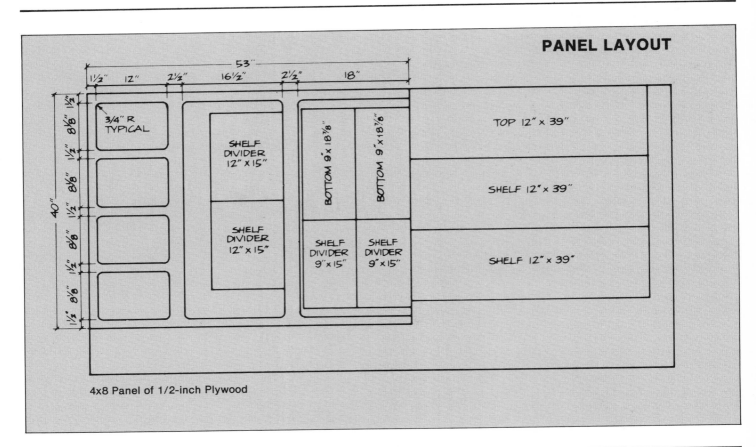

4x8 Panel of 1/2-inch Plywood

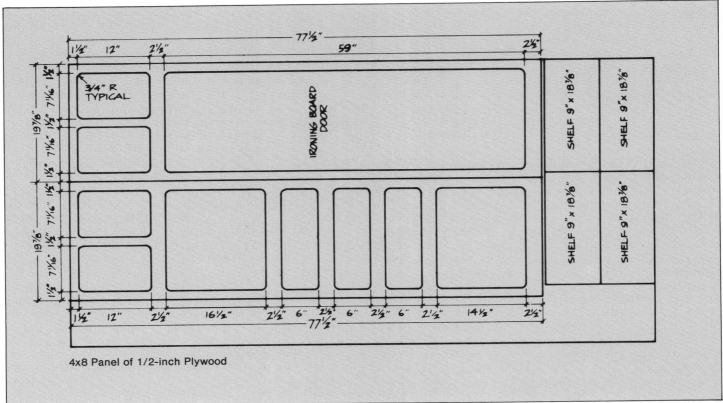

4x8 Panel of 1/2-inch Plywood

PANEL LAYOUT

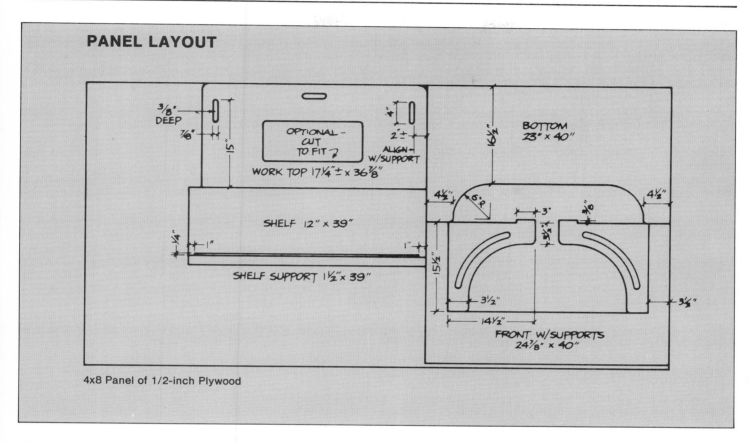

4x8 Panel of 1/2-inch Plywood

OPTIONAL MACHINE BOX

ATTACH COMPLETED BOX TO MACHINE
BY BOLTING IT THROUGH HOLES DRILLED
TO MATCH FITTINGS ON MACHINE BOTTOM
OR USE AN ALUMINUM "L" AS SHOWN
BELOW

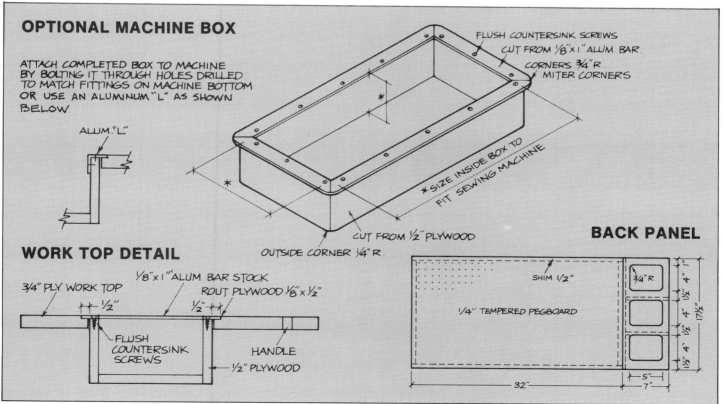

WORK TOP DETAIL

BACK PANEL

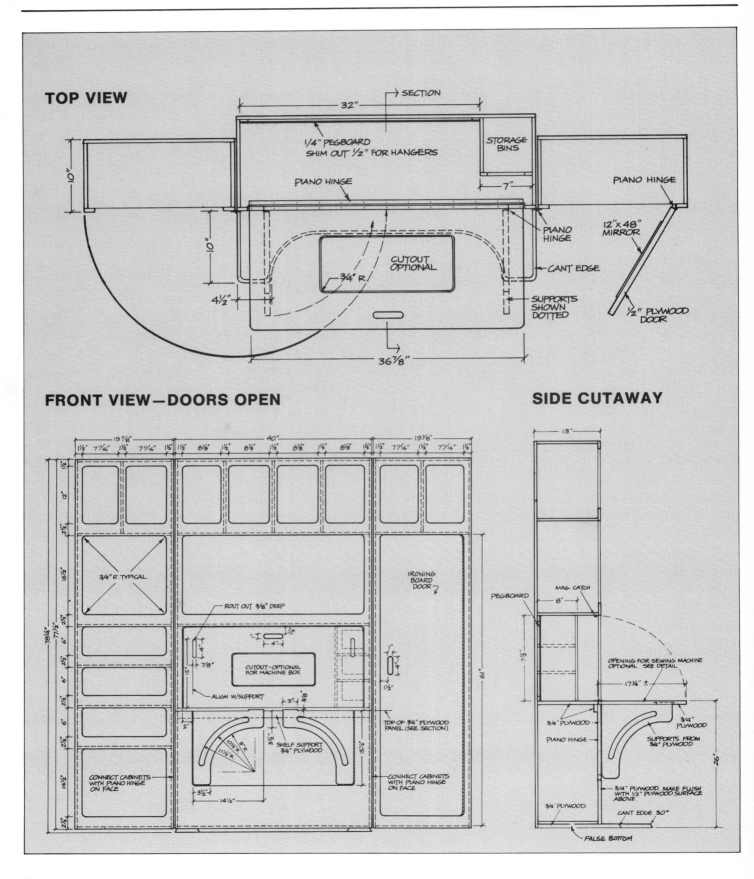

TOP VIEW

SECTION

32"

1/4" PEGBOARD
SHIM OUT 1/2" FOR HANGERS

STORAGE BINS

10"

PIANO HINGE

PIANO HINGE

7"

PIANO HINGE

12"x48" MIRROR

10"

CUTOUT OPTIONAL

3/4" R

CANT EDGE

4 1/2"

SUPPORTS SHOWN DOTTED

36 7/8"

1/2" PLYWOOD DOOR

FRONT VIEW—DOORS OPEN

SIDE CUTAWAY

13"

40"

19 7/8"   19 7/8"

3/4" R. TYPICAL

IRONING BOARD DOOR

PEGBOARD

MAG. CATCH

8"

ROUT OUT 3/8" DEEP

CUTOUT-OPTIONAL FOR MACHINE BOX

ALIGN W/SUPPORT

OPENING FOR SEWING MACHINE OPTIONAL. SEE DETAIL

17 1/4" ±

TOP OF 3/4" PLYWOOD PANEL (SEE SECTION)

3/4" PLYWOOD

3/4" PLYWOOD

SHELF SUPPORT 3/4" PLYWOOD

PIANO HINGE

SUPPORTS FROM 3/4" PLYWOOD

CONNECT CABINETS WITH PIANO HINGE ON FACE

CONNECT CABINETS WITH PIANO HINGE ON FACE

3/4" PLYWOOD. MAKE FLUSH WITH 1/2" PLYWOOD SURFACE ABOVE

61"

15 1/2"

8" R

10 1/2" R

11 1/2" R

3 1/2"

14 1/2"

3/4" PLYWOOD

CANT EDGE 30°

FALSE BOTTOM

26"

78 1/4"

77 1/2"

Dining Table

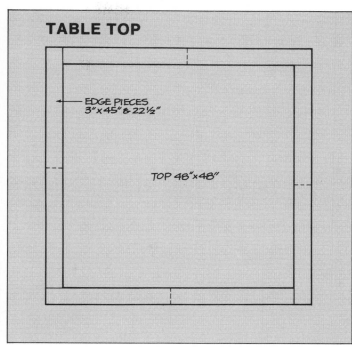

TABLE TOP

EDGE PIECES
3" x 45" & 22½"

TOP 48"x48"

MATERIALS LIST

Quantity	Description
1	4 ft. x 8 ft. plywood panel of 1/2 in. APA grademarked A-B or A-D Interior, A-B or A-C Exterior, or Medium Density Overlay (MDO)
1	4 ft. x 4 ft. plywood panel of 1/2 in. of the same grade
Small can	White glue or powdered resin glue for laminating edge strips. Use waterproof glue if table is for exterior use.
As required	Wood dough for filling any small voids in plywood edges
As required	Fine sandpaper for smoothing edges and cured wood dough
As required	Finishing materials.

CONSTRUCTION NOTES

Draw parts on plywood. Use a compass or make a cardboard template for drawing corner radii. When cutting, center saw cut on layout lines to equalize saw kerf width on all parts.

Make first cut between Parts A and D. Your second cut should include the two edge pieces and a 15-inch scrap piece. Next cut between the B pieces. Now, for accurate cutting of identical A, B, and edge pieces, clamp together the two sections formed by your third cut and cut simultaneously. Cut slots using a saw and chisel or a router. Cut remaining pieces last.

Sand all plywood edges smooth. Lay table top face down and apply glue according to manufacturer's instructions. Stack edge pieces in position as shown and clamp until dry.

Assemble leg pieces to check for fit.

Slip A pieces down on B pieces to form basic four legs.

Slip C into place to form one cross support, and D to form the other. Adjust fit if necessary.

Disassemble legs. Fill any edge voids with wood dough, allow to dry and sand smooth. Sand edges of laminated top and fill in the same manner.

Finish parts as desired. If you use paint, be sure to use a good primer and two coats of a compatible enamel. Or use a synthetic satin-finish varnish to allow the wood grain to show.

Assemble leg pieces and add top. Top will lock legs in place.

SIDES

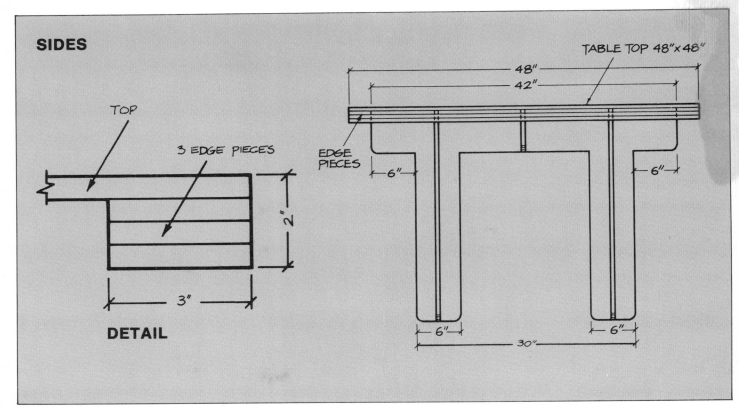

DETAIL

PANEL LAYOUT

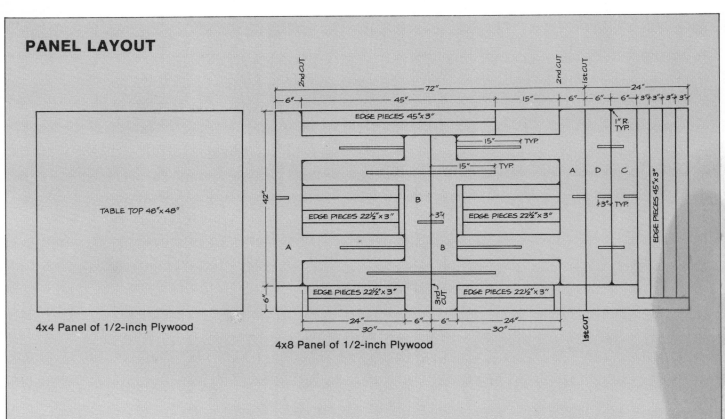

4x4 Panel of 1/2-inch Plywood

4x8 Panel of 1/2-inch Plywood

EXPLODED VIEW

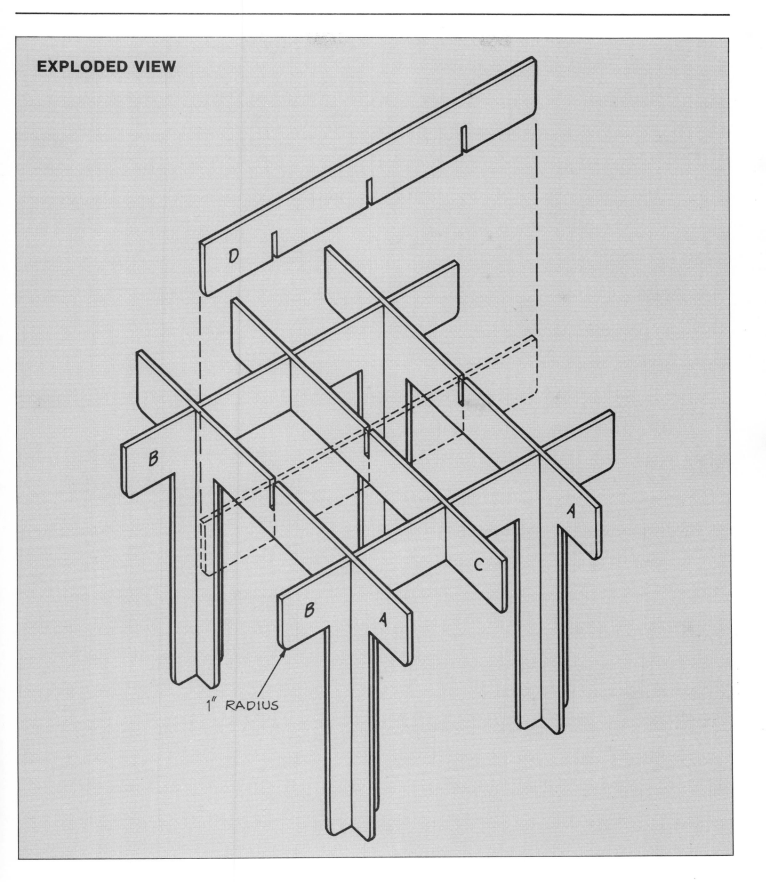

1" RADIUS

A Desk to Grow With

MATERIALS LIST

Quantity	Description
2	4 ft. x 8 ft. plywood panels of 3/4 in. APA grademarked A-B or A-D Interior, A-B or A-C Exterior, or Medium Density Overlay (MDO)
72 (approx.)	1-1/4 in. #8 flathead wood screws for shelves, desk compartment and frame, and chair back
15 (approx.)	1-1/2 in. #8 flathead wood screws for chair legs and fastening chair bottom to legs
1	Continuous piano hinge, 34 in. long, for desk top, plus screws for fastening
2	Magnetic catch and striker sets for desk closure
32 in.	Small-link chain for two 16-inch desk-top supports
4	Eye screws for fastening chains
As required	Wood dough for filling any small voids in plywood cut edges
As required	Fine sandpaper for smoothing edges and cured wood dough
As required	White glue for glue-screw assembly
As required	Primer and paint, antiquing kit or synthetic satin-finish varnish, such as Varathane, with or without stain

CONSTRUCTION NOTES

Draw all parts on plywood panels. Use a compass or cardboard template to draw curved corners. Center saw cut on layout lines to equalize saw kerf width on all parts.

Smooth plywood cut edges with fine sandpaper.

Lay all vertical parts face down, side by side, and draw horizontal lines across them to locate 3/8 inch deep dado cuts. Drill pilot holes for screws through grooves 2 inches in from edges of each part. Make very sure screw holes are spaced exactly equal so that shelves will be interchangeable.

Assemble corner sections with vertical sides and backs, and attach top shelf using glue and screws. Drill pilot holes for screws before installing.

Install piano hinge to join desk top and shelf.

Fill any small gaps in plywood cut edges with wood dough, and sand smooth when dry. Apply desired finish to all parts before completing assembly. Do not apply finish in shelf grooves.

Insert shelves in grooves in desired arrangement. Install shelf-holding screws through pilot holes.

Install 16-3/4-inch by 11-1/2-inch desk compartment side panel and glue and screw to shelf B. Install two screws through shelf above side panel to secure it but DO NOT GLUE unless you plan to leave desk permanently assembled in this configuration.

Install upright front braces and attach desk support chains as shown in exploded views. Install magnetic catches to braces and strikers on matching positions of desk top.

Assemble chair seat: Make dado cuts in seat sides. Glue-screw back in place. Glue-screw seat in place.

Assemble chair bottom in desired configuration using only screws if you expect to change it later. For permanent construction, use glue with screws.

Finish chair seat and bottom assemblies, then mount seat on bottom.

When changing from one desk configuration to the other, it will be necessary to fill unused screw holes with wood dough, sand and apply touch-up finish.

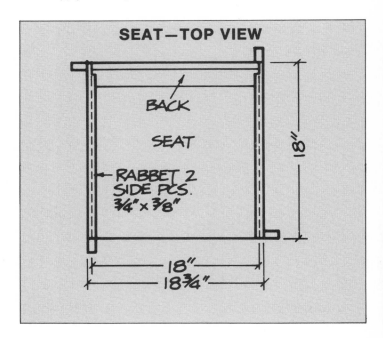

SEAT—TOP VIEW

BACK

SEAT

RABBET 2 SIDE PCS. 3/4" x 3/8"

18"

18"

18 3/4"

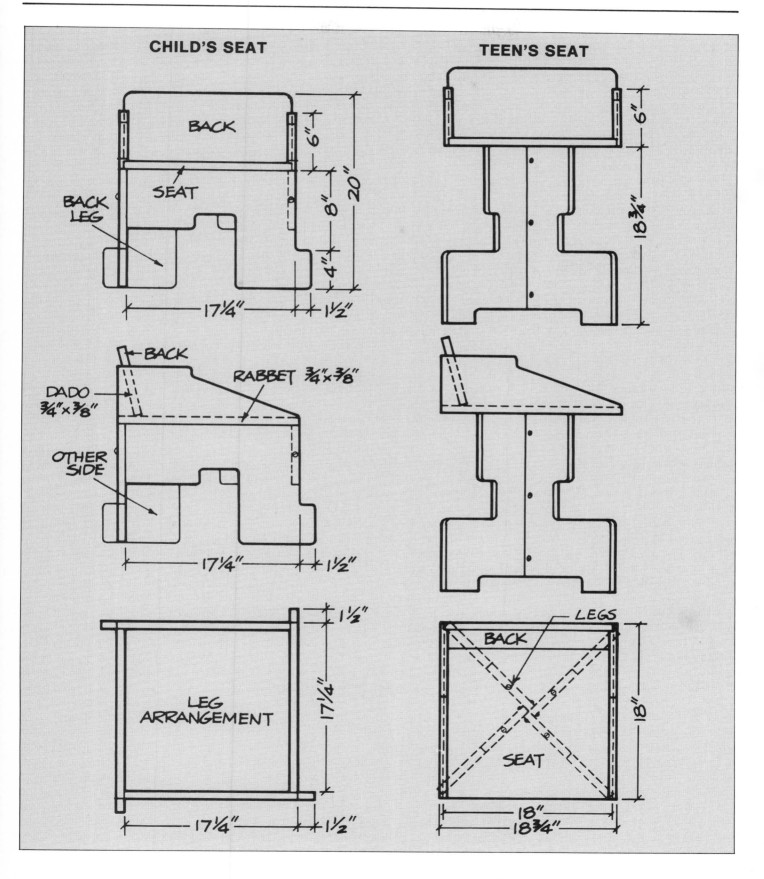

CHILD'S SEAT

BACK

SEAT

BACK LEG

6"

8"

4"

20"

17¼"

1½"

BACK

DADO ¾"×⅜"

RABBET ¾"×⅜"

OTHER SIDE

17¼"

1½"

LEG ARRANGEMENT

1½"

17¼"

17¼"

1½"

TEEN'S SEAT

6"

18¾"

LEGS

BACK

SEAT

18"

18"

18¾"

PANEL LAYOUT

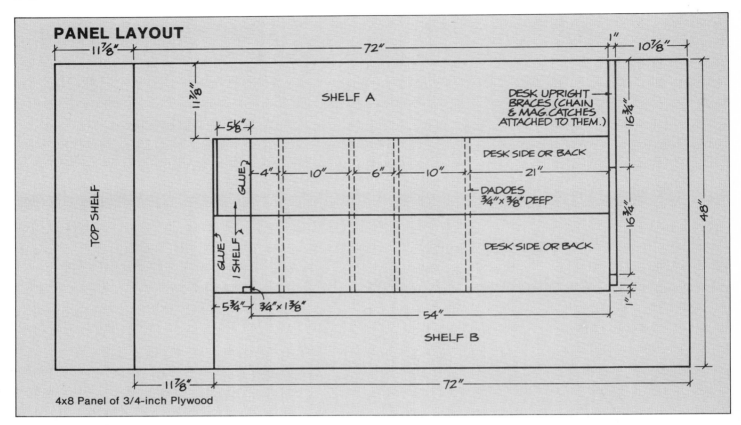

4x8 Panel of 3/4-inch Plywood

PANEL LAYOUT

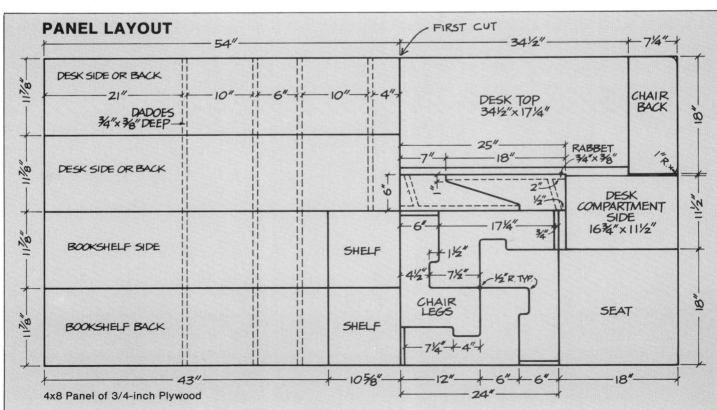

4x8 Panel of 3/4-inch Plywood

DESK

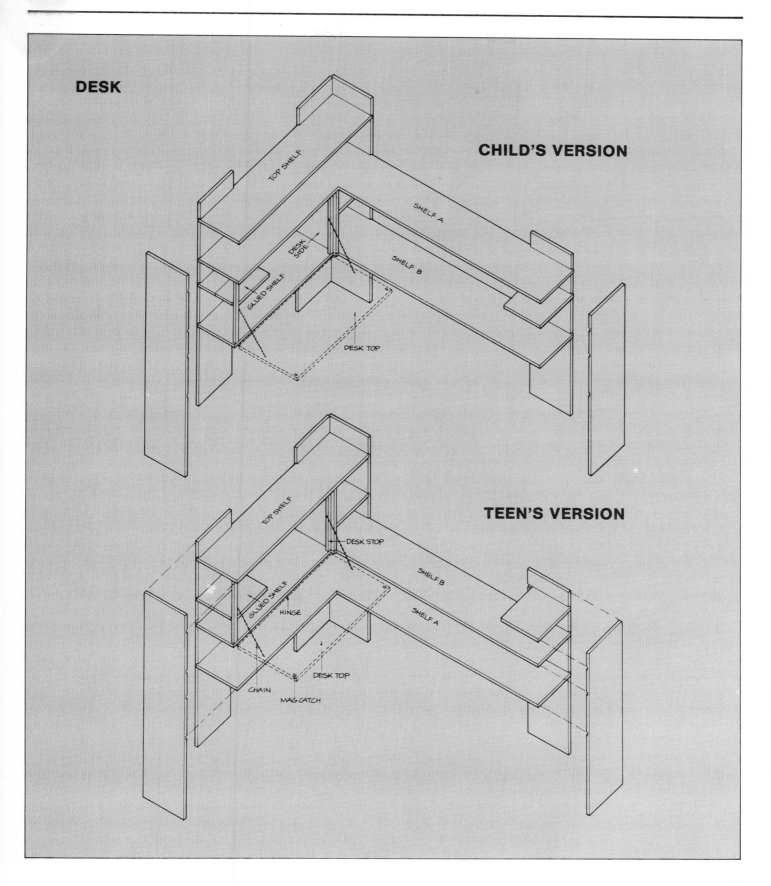

CHILD'S VERSION

TEEN'S VERSION

Convex Cubbyhole Shelf

CONSTRUCTION NOTES

For most accurate layout and cutting, make cardboard template for each size semicircle and trace onto plywood prior to cutting. Fit is very important for unit rigidity.

Center sawblade on pencil layout lines. Cut shelves carefully. **Do not cut slots**.

Stack equal-size shelves and clamp together in sets of four. Fill edge voids and sand or file edges smooth. Sand or feather-chamfer sharp corners to prevent breaking.

Separate stacks. Cut veneer to appropriate lengths leaving 1/2 inch extra on each piece. Glue to shelf edges according to glue manufacturer's instructions. Trim away excess veneer all around.

Clamp shelf sets together again making sure to align all edges and corners.

Use a square to mark exact centerline of back edges of shelves. Mark midlines of first slots 4-1/2 inches on either side of centerline. Mark midlines of additional slots 9 inches on center from first two slots. Mark edges of slots 3/8-inch each side of midlines for total width of 3/4 inch.

Remove clamps. Using a square, lightly carry slot lines along panel faces all the way forward to the curved edges of shelves.

Measure along the midline of each slot and mark 1/2 the length of the midline. See patterns for templates.

Cut slots using saw and chisel or a router. Remember: half the shelves of each size are slotted from the curved edge and half from the back. See panel layout.

Finish with either warm boiled linseed oil rubbed in with clean rag; satin finish polyurethane coating in several coats; or both, allowing oil to dry thoroughly first. Or you can paint. If you paint, you may wish to leave off veneer shelf-edge trim.

MATERIALS LIST

Quantity	Description
1	4 ft. x 8 ft. plywood panel of 3/4 in. APA grademarked A-A or A-B Interior, or Medium Density Overlay (MDO)
3	4 in. x 5 in. shelf brackets and fasteners. If fastening to drywall, Molly bolts or anchor bolts are necessary for the wall connections.
50 ft. (approx.)	1 in. wide wood veneer trim. Use a light color, such as birch.
Small can	Contact cement for applying veneer
As required	Wood dough for filling voids in plywood edges
As required	Fine sandpaper for smoothing plywood cut edges
As required	Finishing materials

PANEL LAYOUT

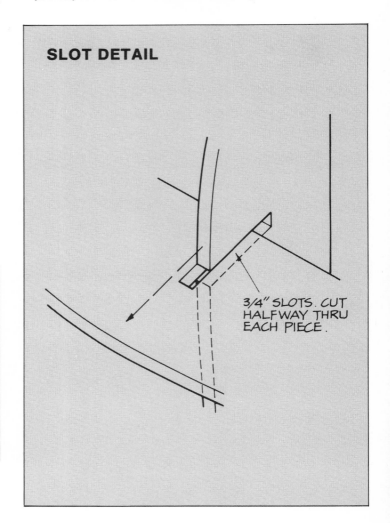

4x8 Panel of 3/4-inch Plywood

SLOT DETAIL

3/4" SLOTS. CUT HALFWAY THRU EACH PIECE.

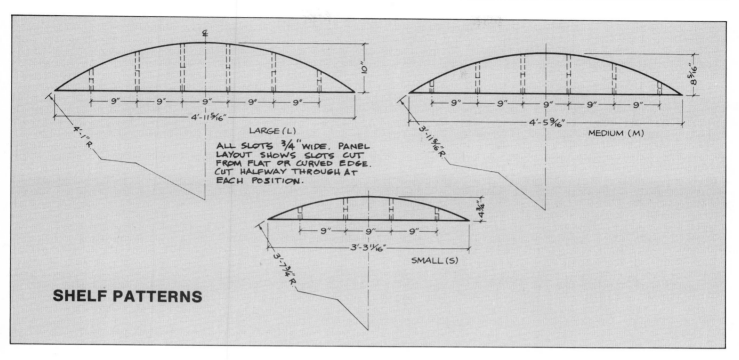

ALL SLOTS 3/4" WIDE. PANEL
LAYOUT SHOWS SLOTS CUT
FROM FLAT OR CURVED EDGE.
CUT HALFWAY THROUGH AT
EACH POSITION.

LARGE (L)

MEDIUM (M)

SMALL (S)

SHELF PATTERNS

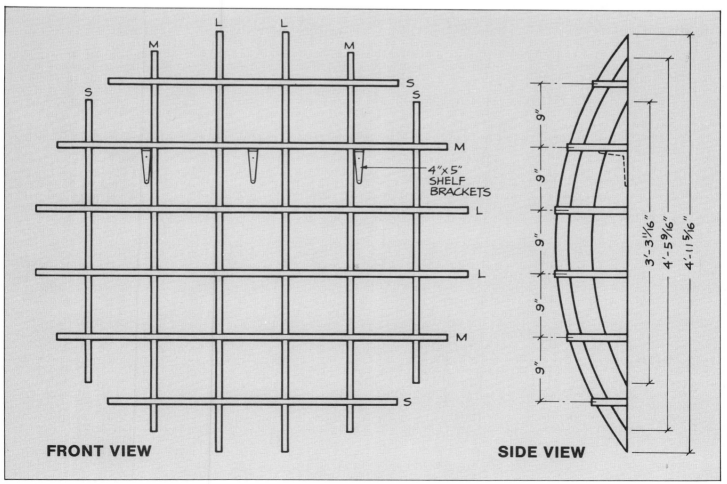

4"x5"
SHELF
BRACKETS

FRONT VIEW

SIDE VIEW

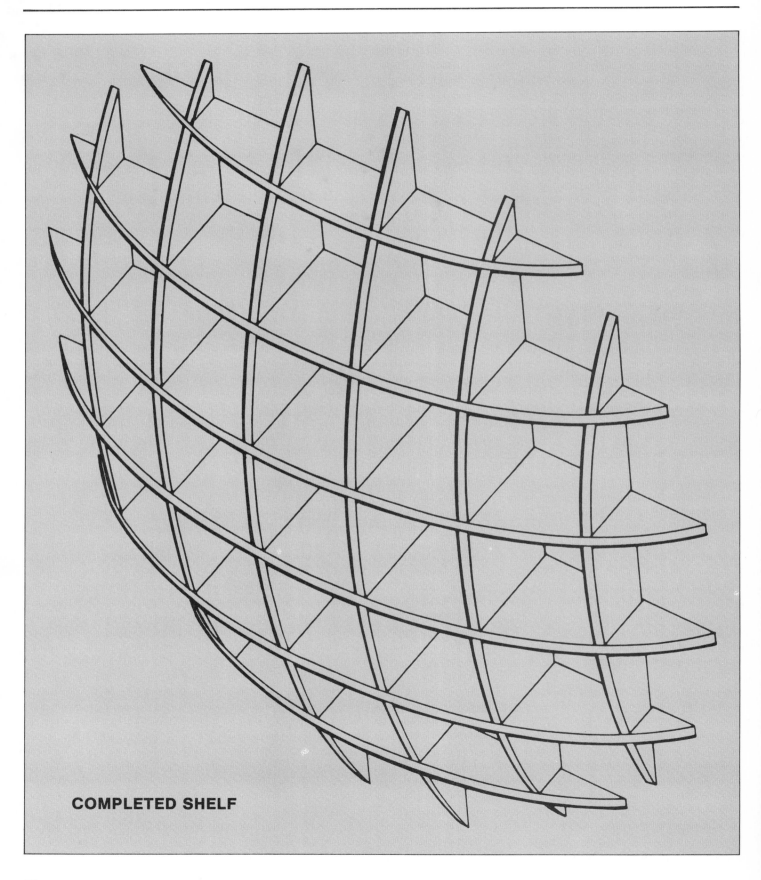

COMPLETED SHELF

Butcher Block Table

MATERIALS LIST

Quantity	Description
1	4 ft. x 8 ft. plywood panel of 3/4 in. APA grademarked A-B or A-D Exterior
2	5-1/2 in. x 33-3/8 in. plywood sheet of 3/8 in. of the same grade for drawer sides
1	5-1/2 in. x 12 in. plywood sheet of 3/8 in. of the same grade for drawer back
4	1x1s, 34 in. long, for drawer and breadboard glides
1	1x1, 10 in. long, for drawer handle. Or use standard drawer handle.
2	35-1/2 in. long continuous hinges, with screws, for drop-leaf installation
4	12 in. folding brackets, with screws, for leaf support
18 ft.	30 in. wide wood-pattern laminate for table top, sides and legs
1/2 pt. (approx.)	Contact cement for installing laminate
1	15-3/8 in. x 24 in. breadboard cut from standard 18 in. x 24 in. breadboard
2	1-1/4 in. #6 roundhead screws for drawer handle
As required	Waterproof glue for glue-nail construction
As required	2d common brads for glue-nail construction of drawer
As required	4d casing or finishing nails for glue-nail construction of table
As required	Wood dough for filling plywood edge voids and countersunk nail holes
As required	Fine sandpaper for smoothing filler and cut edges

CONSTRUCTION NOTES

Cut out pieces according to panel layout.

Because the drawer cutout becomes the drawer front, you may wish to cut all the way across the end piece at top and bottom of the drawer opening as shown in the detail. Then add 1/8 inch of spacer material, or less if needed, to replace the saw kerf when reassembling the end piece. Fill as necessary with wood dough and sand smooth.

Construct legs, then guides for drawer and breadboard, ends, sides and top as indicated in drawings. Use glue-nail construction.

Install 3/4-inch wood scraps in breadboard slots for stops. Breadboard slides into opening on end opposite of drawer.

Sand all edges smooth before applying laminate. Apply according to manufacturer's instructions.

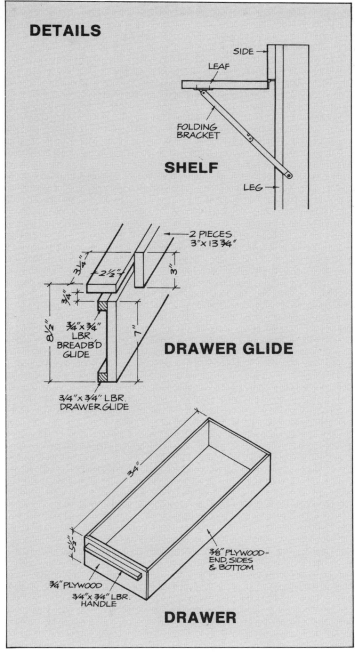

DETAILS

SIDE
LEAF
FOLDING BRACKET
SHELF
LEG

2 PIECES 3" x 13 3/4"
3/4" x 3/4" LBR. BREADB'D GLIDE
3/4" x 3/4" LBR. DRAWER GLIDE
DRAWER GLIDE

34"
3/8" PLYWOOD — END, SIDES & BOTTOM
3/4" PLYWOOD
3/4" x 3/4" LBR. HANDLE
DRAWER

TABLE FRONT DETAIL

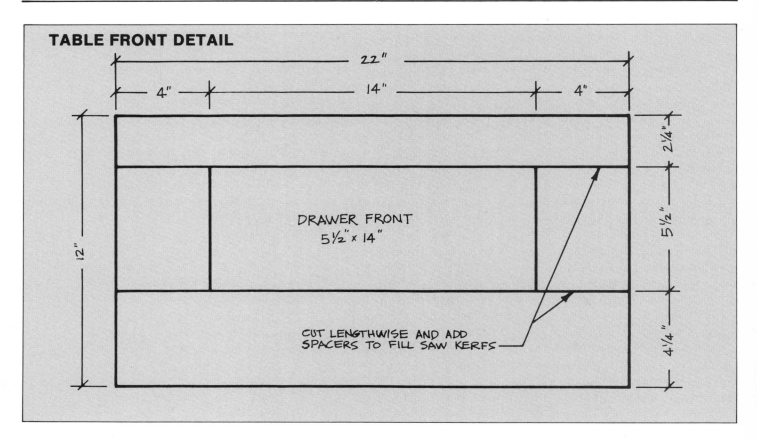

22"

4"   14"   4"

12"

2¼"

5½"

4¼"

DRAWER FRONT
5½" x 14"

CUT LENGTHWISE AND ADD
SPACERS TO FILL SAW KERFS

PANEL LAYOUT

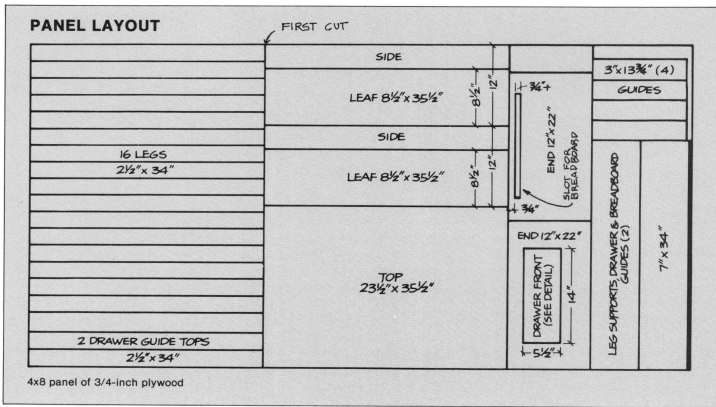

FIRST CUT

SIDE

LEAF 8½" x 35½"

12"

8½"

SIDE

LEAF 8½" x 35½"

8½"

12"

16 LEGS
2½" x 34"

3" x 13¾" (4)
GUIDES

¾"+

END 12" x 22"

SLOT FOR BREADBOARD

¾"

TOP
23½" x 35½"

END 12" x 22"

DRAWER FRONT
(SEE DETAIL)

14"

5½"

LEG SUPPORTS, DRAWER & BREADBOARD GUIDES (2)

7" x 34"

2 DRAWER GUIDE TOPS
2½" x 34"

4x8 panel of 3/4-inch plywood

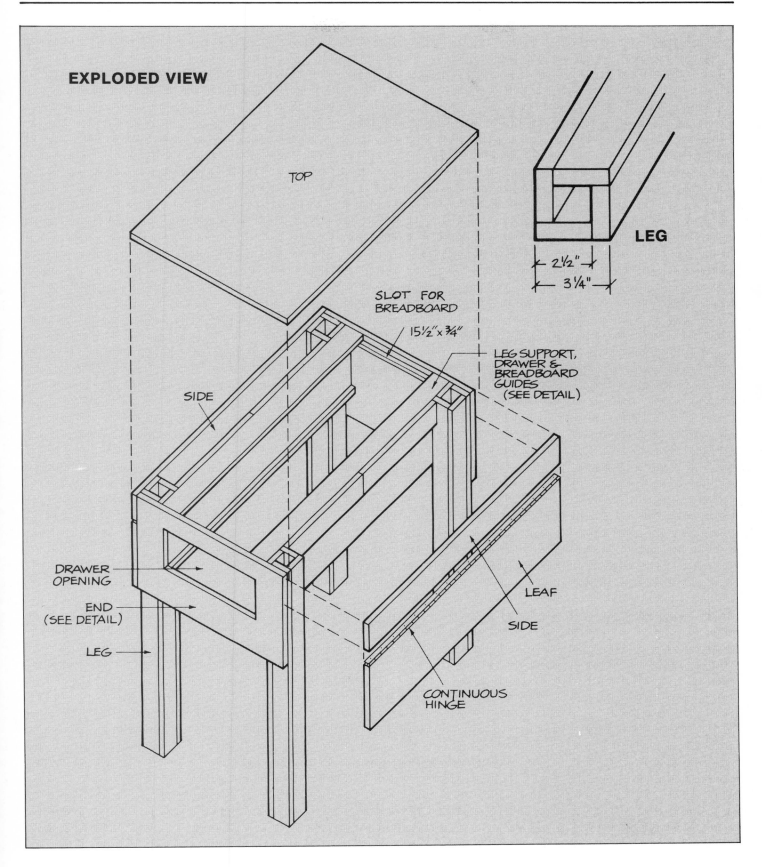

EXPLODED VIEW

TOP

LEG

2½"

3¼"

SLOT FOR
BREADBOARD

15½" x ¾"

SIDE

LEG SUPPORT,
DRAWER &
BREADBOARD
GUIDES
(SEE DETAIL)

LEAF

SIDE

DRAWER
OPENING

END
(SEE DETAIL)

LEG

CONTINUOUS
HINGE

Dihedral Table

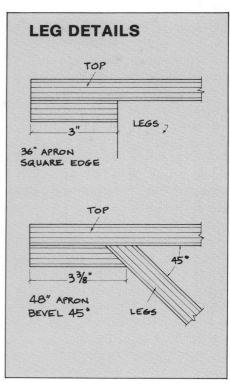

LEG DETAILS

TOP

3"

LEGS

36" APRON
SQUARE EDGE

TOP

3 3/8"

45°

48" APRON
BEVEL 45°

LEGS

MATERIALS LIST

Quantity	Description
1	4 ft. x 8 ft. plywood panel of 3/4 in. APA grademarked Medium Density Overlay (MDO), A-B or A-D Interior, or A-B or A-C Exterior
As required	3d finishing nails for glue-nailing apron to table top
As required	Urea-resin glue for glue-nail assembly of apron
As required	Wood dough or other filler for filling any voids in cut edges
As required	Fine sandpaper for smoothing edges and filler
As required	Primer and enamel for finishing

CONSTRUCTION NOTES

Lay out parts as shown in panel layout. Allow for saw kerf width when plotting dimensions.

Cut out parts.

Cut out 3/4-inch slots in legs as shown in panel layout. A saber saw will make this task simple.

Bevel top ends of legs to 45°.

Bevel inside edge of 48-inch apron pieces to 45°.

Glue-nail apron to table bottom. Space nails 6 to 8 inches apart in staggered rows along edges of apron pieces. Place nails far enough from inside edge so they do not interfere with leg space. Be sure to slant beveled sides of 48-inch apron pieces as shown in detail.

Paint pieces as desired.

Assemble by locking legs together and placing top on. Lock table together by sliding legs into apron bevel.

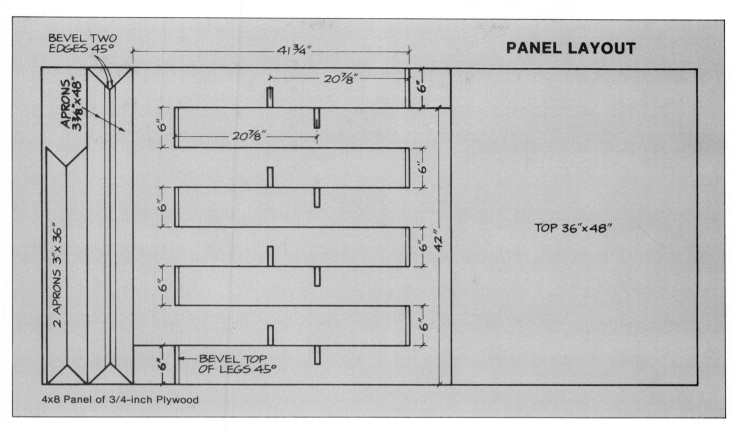

PANEL LAYOUT

BEVEL TWO EDGES 45°

41¾"

20⅞"

6"

APRONS 3⅜"×48"

6"

20⅞"

6"

2 APRONS 3"×36"

6"

6"

42"

TOP 36"×48"

6"

6"

6"

6"

BEVEL TOP OF LEGS 45°

4x8 Panel of 3/4-inch Plywood

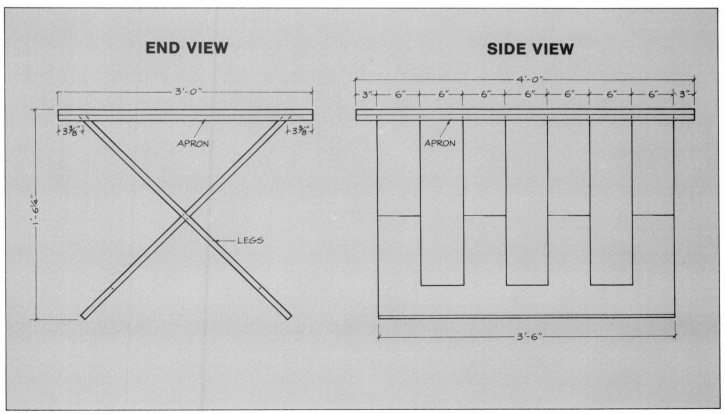

END VIEW

3'-0"

3⅜"

APRON

3⅜"

1'-6¼"

LEGS

SIDE VIEW

4'-0"

3" 6" 6" 6" 6" 6" 6" 6" 3"

APRON

3'-6"

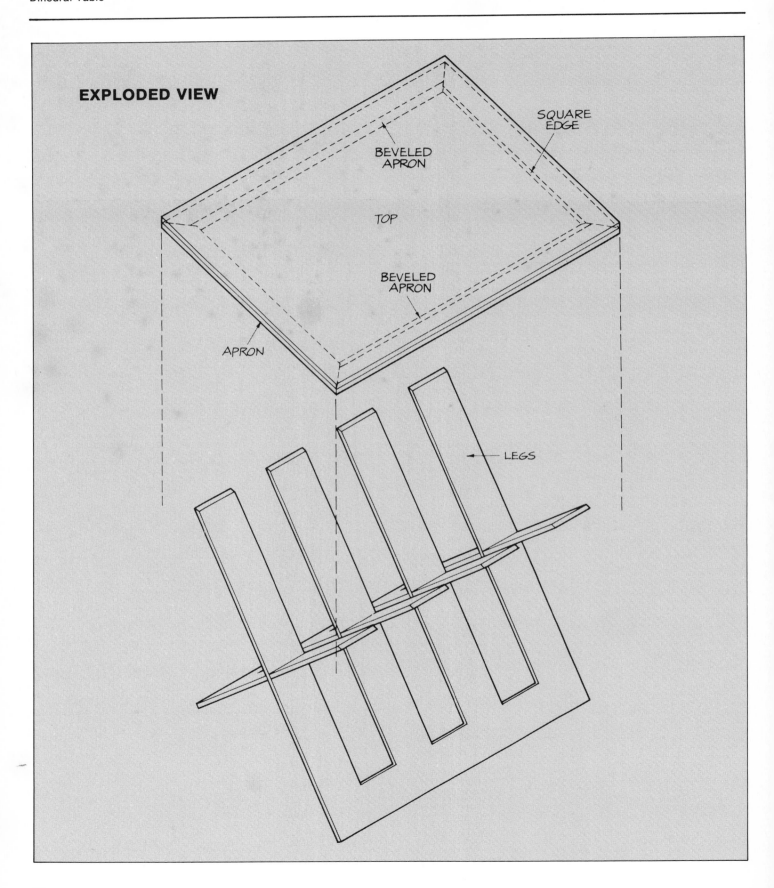

EXPLODED VIEW

SQUARE EDGE

BEVELED APRON

TOP

BEVELED APRON

APRON

LEGS

Bird House

CONSTRUCTION NOTES

From 3/8 inch plywood, cut 4 pieces 7-15/16 inches by 7-15/16 inches. These pieces are the front and back, parts F and F-1, and the bottom sides, parts B and B-1, in the cutting diagram.

Drill entrance hole to accommodate type of bird desired:

House Wren	7/8 in. dia.
Bewick Wren	
Carolina Wren	1-1/8 in. dia.
Chickadee	
Tufted Titmouse	1-1/2 in. dia.
White Breasted Nuthatch	
Bluebird	1-1/2 in. dia.
Swallow	

Cut one top piece 9-1/2 inches by 7-15/16 inches, part T.

Cut the other top piece 10-1/2 inches by 7-15/16 inches, part T-1.

From 3/4 inch wood cut four 6-3/16-inch wood strips.

Glue-nail 3/4-inch wood strips to parts B and B-1. Set them flush with the edge as shown in the plans.

Position remaining wood strip as illustrated on part T and glue-nail in place.

Glue-nail part B-1 to part B.

Fasten front and back, parts F and F-1, to parts B and B-1 with 3/4 inch wood screws.

Glue-nail top T in place.

Glue-nail top T-1 in place. Nail through T-1 into wood strips attached to top T and bottom B-1.

Drill 1/8-inch hole for hanging.

Finish as desired.

MATERIALS LIST

Quantity	Description
1	16 in. x 32 in. plywood panel of 3/8 in. APA grademarked A-C or B-C Exterior, or Medium Density Overlay (MDO)
2-1/2 linear ft	3/4 in. x 3/4 in. board to cut for nailing strips
32 (approx.)	2d galvanized nails
8	1 in. #8 flathead wood screws
As required	White glue for wood strips
As required	Hanging wire

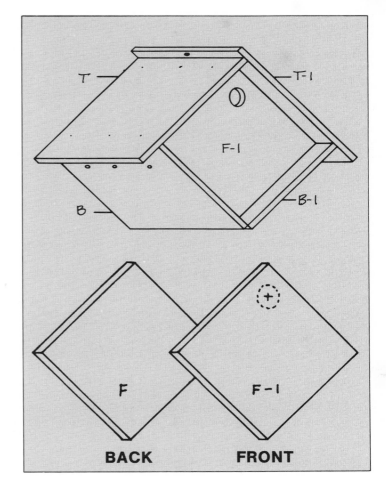

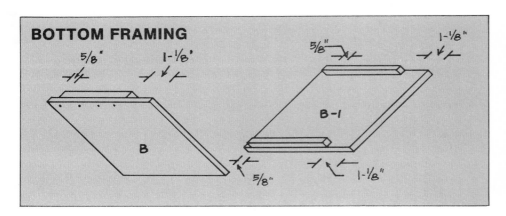

BOTTOM FRAMING

5/8" 1-1/8'

B

5/8" 1-1/8"

B-1

5/8" 1-1/8"

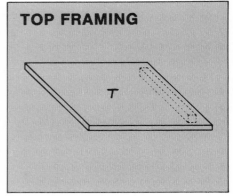

TOP FRAMING

T

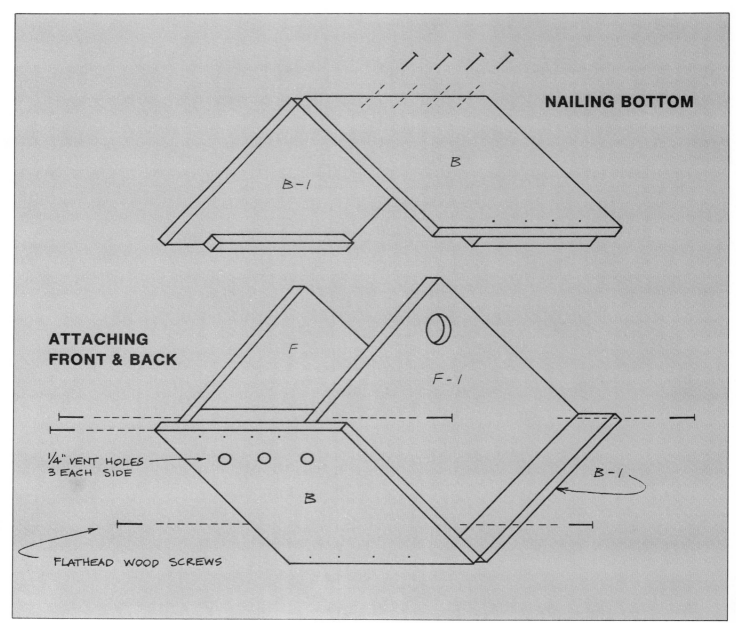

NAILING BOTTOM

B-1

B

**ATTACHING
FRONT & BACK**

F

F-1

1/4" VENT HOLES
3 EACH SIDE

B

B-1

FLATHEAD WOOD SCREWS

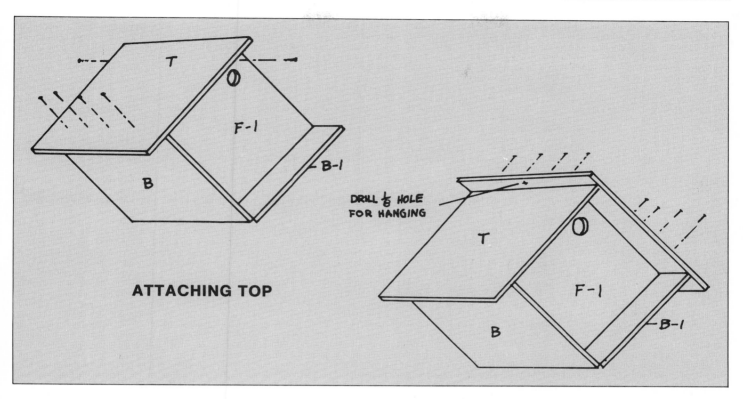

ATTACHING TOP

DRILL ⅛ HOLE FOR HANGING

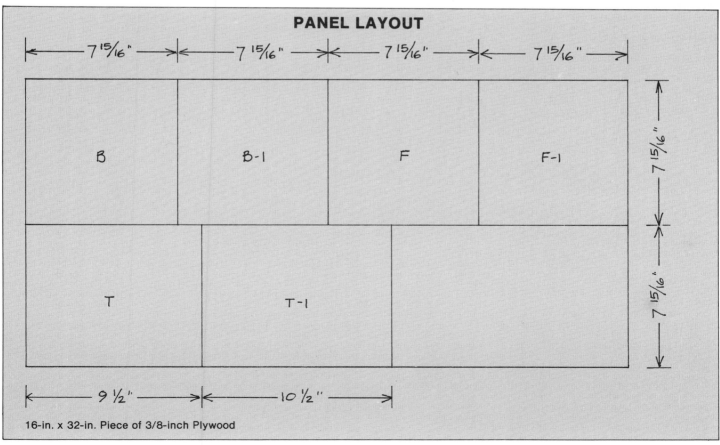

PANEL LAYOUT

16-in. x 32-in. Piece of 3/8-inch Plywood

Slot-Together Patio Chairs

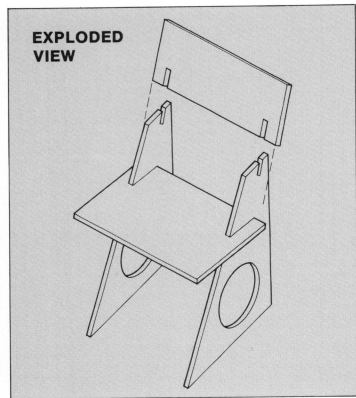

EXPLODED VIEW

MATERIALS LIST

Quantity	Description
1	4 ft. x 8 ft. plywood panel of 3/4 in. APA grademarked Medium Density Overlay (MDO), or A-B or A-C Exterior. Makes 4 chairs
As required	Wood dough or other filler for filling cut-edge voids
As required	Fine sandpaper for smoothing plywood cut and filled edges
As required	Exterior primer and paint

CONSTRUCTION NOTES

Cut out parts according to plans. Be sure to allow for the saw kerf width.

Round all corners to eliminate sharp corners. Fill all edge voids with wood dough and sand smooth.

Circular cutouts shown in plans are optional. They are included for appearance and to reduce weight slightly. Cutouts may be the shape of your choice. Be sure no cutout is closer to any cut edge than 2-1/2 inches.

Fit pieces together to check fit. Take apart and finish as desired.

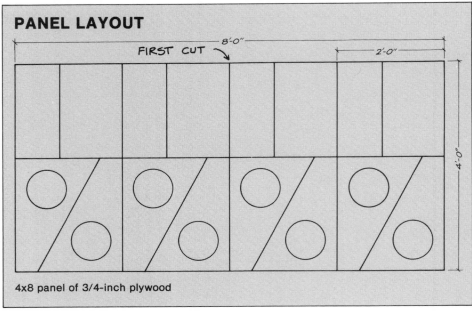

PANEL LAYOUT

FIRST CUT

8'-0"

2'-0"

4'-0"

4x8 panel of 3/4-inch plywood

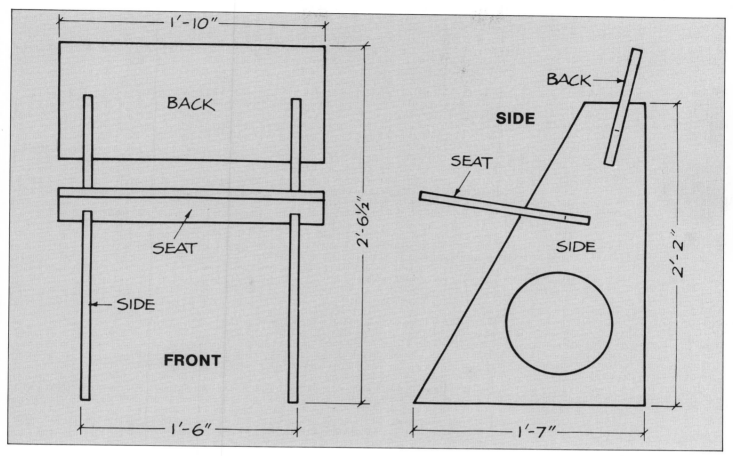

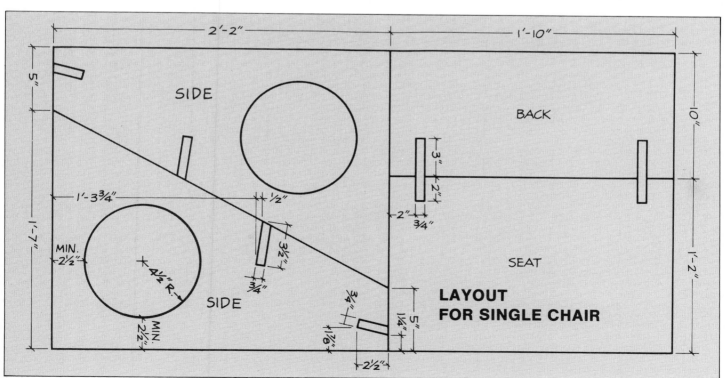

Patio Side Cart

MATERIALS LIST

Quantity	Description
1	4 ft. x 8 ft. plywood panel of 5/8 in. APA gra-demarked A-B, A-C or B-C Exterior, or Medium Density Overlay (MDO)
1	1/4 in. diameter steel rod, 20-1/2 in. long, for axle. Drill 1/8 in. diameter holes through, 1/4 in. from ends
2	Cotter pins to fit 1/8-inch holes
4	1-1/2 in washers with 1/4 in. holes for wheel protection
2	1 in. x 1/8 in. angle iron for wheel stops with sawn and filed axle width slots, as shown in plan
2	Axle straps or cable clamps, with screws
8	1-1/2 in. (3 in. overall length) angles with screws, for bracing bottom-shelf assembly
As required	4d finishing nails for glue-nail assembly
As required	Waterproof glue for glue-nail assembly
As required	Wood dough or other filler for countersunk nail holes
As required	Fine sandpaper
As required	Exterior primer and paint

CONSTRUCTION NOTES

Lay out all parts on plywood panel. Use a compass or cardboard template to draw curved corners. Center saw on layout lines to equalize saw kerf width on all parts.

Fill all voids in exposed edges with wood dough and sand smooth.

Screw 4 corner braces to bottom to support sides as shown in exploded view.

Screw corner braces to bottom backing strips. Make sure they are high enough so they will not interfere with corner braces on bottom when backing strips are put in place.

Sides can be prepared for shelves by routing 5/8-inch grooves 5/16 inch deep. If a router is not available, shelves can be supported by 1x1 wood strips or molding as shown in the details.

Glue-nail backing strips to bottom.

Attach sides to bottom and backing strips using corner braces and glue-nailing joints. Countersink all nails.

Attach shelves working from bottom up. Glue-nail all joints for extra strength. Countersink all nails.

Attach wheels as shown in detail. Glue-nail legs in place.

Fill all nail holes and sand smooth.

Finish as desired with exterior paint.

PANEL LAYOUT

4 BACKING STRIPS 3"x4'

TOP 6"x4'

UPPER SHELF 6"x4'

WORKING SURFACE 1'-6"x4'

BOTTOM 1'-6"x4'

3⅛"   3⅛"

6"

6" — 6⅜"   6"—|—6"

8¼6"R.

2 SHELF SUPPORTS

3¼"R. WHEEL

1¼" FEET (2)

3¼"R. WHEEL

9"R. SHELF

1'-11⅝"

SIDE 1'-6"x4'

SIDE 1'-6"x4'

SHELF 9"R.

3⅛"   3⅛"

DOTTED LINES REPRESENT ROUTING 5/8"x 5/16" DEEP.

4x8 Panel of 5/8-inch Plywood

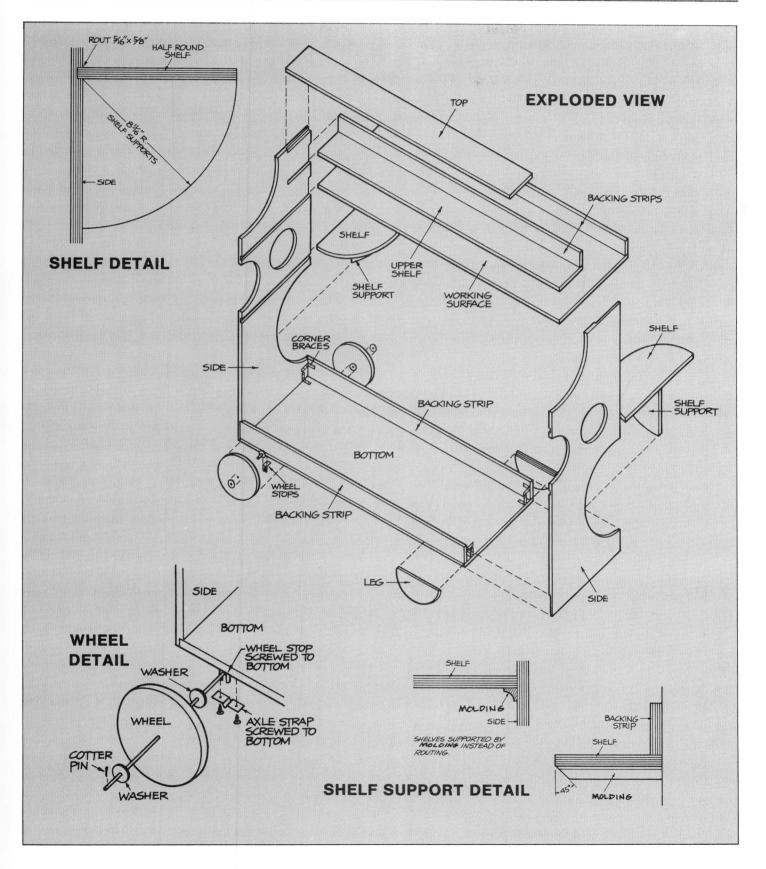

ROUT 5/16" x 5/8" HALF ROUND SHELF

8½" R SHELF SUPPORTS

SIDE

SHELF DETAIL

EXPLODED VIEW

TOP

BACKING STRIPS

SHELF

UPPER SHELF

SHELF SUPPORT

WORKING SURFACE

SHELF

SIDE

CORNER BRACES

SHELF SUPPORT

BACKING STRIP

BOTTOM

WHEEL STOPS

BACKING STRIP

LEG

SIDE

SIDE

BOTTOM

WHEEL DETAIL

WASHER

WHEEL STOP SCREWED TO BOTTOM

WHEEL

AXLE STRAP SCREWED TO BOTTOM

COTTER PIN

WASHER

SHELF

MOLDING

SIDE

SHELVES SUPPORTED BY *MOLDING* INSTEAD OF ROUTING.

BACKING STRIP

SHELF

45°

MOLDING

SHELF SUPPORT DETAIL

Whale Rocker & Desk

MATERIALS LIST

Quantity	Description
1	4 ft. x 4 ft. plywood panel of 1/2 in. APA grademarked A-B Interior, A-B or A-C Exterior, or Medium Density Overlay (MDO)
1	3/4 in x 3/4 in board, 5 ft. long, for seat supports
30	1-1/2 in. #8 flathead wood screws for installing Parts C, D, E and assembly J-K
6	6d casing or finishing nails for assembling steering wheel
As required	White glue for assembly
As required	Wood dough for filling any small voids in plywood edges
As required	Fine sandpaper for smoothing edges and cured wood dough
As required	Primer and paint

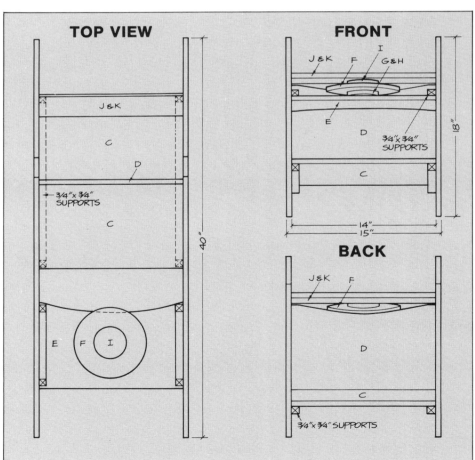

CONSTRUCTION NOTES

Draw whale parts on plywood. To draw whale sides, lightly pencil in a grid of 2-inch squares on the plywood. Then draw the outline on the grid, following the scale guide given in the plan.

Cut out parts with a saber saw or jigsaw. To make cutting of like parts more accurate, rough-cut the areas of Parts A and B, clamp them together, then cut them simultaneously. Do the same with Parts D and E. Be sure the saw cuts the same on all layout lines to equalize saw kerf on all parts.

Glue parts J and K together, following glue manufacturer's instructions. Clamp and let dry. Sand any rough edges.

Sand all exposed plywood cut edges. Fill any voids in the edges with wood dough, allow to dry, and sand smooth.

Apply glue to Parts F, G, H and I. Assemble steering assembly, nailing together with equally spaced nails.

Mount steering assembly on Part E using glue and nails.

Glue-nail 3/4 x 3/4-inch supports in place on Parts C and E as shown in the support detail and in the top and end views. Note that when the whale sits right-side-up, supports will be on top of Part E and underneath Part C (the seat). But when the whale is turned over to function as a desk, Part E will become the seat and will then be supported from beneath.

Glue and screw Parts C, D, E and J-K into position between Parts A and B. Drill pilot holes for the screws first. Locations are shown by dotted lines on the panel layout grid diagram. In the case of Parts C and E, run the screws into the support pieces rather than the plywood edges.

Paint whale with non-toxic primer and enamel, vinyl lacquer, or equivalent.

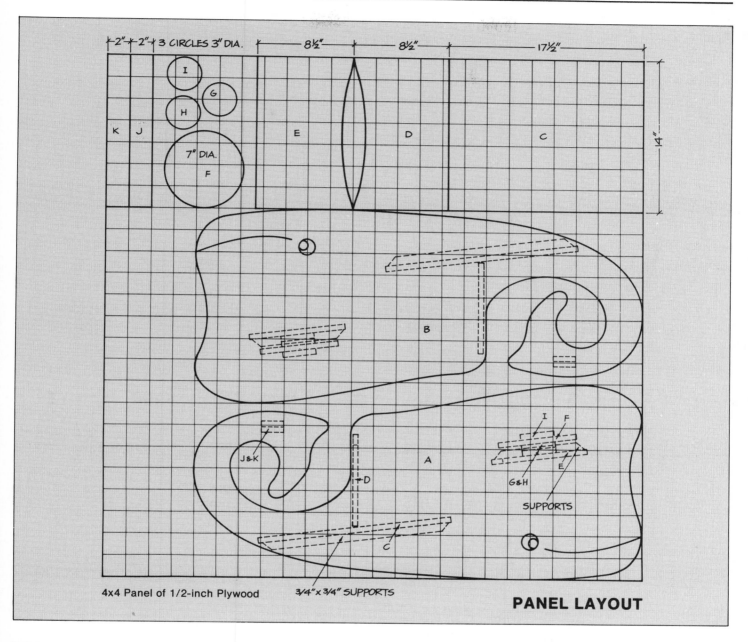

4x4 Panel of 1/2-inch Plywood

3/4"x 3/4" SUPPORTS

PANEL LAYOUT

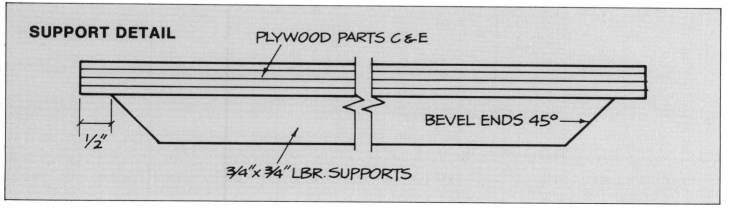

SUPPORT DETAIL

PLYWOOD PARTS C & E

BEVEL ENDS 45°

1/2"

3/4" x 3/4" LBR. SUPPORTS

EXPLODED VIEW

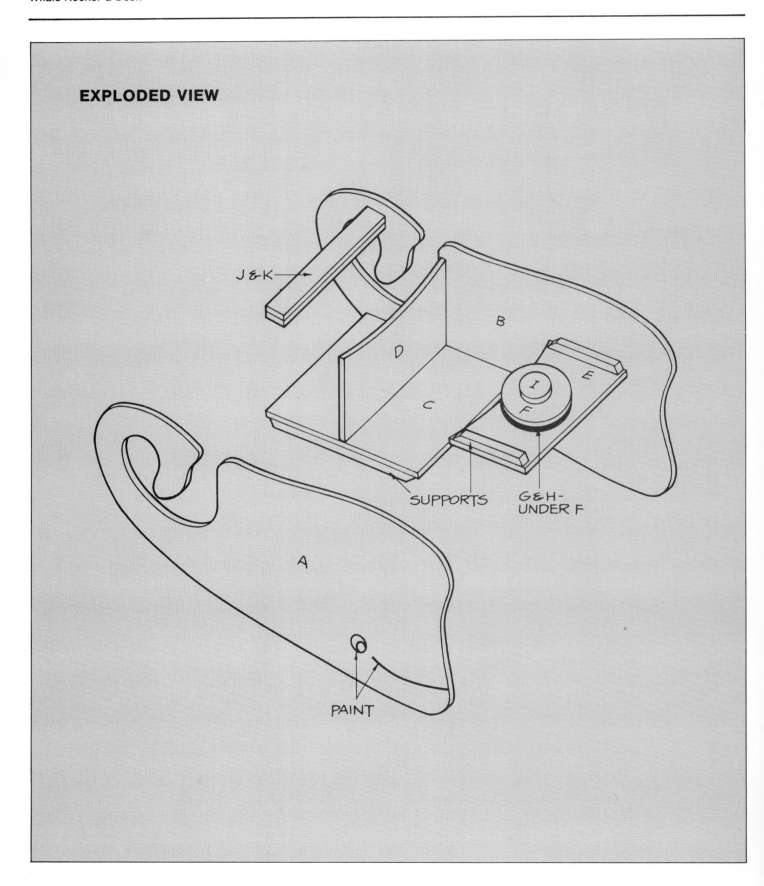

J & K

B

D

C

I

E

F

SUPPORTS

G & H -
UNDER F

A

PAINT

Truck Toybox

CONSTRUCTION NOTES

Lay out parts as shown in cutting diagram. Dimensions are finished sizes. Allow for saw kerf width when measuring.

Cut out parts. Make cut along box sides and chassis rails first. Mark parts for easy identification.

Lay out chassis rails A as shown in detail. Use a 6-5/8-inch radius for curves to hold wheels. Cut out one part A and use it to lay out second part. After cutting, clamp together and smooth both parts A so they will be equal. Drill holes for axles while parts A are clamped together.

Glue-screw chassis front B and back B to rails A to form chassis.

Glue-nail 25-3/8-inch 1x1s side rails to chassis as shown in exploded view on page 65.

Cut six wheels and two wheel spacers from 2x10 board. Glue two wheels together to form rear wheels. Glue wheel spacer to another wheel to form front wheels and clamp until glue dries. Drill 7/8-inch hole for axle through both parts while clamped.

Paint wheels as desired.

Cut out wheel covers and paint as desired.

Attach wheels to chassis with dowel axles. Glue wheel covers in place.

Cut out fenders, headlights and grill from 1x10.

Paint fenders, headlights and grill, and 2x4 bumper as desired.

Glue-screw parts F, H, I, J and K together to form cab. Attach cab top G with continuous hinge. Attach window trim if desired.

Paint cab. When dry, glue fenders, headlights, grill and bumper in place.

Glue-screw box sides C, ends D and bottom E to form box. Paint as desired.

Cut and paint trim as desired for box.

Glue trim as shown.

Glue box and cab to chassis.

Touch up screw heads after assembly.

Fuel tanks in photo are optional. They were cut from a cardboard tube, ends covered, and painted.

MATERIALS LIST

Quantity	Description
1	4 ft. x 8 ft. plywood panel of 3/4 in. APA gra-demarked A-B or A-D Interior or Medium Density Overlaid (MDO)
1	7/8 in. diameter dowel, 36 in. long. Cut front axle 17-1/2 in. long, rear axle 17 in. long.
2	1x1s, 25-3/8 in. long, for chassis side rails
1	2x10, 6 ft. long. Cut into 6 wheels and 2 front wheel spacers.
1	1/4 in. x 12 in. x 12 in. scrap plywood for wheel covers
1	2x4, 18 in. long, for bumper
1	1x10, 36 in. long. Cut into fenders, headlights and grill
10	1x1s, 9-1/2 in. long, for box vertical trim
2	1x1s, 16-1/2-in. long for front & back horizontal trim. Cut to fit.
2	1x1s, 24-1/2 in. long, for horizontal side trim. Cut to fit.
4	13-1/2 in. long 2x2s for outside corner molding on box. Cut to fit and cut away 3/4 in. x 3/4 in. corner in each.
2	1x2s, 28 in. long, mitered 45 degrees as shown in exploded view for box-top molding.
4	1x2s, 20 in. long, mitered 45 degrees as shown in exploded view for box-top & box-bottom molding
2	1x2s, 28 in. long, mitered 45 degrees as shown in exploded view for box-bottom molding
1	Continuous hinge, 18 in. long, for cab top
1	1/4 in. x 3/4 in. x 48 in. trim. Cut to fit for 3 sides of cab top
2 (optional)	8 in. x 10 in. sheets of Plexiglas, or equivalent, for side windows. Cut to dimensions
1 (optional)	8 in. x 17 in. sheet of Plexiglass or equivalent for windshield. Cut to dimensions
10 linear ft. (optional)	5/4 in. outside corner molding for framing windows. Cut to dimensions shown in detail. Cut lengths to size for windows.
170 (approx.)	1-1/2 in. #8 flathead wood screws for glue-screw assembly
As required	2d finishing nails for glue-nail assembly of trim and molding
20	1/2 in. #8 panhead sheet metal screws for attaching wheel covers
4	1/4 in. diameter hex-head lag screws, 1-1/2 in. long, for attaching wheels to axles
As required	White glue for glue-screw assembly of all joints
As required	Fine sandpaper for smoothing plywood cut edges
As required	Wood dough, if desired, for filling any edge voids
As required	Finishing materials. Pictured toybox used black, red and white gloss enamel

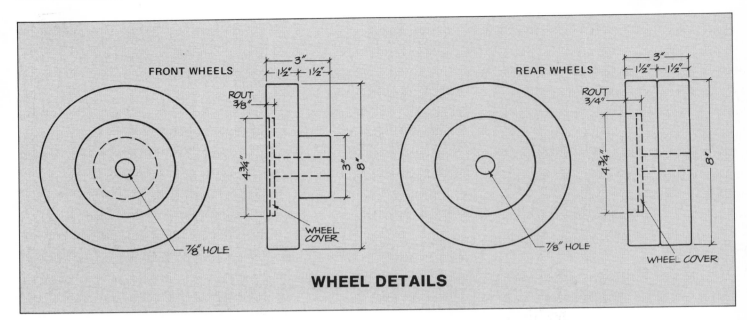

WHEEL DETAILS

PANEL LAYOUT

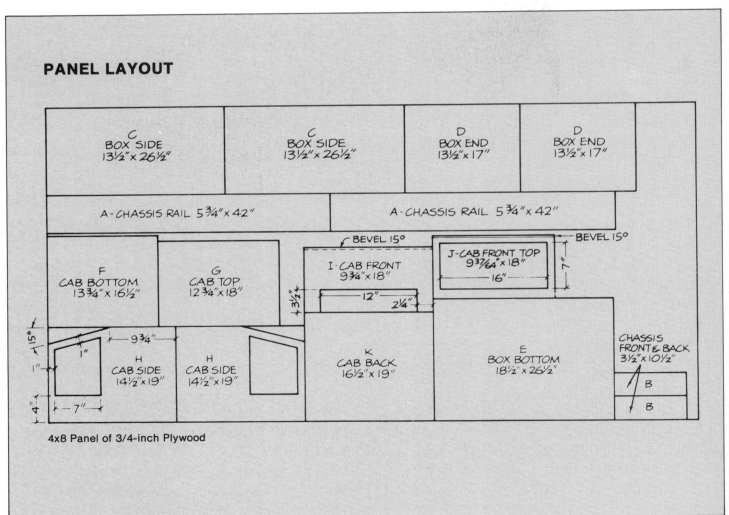

4x8 Panel of 3/4-inch Plywood

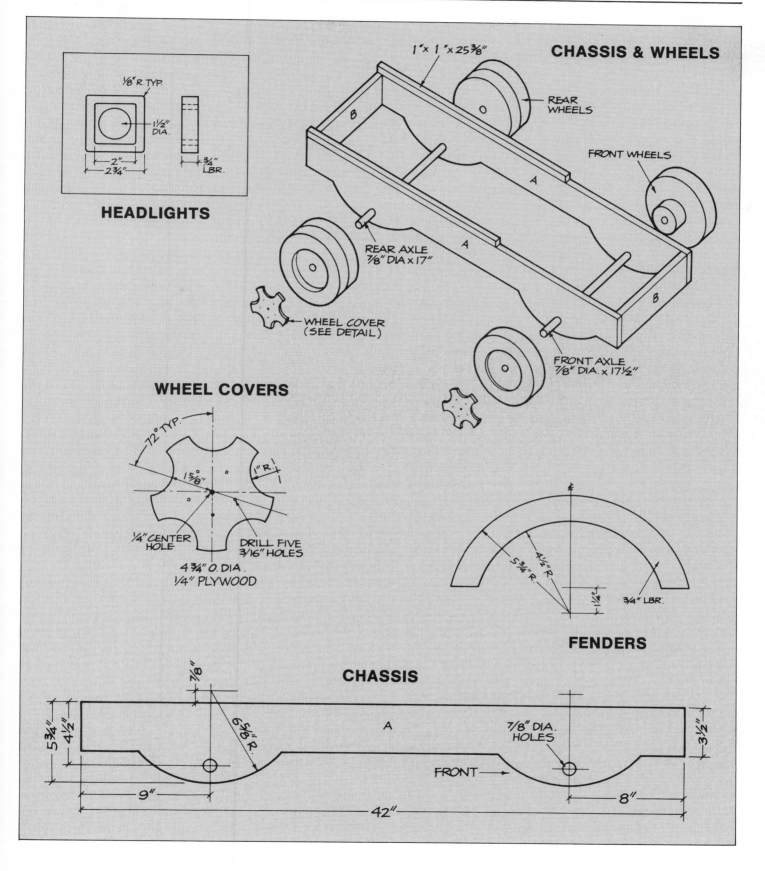

HEADLIGHTS

1/8" R. TYP.

1 1/2" DIA.

2"
2 3/4"

3/4" LBR.

CHASSIS & WHEELS

1" x 1" x 25 3/8"

B

REAR WHEELS

FRONT WHEELS

A

A

REAR AXLE 7/8" DIA x 17"

WHEEL COVER (SEE DETAIL)

B

FRONT AXLE 7/8" DIA. x 17 1/2"

WHEEL COVERS

72° TYP.

1" R.

1 5/8"

1/4" CENTER HOLE

DRILL FIVE 3/16" HOLES

4 3/4" O. DIA. 1/4" PLYWOOD

4 1/2" R.

5 3/4" R.

1/4"

3/4" LBR.

FENDERS

CHASSIS

7/8"

5 3/4"
4 1/2"

6 5/8" R.

A

7/8" DIA. HOLES

3 1/2"

FRONT →

9"

8"

42"

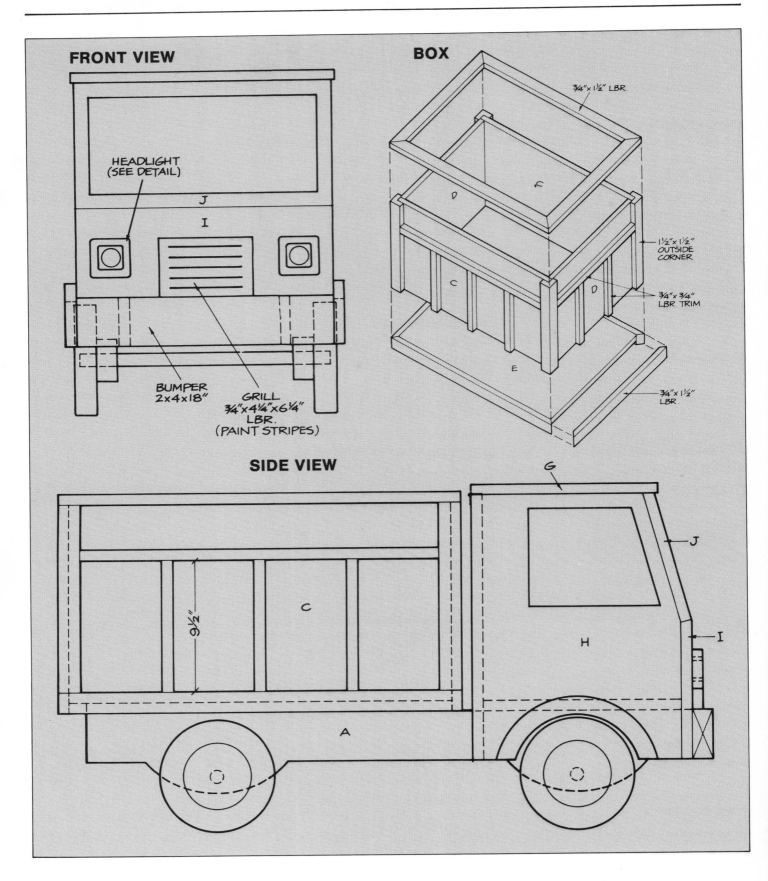

FRONT VIEW

HEADLIGHT
(SEE DETAIL)

J

I

BUMPER
2x4x18"

GRILL
3/4"x4 1/4"x6 1/4"
LBR.
(PAINT STRIPES)

BOX

3/4"x1 1/2" LBR.

F

D

1 1/2"x1 1/2"
OUTSIDE
CORNER

C

D

3/4"x 3/4"
LBR. TRIM

E

3/4"x1 1/2"
LBR.

SIDE VIEW

G

J

9 1/2"

C

H

I

A

CAB

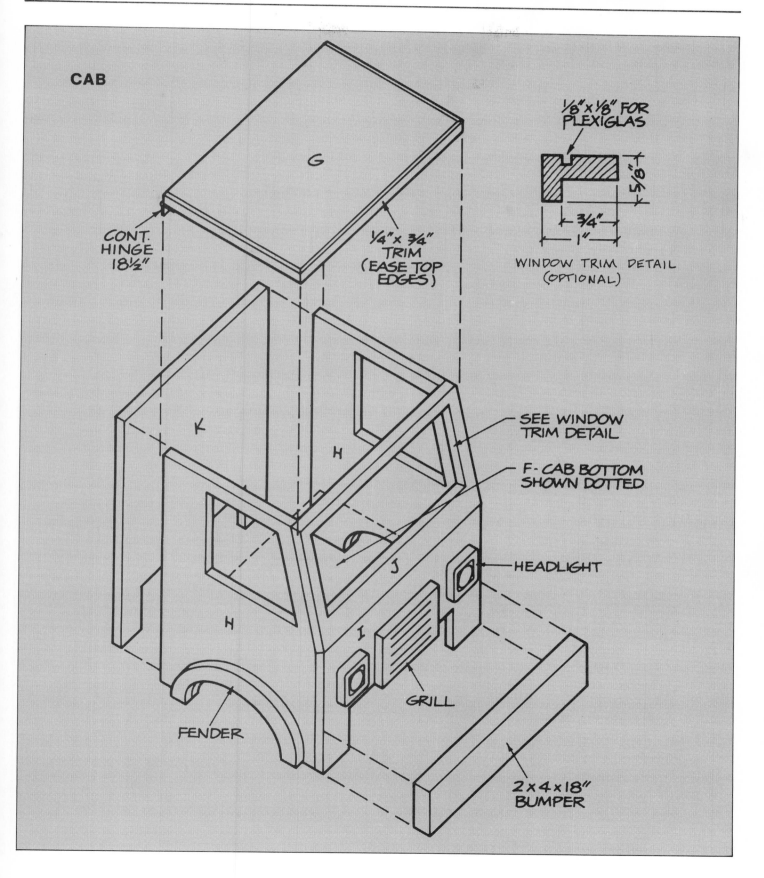

CONT. HINGE 18½"

G

¼" × ¾" TRIM (EASE TOP EDGES)

⅛"×⅛" FOR PLEXIGLAS

5/8"

¾"

1"

WINDOW TRIM DETAIL (OPTIONAL)

SEE WINDOW TRIM DETAIL

F· CAB BOTTOM SHOWN DOTTED

HEADLIGHT

K

H

J

H

I

GRILL

FENDER

2×4×18" BUMPER

Potter's Kick Wheel

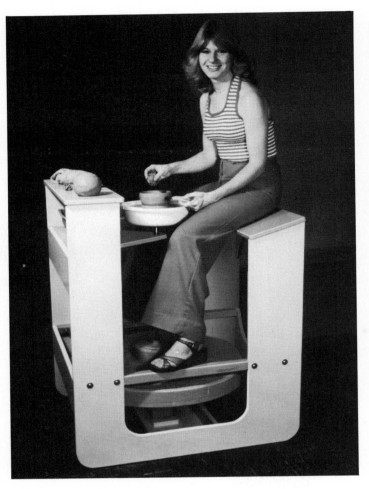

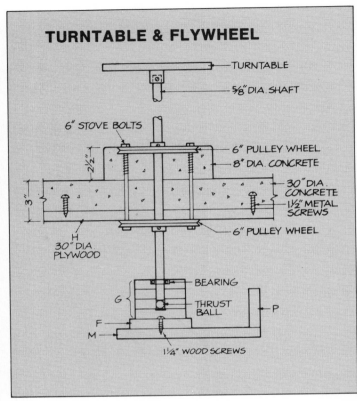

TURNTABLE & FLYWHEEL

- TURNTABLE
- 5/8" DIA. SHAFT
- 6" STOVE BOLTS
- 6" PULLEY WHEEL
- 8" DIA. CONCRETE
- 30" DIA. CONCRETE
- 1½" METAL SCREWS
- 6" PULLEY WHEEL
- 30" DIA PLYWOOD
- BEARING
- THRUST BALL
- 1¼" WOOD SCREWS

MATERIALS LIST

Quantity	Description
1	4 ft. x 8 ft. plywood panel of 3/4 in. APA grademarked A-B or A-D Interior, A-B or A-C Exterior, or Medium Density Overlay (MDO)
1 bag	1 cu. ft. concrete mix for wheel
8 linear ft.	3 in. wide aluminum flashing, or equivalent, for wheel form
60 to 70	1-/2 in. #8 flathead wood screws for glue-screw assembly
8	1-1/2 in. #10 sheet metal screws to attach wheelbase and concrete tie
2	1/4 in. diameter stove bolts, 6 in. long with washers, for pulley and kick wheel assembly
2	1/4 in. diameter lag bolts, 3-1/2 in. long with washers, for bearing-block assembly

Quantity	Description
8	1/4 in. diameter stove bolts, 2 in. long with washers, for attaching footrests
1	5/8 in. diameter thrust ball
1	5/8 in. diameter metal disc for thrust-ball mount
2	5/8 in. flanged ball bearings (Cat. No. 4x728, W.W. Grainger Co., 5959 W. Howard St., Chicago, IL 60648, or equivalent)
2	6 in. diameter pulley wheels (Cat. No. 3x919, W.W. Grainger Co., or equivalent)
1	5/8 in. diameter steel line shaft, 36 in. long (Sears Cat. No. 9H 2830C, cut to length)
1	8 in. sanding disc for throwing head (Cat. No. AD85-C13, Silvo Hardware Co., 1019 Walnut St., Philadelphia, PA 19106, or equivalent)

Quantity	Description
1 (optional)	Plastic wash basin with 5/8-inch collar to act as a splash quard
As required	Waterproof glue for glue-screw assembly
As required	Wood dough or other filler for filling countersunk screw holes and voids in plywood edges
As required	Fine sandpaper for smoothing plywood edges and filler
As required	Exterior primer and enamel for finishing

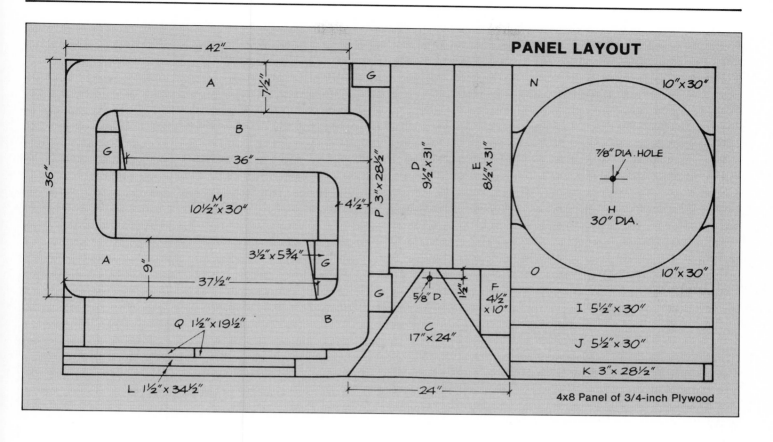

PANEL LAYOUT

4x8 Panel of 3/4-inch Plywood

CONSTRUCTION NOTES

Draw all parts on plywood according to measurements given.

Cut out parts. Be sure to center saw blade on layout lines to equalize the kerf width on all parts.

If desired, the angle and height of seat can be modified prior to construction to suit user.

Draw an 11-inch diameter circle centered on the wheel base (part H) and mark location for the 8 equally spaced sheet metal screws. Drive screws into plywood to a depth of 5/8 inches Remainder protruding from the wood will permanently anchor concrete to wheel base.

Cast the flywheel with the following steps:

Drill pulley wheels for 6-inch stove bolts. See turntable/flywheel detail.

Set wheelbase level on three bricks or 2x4s on edge. Insert shaft through wheelbase to floor. Be sure it is well greased to prevent concrete from sticking. Slide upper pulley wheel on shaft and let rest on wheelbase.

Align shaft exactly perpendicular to the wheelbase and brace securely.

Space pulleys on shaft using set screws. They should be set 5-1/4 inches apart measured centerline to centerline with bottom pulley flush beneath wheelbase. Install stove bolts.

Tack concrete form made of flashing to wheelbase around its perimeter and fill with 2-inch depth of concrete.

Center another piece of flashing in an 8-inch diameter circle around the shaft and on top of the wheelbase concrete. Push into wheelbase concrete about 1/16 inch.

Pour 2-1/2 inches deep for hub. Hub concrete will nearly cover the upper pulley wheel.

Loosen pulley wheel set screws and make sure shaft will turn as concrete begins to set.

As concrete sets, remove flashing and round top edges of concrete using trowel.

Glue-screw plywood unit together as shown in drawings. Finish as desired with enamel.

Mount kick wheel/throwing head assembly. Place shaft through bearing in part C and align the shaft plumb by moving bearing block assembly. Attach bearing block assembly to base M with 1-1/4-inch wood screws. Set kick wheel to correct height on shaft and lock in place with set screws. It may be desirable to make indentations with a drill on shaft at appropriate locations for kick wheel set screws to increase their holding power.

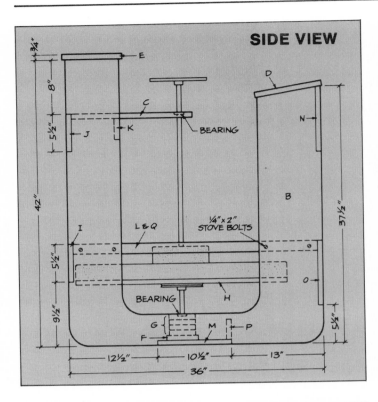

SIDE VIEW

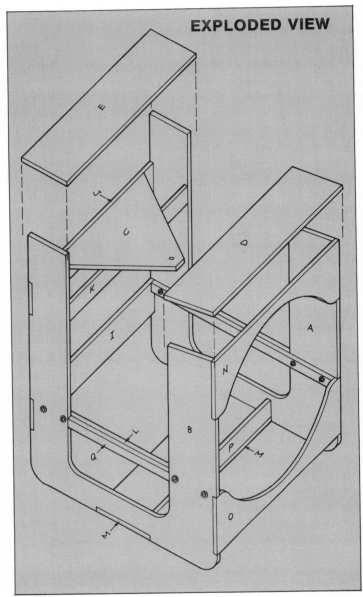

EXPLODED VIEW

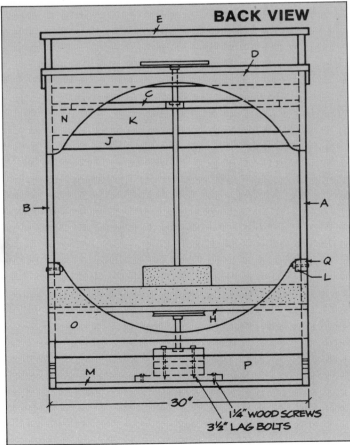

BACK VIEW

Sketch Bench

MATERIALS LIST

Quantity	Description
1	4 ft. x 8 ft. plywood panel of 1/2 in. APA grademarked A-B Interior, A-C Exterior, or Medium Density Overlay (MDO)
1	4 ft. x 8 ft. plywood panel of 3/4 in. of the same grade
2	2x4s, 72-1/2 in. long
2	2x4s, 46-1/2 in. long
4	2x4s, 13-1/2 in. long
5	2x2s, 15 in. long
1	3 ft. x 4 ft. chalkboard, available from school supply or stationery outlets
1	72 in. x 18 in. corkboard
3	1/8 in. x 1 in. x 2-1/4 in. metal strips for drawer catches
6	1/16 in. x 1 in. x 16-1/4 in. plastic laminate strips for drawer slides
4	3-1/2 in. #12 wood screws for fastening vertical 2x4 framing to bench
8	2 in. #8 wood screws for fastening vertical 2x4 framing to upper back of plywood and to chalkboard frame
3	1 in. wood screws for fastening metal drawer catches
As required	8d finishing nails
As required	White or urea-resin glue
As required	Wood dough or synthetic filler
As required	Fine sandpaper
As required	Top-quality latex paint

CONSTRUCTION NOTES

Glue and nail 2x4 base frame together for bench.

Lay out panels for cut as shown in the cutting diagram. Use a straight edge and carpenter's square for accuracy. Allow for saw kerf width when plotting dimensions. Mark each piece with its name to avoid confusion.

Cut out pieces and true edges with a sanding block.

Fill and smooth all exposed edges.

Nail bottom to base frame.

Glue-nail lower back, two dividers and sides to base frame.

Glue-nail 2x2s into place as shown in plans.

Glue plastic laminate drawer slides into place.

Glue plywood drawer stops in place.

Drill pilot holes in 2x2 frame and attach drawer catches with 1-inch wood screws as shown in detail.

Glue-nail plywood facing into place.

Glue-nail seat in place.

Glue-nail upper back in place.

Drill pilot holes and attach vertical 2x4s to bench with #12 wood screws. Drill pilot holes for attaching 2x4s to upper back and chalk board with #8 wood screws.

Attach 2x4s to upper back with #8 wood screws.

Sand and paint assembly as desired.

Place and attach chalk board with #8 wood screws.

Cut notch in tower corners of corkboard to match upper back. Glue corkboard to upper back.

Assemble drawers by gluing and nailing back, sides and inner face to bottom.

Finish drawer face to match assembly. Glue face to drawer inner face.

Insert drawers by lifting front to allow back to fit under drawer stop.

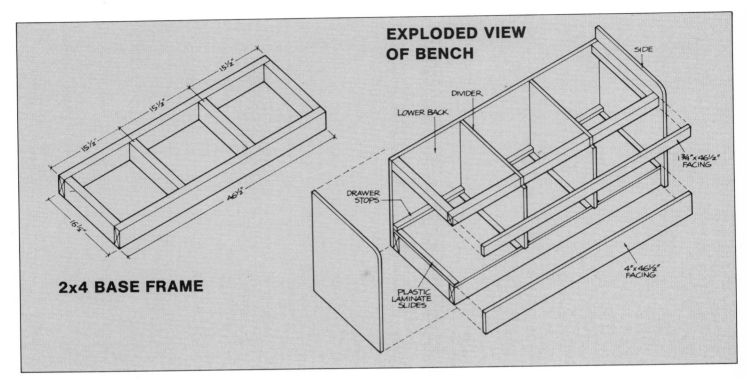

EXPLODED VIEW OF BENCH

2x4 BASE FRAME

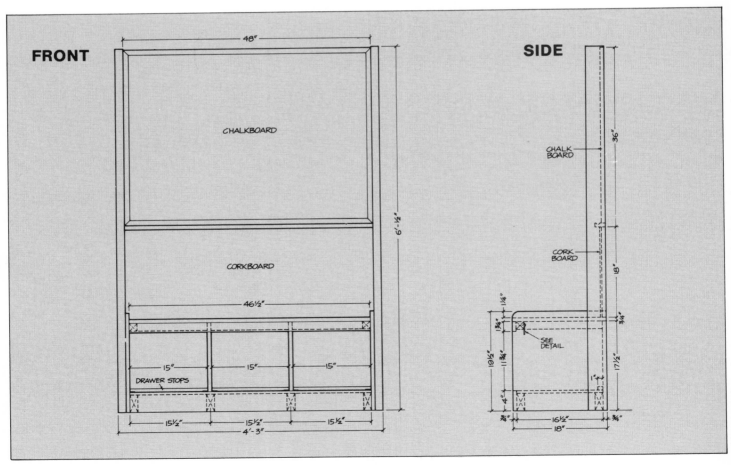

FRONT

CHALKBOARD

CORKBOARD

DRAWER STOPS

SIDE

PANEL LAYOUT

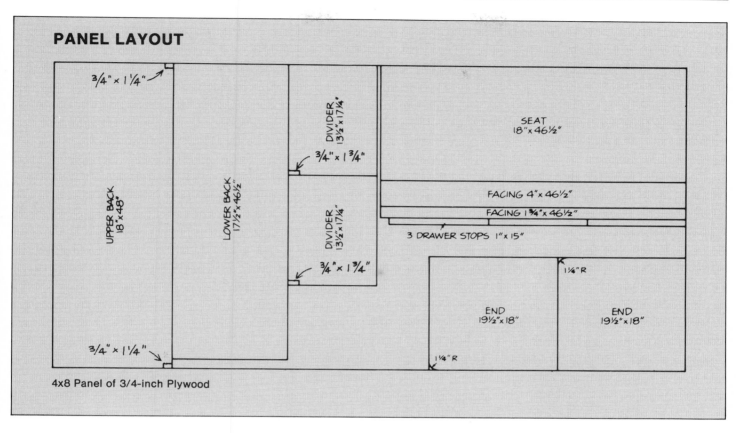

4x8 Panel of 3/4-inch Plywood

PANEL LAYOUT

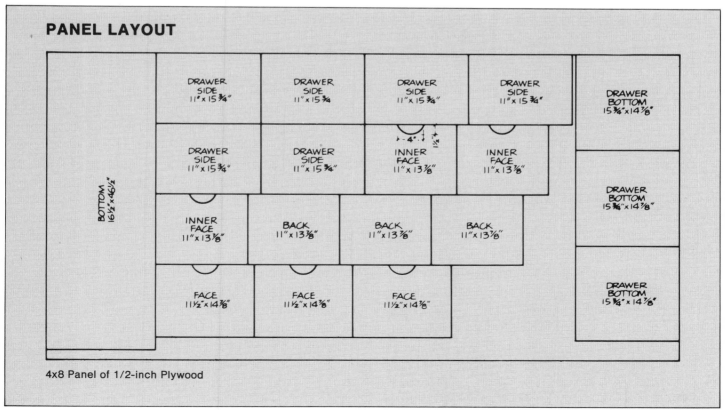

4x8 Panel of 1/2-inch Plywood

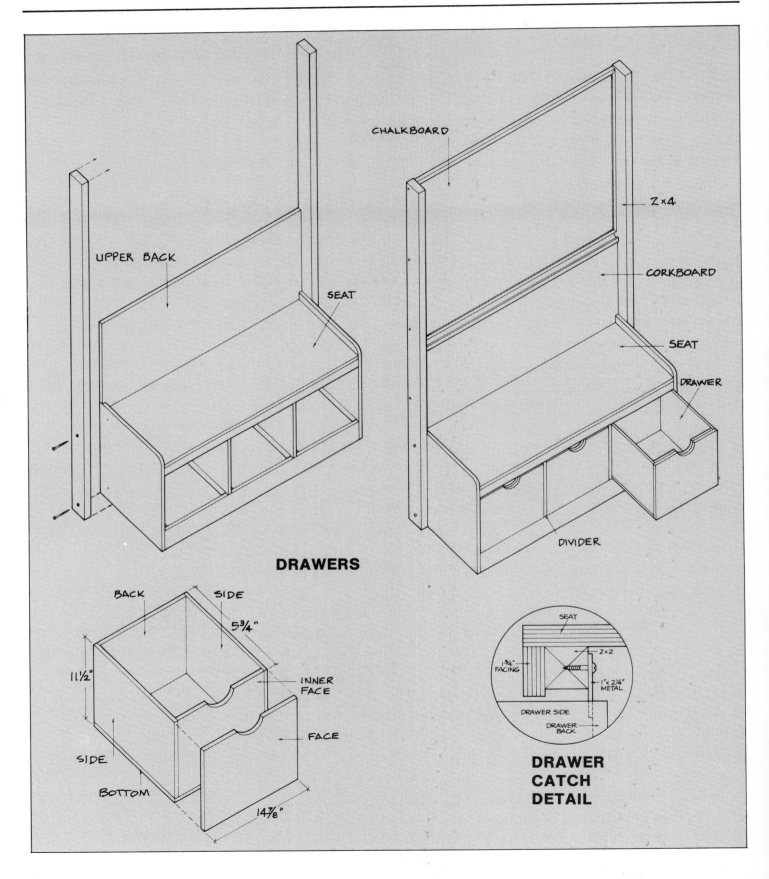

CHALKBOARD

UPPER BACK

SEAT

2×4

CORKBOARD

SEAT

DRAWER

DIVIDER

DRAWERS

BACK

SIDE

5¾"

11½"

INNER FACE

FACE

SIDE

BOTTOM

14⅞"

SEAT

1¾" FACING

2×2

1" x 2¼" METAL

DRAWER SIDE

DRAWER BACK

DRAWER CATCH DETAIL

Fire Engine Bunkbed

MATERIALS LIST

Quantity	Description
5	4 ft. x 8 ft. plywood panels of 1/2 in. APA grademarked Medium Density Overlay (MDO), A-B Interior, or A-C Exterior plywood
8	2x4s, 8 ft. long
5	2x4s, 12 ft. long
7	2x2s, 8 ft. long
1	1 in. diameter dowel, 5 ft. long
48	1/4 in. diameter carriage bolts, 2-1/4 in. long
12	1-1/4 in. long #8 flathead wood screws
2	Continuous piano hinges, 20-1/2 in. long
2	30 x 75 in. mattresses, bunk-size
As required	Top quality paints

CONSTRUCTION NOTES

Glue-nail 2x4 frame as shown in plan. Use half-lap joints for inside cross pieces. Glue-nail legs of bed to frame as shown.

Lay out and cut out bottom bunk as shown on panel layout. Glue-nail bottom bunk to frame.

Lay out and cut out six fender sides, two fender fronts and two running boards. Bevel edges as shown in wheel details. Note that front wheels require fender fronts. Countersink nails and conceal holes with wood dough.

Lay out other parts as shown on panel layouts. Allow for kerf width when measuring to insure a proper fit.

Paint wheels as shown in detail and glue-nail in place.

Glue-nail 2x2 framing as shown in plan. See toy storage/hood detail for framing.

Attach inside trim with glue, nails and carriage bolts to 2x2 frame.

Attach sides to 2x2 frame with glue and carriage bolts. Nail sides to 2x4 frame along bottom.

Attach back with glue, nails and carriage bolts to frame.

Glue upper bunk in place. Secure with 6-inch 2x2s held with carriage bolts at corners as shown in plan.

Attach two lids to top with continuous hinges. Attach assembly to 2x2 frame with four carriage bolts through top.

Fill any voids in plywood edges and sand smooth. Paint as desired.

Round ends of 2x4 bumpers and paint black. Glue-nail to front and rear.

Assemble headlights and paint gold. Glue in place as shown in detail.

Cut 2x2s into two 44-inch lengths for ladder. Drill centered holes as shown in detail for 1-inch dowels. Glue ladder together and paint yellow.

Fasten ladder to side with screws as shown in plan.

LADDER

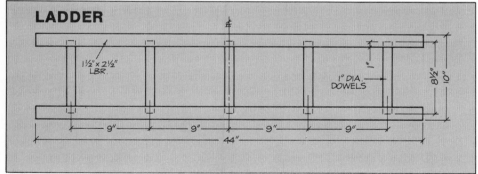

TOY STORAGE COMPARTMENT—HOOD

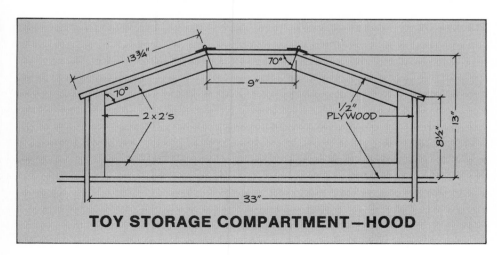

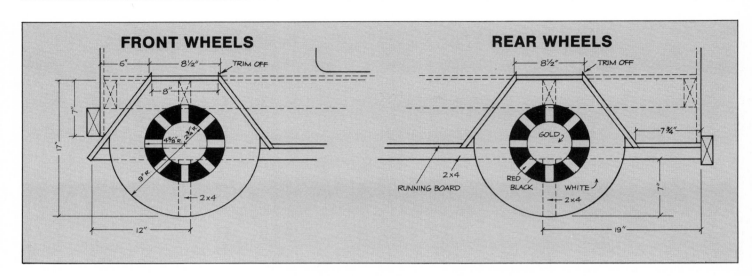

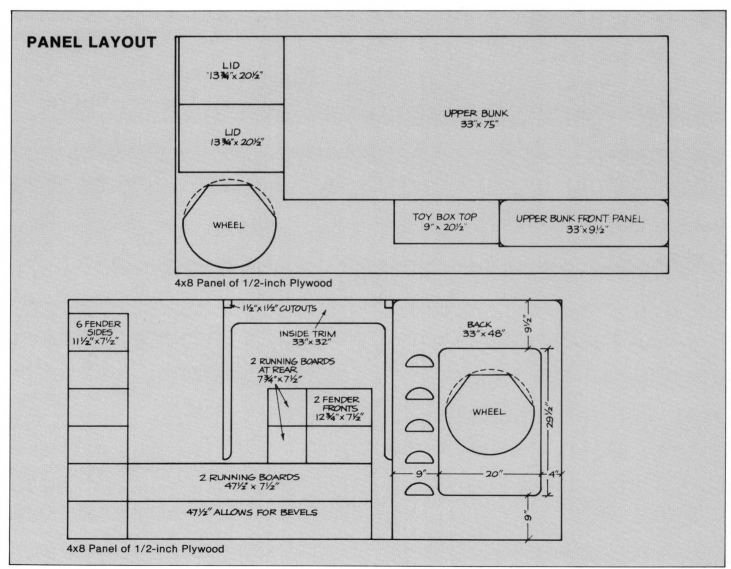

PANEL LAYOUT

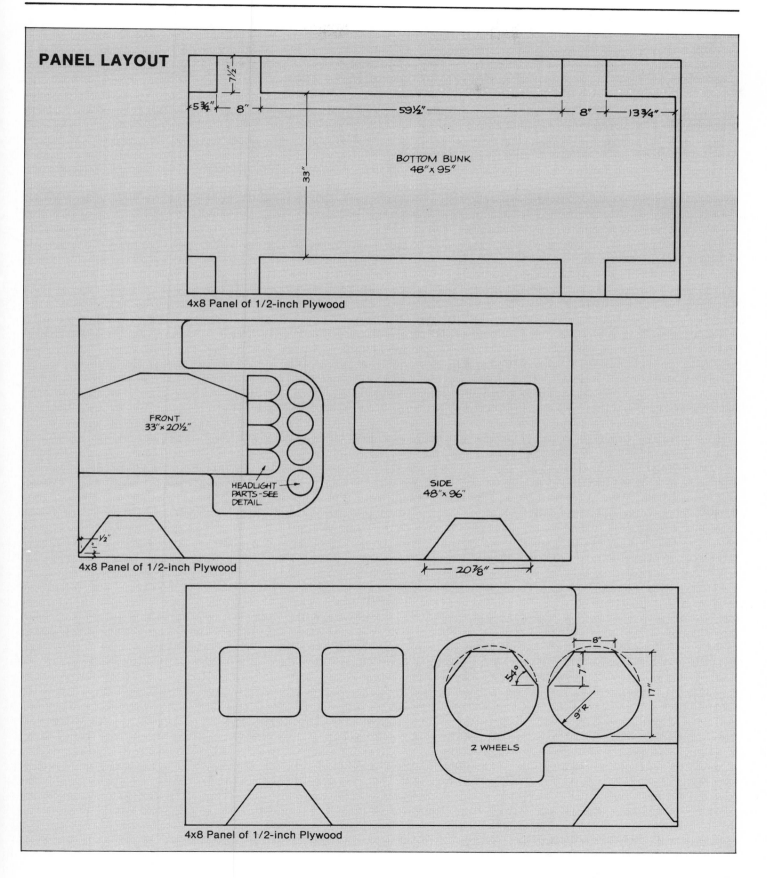

4x8 Panel of 1/2-inch Plywood

4x8 Panel of 1/2-inch Plywood

4x8 Panel of 1/2-inch Plywood

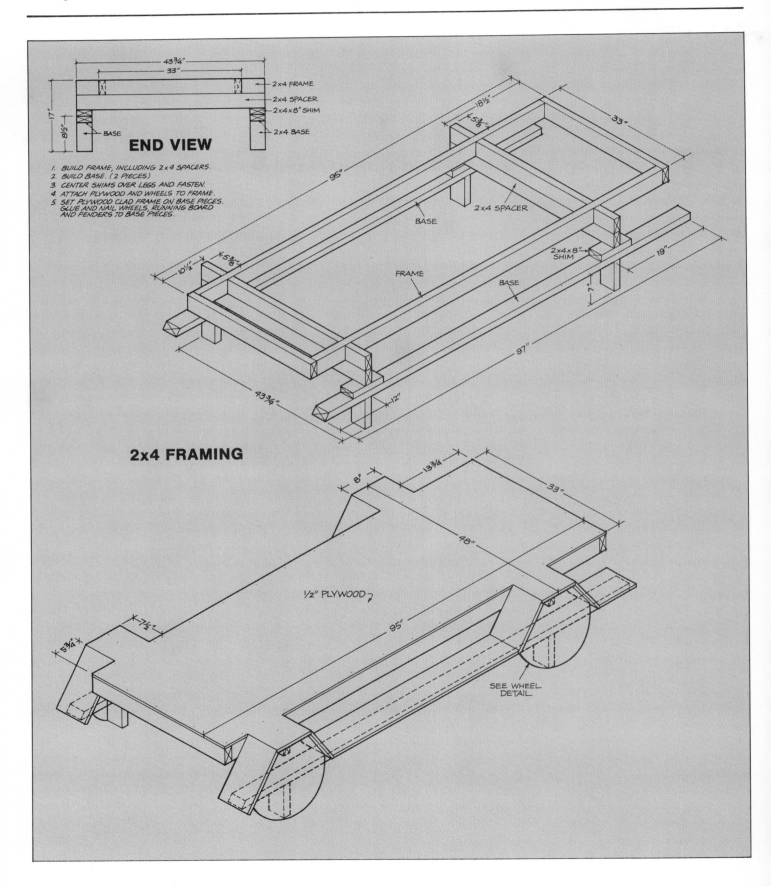

END VIEW

43¾"
33"
2x4 FRAME
2x4 SPACER
2x4x8" SHIM
BASE
2x4 BASE
17"
8½"

1. BUILD FRAME, INCLUDING 2x4 SPACERS.
2. BUILD BASE. (2 PIECES)
3. CENTER SHIMS OVER LEGS AND FASTEN.
4. ATTACH PLYWOOD AND WHEELS TO FRAME.
5. SET PLYWOOD CLAD FRAME ON BASE PIECES.
   GLUE AND NAIL WHEELS, RUNNING BOARD
   AND FENDERS TO BASE PIECES.

2x4 FRAMING

18½"
5⅜"
33"
95"
2x4 SPACER
BASE
10½"
5⅜"
FRAME
BASE
2x4x8"
SHIM
19"
7"
43¾"
12"
97"

½" PLYWOOD
8"
13¾"
33"
48"
7½"
95"
5¾"
SEE WHEEL
DETAIL.

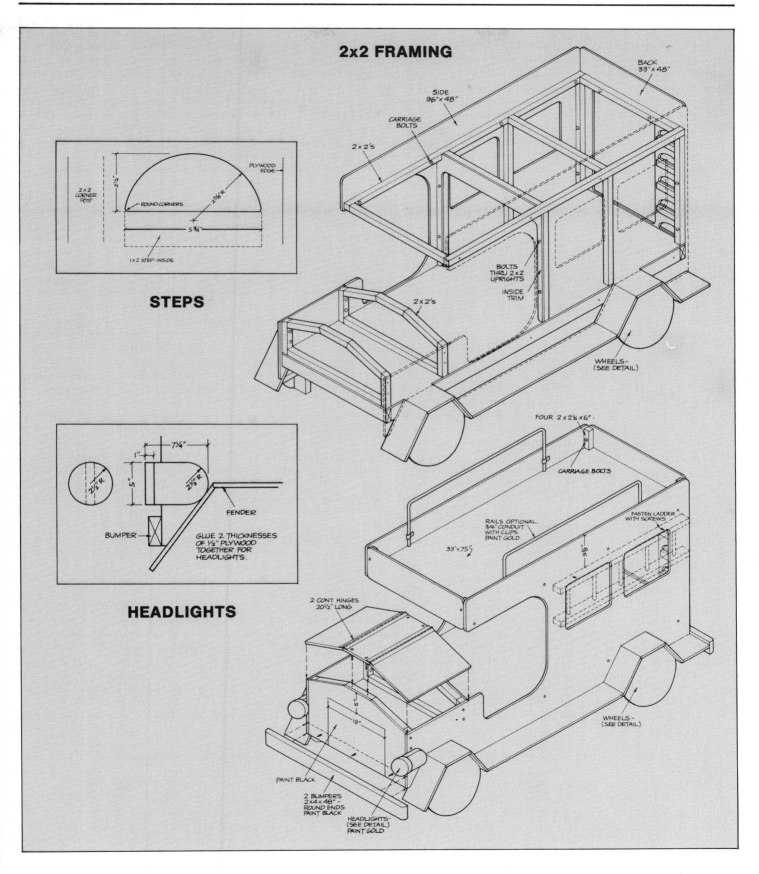

2x2 FRAMING

SIDE 96"x 48"

BACK 33"x 48"

CARRIAGE BOLTS

2 x 2's

BOLTS THRU 2 x 2 UPRIGHTS

INSIDE TRIM

2 x 2's

WHEELS— (SEE DETAIL)

PLYWOOD EDGE

2 x 2 CORNER POST

ROUND CORNERS

2½6"R

5¾"

1 x 2 STEP-INSIDE

STEPS

FOUR 2 x 2's x 6".

CARRIAGE BOLTS

RAILS OPTIONAL. ¾" CONDUIT WITH CLIPS. PAINT GOLD

FASTEN LADDER WITH SCREWS

33"x 75"

7¼"

1"

5"

2½" R

2½" R

FENDER

BUMPER

GLUE 2 THICKNESSES OF ½" PLYWOOD TOGETHER FOR HEADLIGHTS.

HEADLIGHTS

2 CONT. HINGES 20½" LONG

6"

19"

PAINT BLACK

2 BUMPERS 2 x 4 x 48" ROUND ENDS PAINT BLACK

HEADLIGHTS— (SEE DETAIL) PAINT GOLD

WHEELS — (SEE DETAIL)

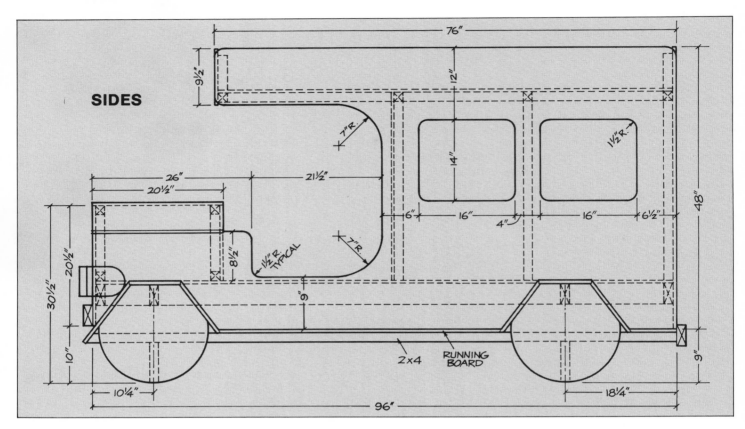

SIDES

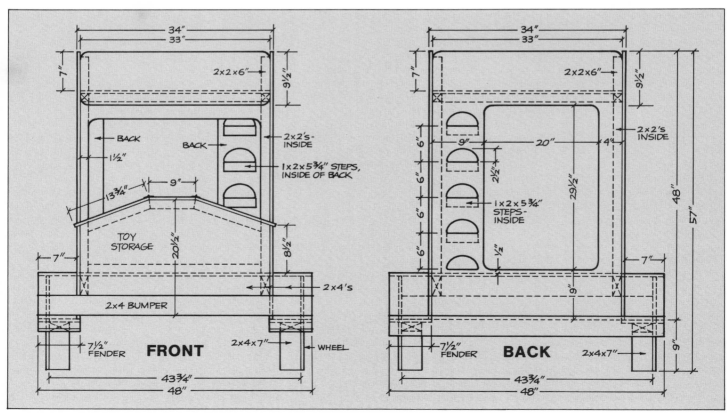

Wine Storage Rack

MATERIALS LIST

Quantity	Description
1	2 ft. x 4 ft. plywood panel of 5/8 in. APA grademarked A-A Interior, Medium Density Overlay (MDO), or textured siding panel.
4-1/2 linear ft.	3/4 in. or 1 in. diameter dowel
3 linear ft.	1/4 in. diameter dowel
4	Rubber glides
As required	Fine sandpaper for smoothing cut edges of plywood and dowel
As required	Wood filler or surfacing putty to fill any small gaps in plywood edges
As required	Paint or stain for finishing

CONSTRUCTION NOTES

Lay out front on plywood using a grid to ensure proper shape.

Cut out front and use it to layout back.

Cut out back. Clamp front and back together for final smoothing. Fill and sand edges.

Cut 3/4-inch dowels into five 10-1/2-inch lengths. Drill dowels as shown on plans.

Cut holes for bottles on front and back as shown in plans. Drill holes for dowels. 3/4-inch dowels should fit tightly in holes.

Cut 1/4-inch dowels into twenty 1-1/2-inch pins.

Fit 3/4-inch dowels into front and back and pin with 1/4-inch dowel pins.

Paint or stain as desired.

Attach rubber glides to bottom.

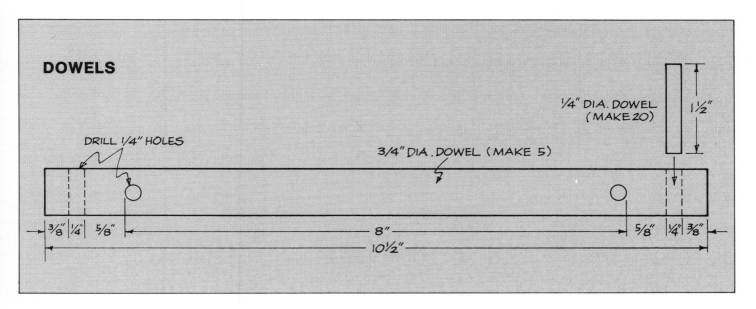

DOWELS

DRILL 1/4" HOLES

3/4" DIA. DOWEL (MAKE 5)

1/4" DIA. DOWEL (MAKE 20)

1 1/2"

3/8" 1/4" 5/8" 8" 5/8" 1/4" 3/8"

10 1/2"

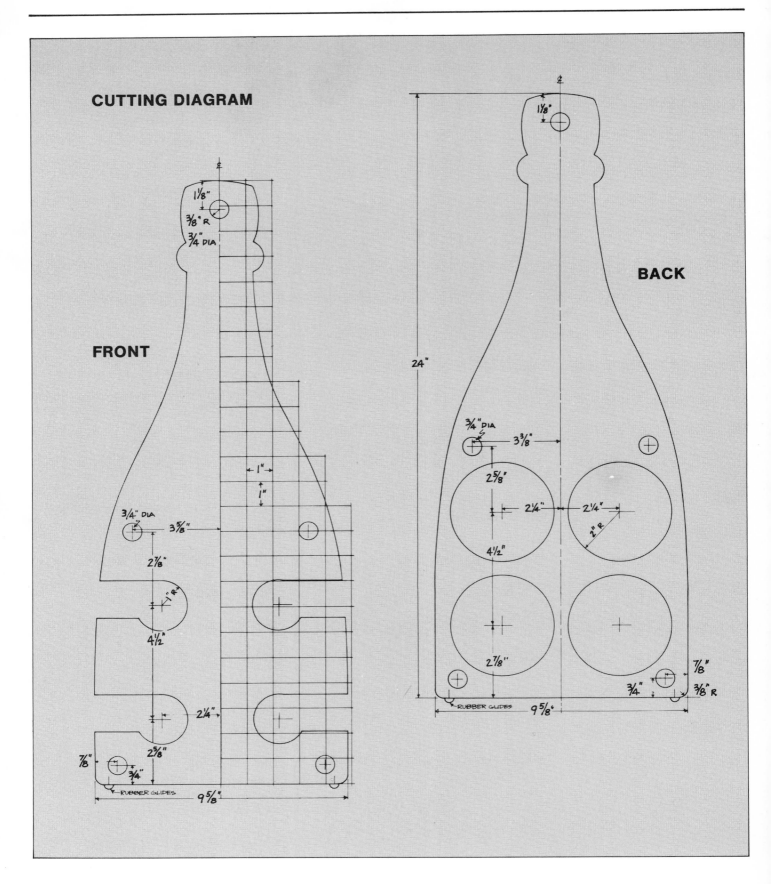

CUTTING DIAGRAM

FRONT

BACK

EXPLODED VIEW

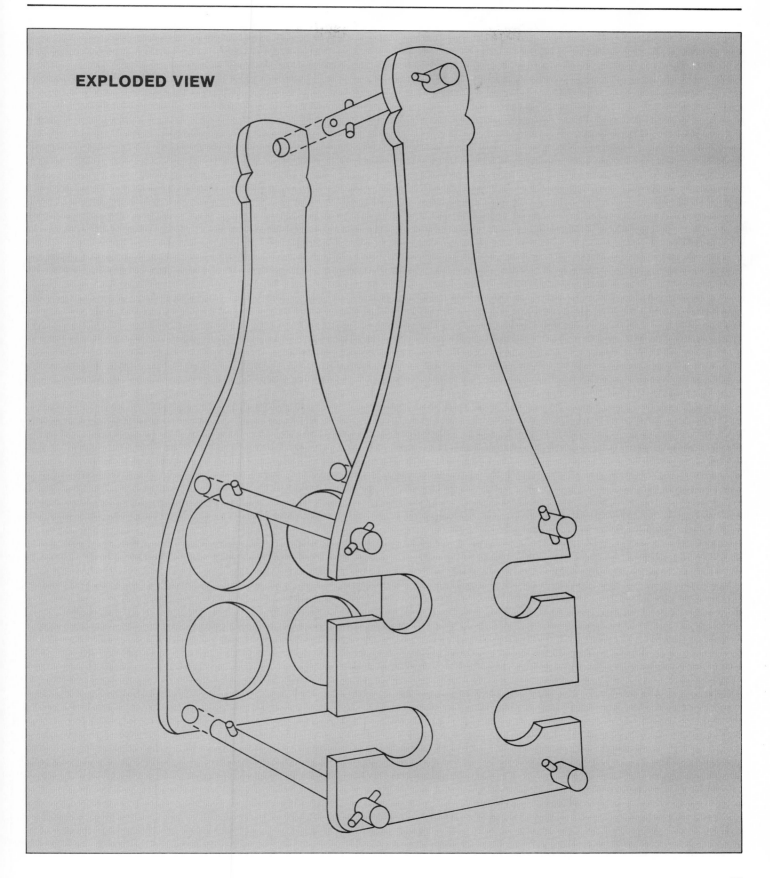

Fold Away Vise Table & Sawhorse

MATERIALS LIST

Quantity	Description
1	4 ft. x 8 ft. plywood panel of 3/4 in. APA grademarked A-B or A-D Interior, A-B or A-C Exterior, or Medium Density Overlay (MDO)
12	Strap hinges, 1-1/2 in. with screws
4 pieces	Angle iron, 1-1/2 in. x 2 in.
2 pieces	Threaded rod, 3/8 in. diameter x 18 in. long
4	Nuts, to fit 3/8 in. diameter threaded rod
2	Bolts, 1/4 in. diameter x 5 in. long
2	Lock nuts, 3/8 in. diameter x 1/2 in. deep
20 (approx.)	1-1/4 in. #8 flathead wood screws
8 (approx.)	2 in. #8 flathead wood screws
8	1-1/4 in. #8 roundhead wood screws
2	Carriage bolts, 1/4 in. diameter x 2 in. long, with wing nuts
4	Compression pins, 1/8 in. diameter x 1/2 in. long
As required	Wood dough for filling any small voids in plywood edges
As required	Fine sandpaper for smoothing edges and cured wood dough
As required	White glue for glue-screw assembly
As required	Finishing materials

CONSTRUCTION NOTES

Lay out parts on plywood. Center saw cuts on layout lines to equalize saw kerf width on all parts.

Cut off the table top section and cut it in half. Set these two sections aside. Cut out other parts.

Clamp sawhorse legs together and cut slots simultaneously, either using a router or making parallel cuts along sides and removing slot material with hammer and chisel. Repeat for sawhorse ends.

Lightly sand cut edges smooth.

Slide sawhorse ends into leg slots to check fit. Adjust if necessary. Fasten ends to top with hinges.

Laminate the two table top sections together using glue according to manufacturer's instructions. Clamp until dry. Cut the laminated piece lengthwise into two 12-inch wide sections.

Assemble runner channels on side and bottom plates and fasten to the stationary section of the table top, as shown in detail. Be careful to align channels so slides will not bind. Use glue and 2-inch #8 flatheat screws where channels fasten to top. Use 1-1/4-inch #8 flathead screws on other half. Attach spacer plate using glue and 1-1/4-inch #8 screws.

Place runner slides in runner channels and lay movable table section in position on top of slides. Mark position of slides on underside of movable table section and then, using 1-1/4-inch #8 flathead screws, glue-screw slides to movable table section as shown in exploded view. This assures that slides will run true within channels.

Hinge legs to stationary table top assembly as shown in bottom and front views. Note that the spacer plate on one side allows legs to fold flat. Also install hinges that fasten cross braces to legs. Note placement in end and front views. Where cross braces overlap, drill a 5/16-inch hole through cross braces. Insert carriage bolts and wing nuts. These remove for storing table.

Drill a 3/16-inch hole through a lock nut and tap it with 1/4 inch thread. If you do not have the proper equipment a machine shop can do this and the drilling below for you. Place nut to act as handle/rod connector on one end on the threaded rod and insert one of the 5-inch bolts. Bend end of bolt to form a handle. Repeat for second rod.

Drill two 3/16-inch holes in one flange of each angle iron to accommodate 1-1/4-inch #8 roundhead mounting screws. Center a 5/16-inch hole in remaining flanges of angle irons to be installed on movable table section and tap it fit the threaded rod. Center a 7/16-inch hole in remaining flanges of angle irons to be installed on stationary table section as shown in the detail.

Using 1-1/4-inch roundhead screws, fasten angle irons beneath table sections as shown in the bottom view and detail. Set irons flush against inside edges of runner channels. 7/16-inch and 5/16-inch holes drilled in flanges should align, front to rear.

Install threaded 3/8-inch diameter rods and hardware as shown in detail. Drill 1/8-inch holes through retaining nuts and rod. Insert compressing pins to lock in place.

Woodworkers may want to drill a configuration of 5/8-inch holes in the vise-table top and use dowels to hold a wide variety of shapes and sizes of woodwork.

Remove movable section and carriage bolts before finishing. Fill any small voids in plywood cut edges with wood dough. Let dry and sand smooth. If desired, finish with primer and paint according to manufacturer's directions. Do not paint runner channels or slides. Wax runner slides before reassembling the vise table.

PANEL LAYOUT

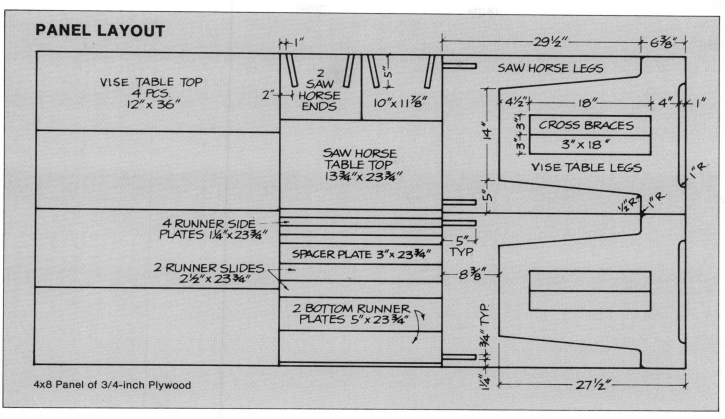

VISE TABLE TOP
4 PCS.
12" x 36"

2 SAW HORSE ENDS

10" x 11⅜"

SAW HORSE TABLE TOP
13¾" x 23¾"

4 RUNNER SIDE PLATES 1¼" x 23¾"

SPACER PLATE 3" x 23¾"

2 RUNNER SLIDES 2½" x 23¾"

2 BOTTOM RUNNER PLATES 5" x 23¾"

SAW HORSE LEGS

CROSS BRACES
3" x 18"

VISE TABLE LEGS

4x8 Panel of 3/4-inch Plywood

SAWHORSE

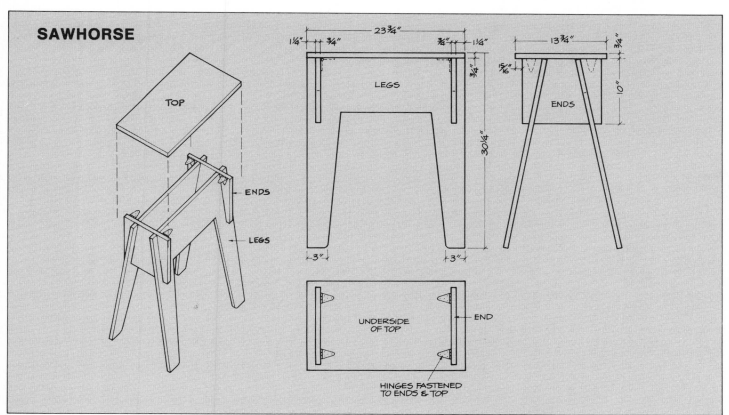

TOP

ENDS

LEGS

LEGS

ENDS

UNDERSIDE OF TOP

END

HINGES FASTENED TO ENDS & TOP

VISE TABLE

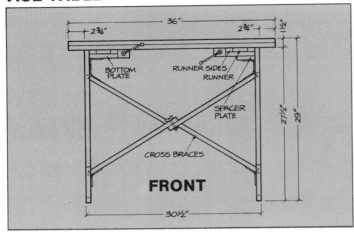

FRONT

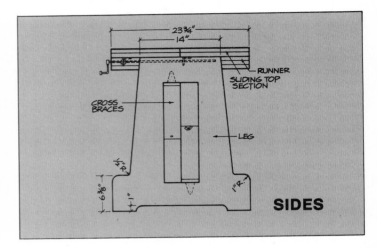

SIDES

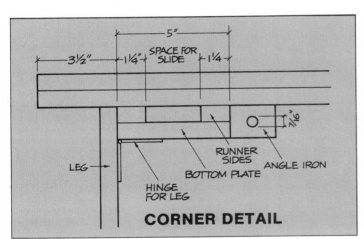

CORNER DETAIL

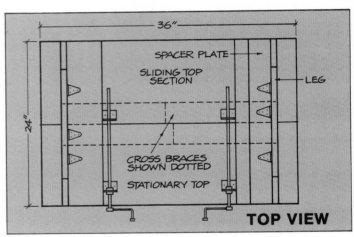

TOP VIEW

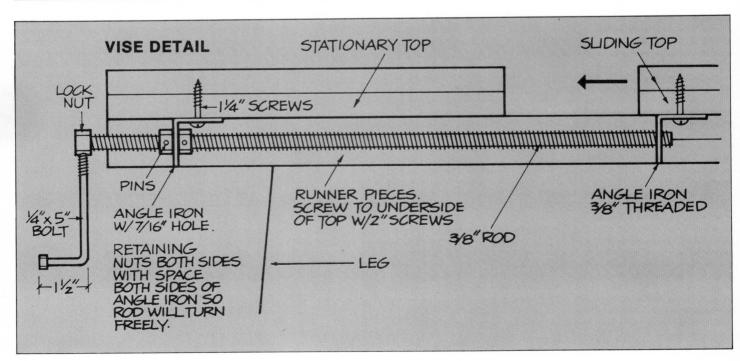

VISE DETAIL

STATIONARY TOP

SLIDING TOP

LOCK NUT

1¼" SCREWS

PINS

¼" x 5" BOLT

1½"

ANGLE IRON W/ 7/16" HOLE.

RETAINING NUTS BOTH SIDES WITH SPACE BOTH SIDES OF ANGLE IRON SO ROD WILL TURN FREELY.

RUNNER PIECES. SCREW TO UNDERSIDE OF TOP W/2" SCREWS

LEG

3/8" ROD

ANGLE IRON 3/8" THREADED

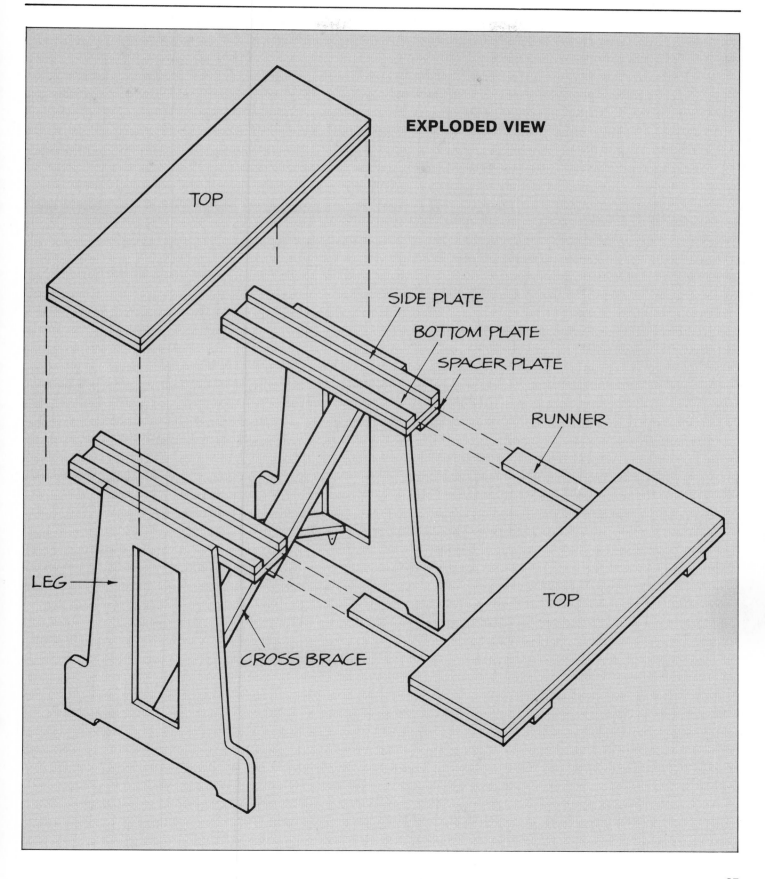

EXPLODED VIEW

TOP

SIDE PLATE

BOTTOM PLATE

SPACER PLATE

RUNNER

TOP

LEG

CROSS BRACE

Wine & Glass Rack

MATERIALS LIST

Quantity	Description
1	4 ft. x 8 ft. plywood panel of 1/2 in. APA grademarked A-B or A-D Interior, A-B or A-C Exterior, or Medium Density Overlay (MDO)
4	1x2s, 25 in. long, for face trim. Miter at corners.
2 (optional)	12 in. x 12 in. mirror tiles
20 ft. (approx.)	1/2 in. wide wood veneer trim for bottle-rack edges.
1/2 lb. (approx.)	4d finishing nails for glue-nail assembly
As required	White glue, approximately 8 oz. bottle, for glue-nail assembly
As required	Fine sandpaper for plywood edges
As required	Wood dough for plywood edges
As required	Finishing materials

CONSTRUCTION NOTES

Draw all parts on plywood.

Cut out all parts. Center saw cut on layout lines to equalize saw kerf on all parts.

Clamp shelves together in stacks: four 6 x 16 inch shelves with three slots each, two 6 x 16 inch shelves with one slot each, and and so forth. Mark exact centerline of slots on panel edges.

Unclamp and mark half the slot width, 1/4 inch, on each side of the matched centerline markings. Draw slots accurately on each piece and cut out, using saw and chisel or a router. To cut glass-hanger slots, draw each one on the panel pieces. Rounded ends may be shaped with a jigsaw or router; or with a 5/8-inch drill bit, then sand or file to final configuration.

Lightly smooth plywood cut edges with fine sandpaper.

Assemble bottle unit to check fit, adjusting if necessary. Disassemble. Apply glue to slots according to manufacturer's directions and reassemble. Secure ends with nails. Set nails, fill holes with wood dough, and sand smooth.

Lay side and back pieces side by side and draw lines across them to mark shelf and glass rack locations. Using glue and nails, join back, sides, bottom and top as shown in exploded view.

Glue and nail glass-hanger rack and shelf in place, and install mirror tiles. Set all exterior nail holes, fill and sand.

Finish bottle rack and cabinet interior as desired. Set bottle rack in place. Apply glue to corner fittings.

Install 1x2 face trim, using glue and nails.

Finish exterior as desired. You may apply wood veneer to bottle rack edges; or fill any edge voids with wood dough, sand smooth when dry and varnish or paint.

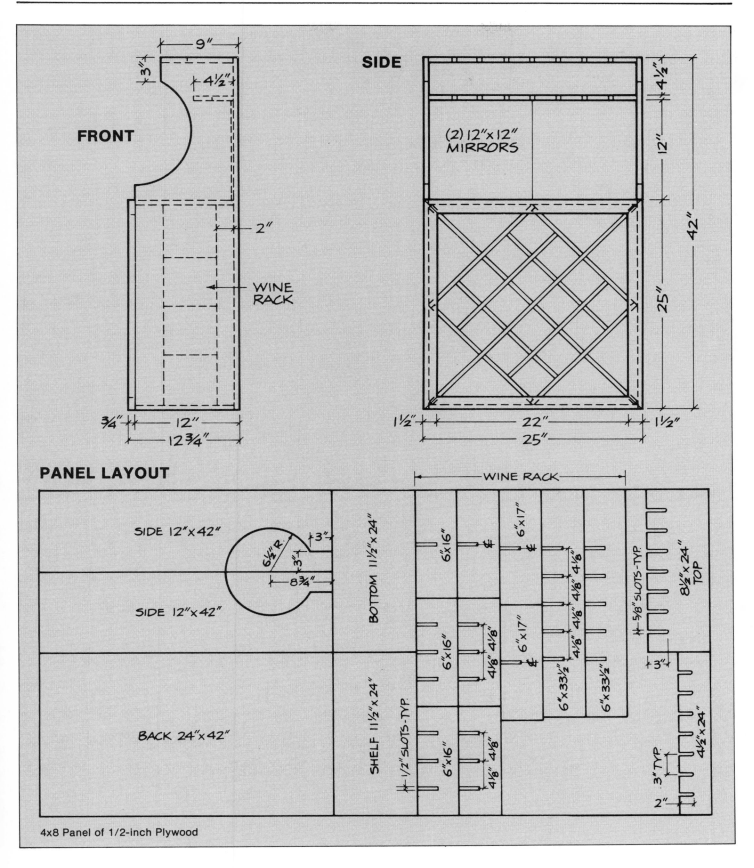

FRONT

9"
3"
4½"
2"
WINE RACK
¾"
12"
12¾"

SIDE

(2) 12"x12" MIRRORS
4½"
12"
42"
25"
1½"
22"
1½"
25"

PANEL LAYOUT

WINE RACK

SIDE 12"x42"
6½" R.
3"
3"
8¾"

SIDE 12"x42"

BACK 24"x42"

BOTTOM 11½"x24"

SHELF 11½"x24"

½" SLOTS-TYP.

6"x16"
6"x16"
6"x16"
4⅛"
4⅛"
4⅛"

6"x17"
6"x17"

6"x33½"
6"x33½"

4⅛" 4⅛" 4⅛"
4⅛" 4⅛" 4⅛"

⅝" SLOTS-TYP.

8½"x24" TOP

3"

4½"x24"

3" TYP.

2"

4x8 Panel of 1/2-inch Plywood

EXPLODED VIEW

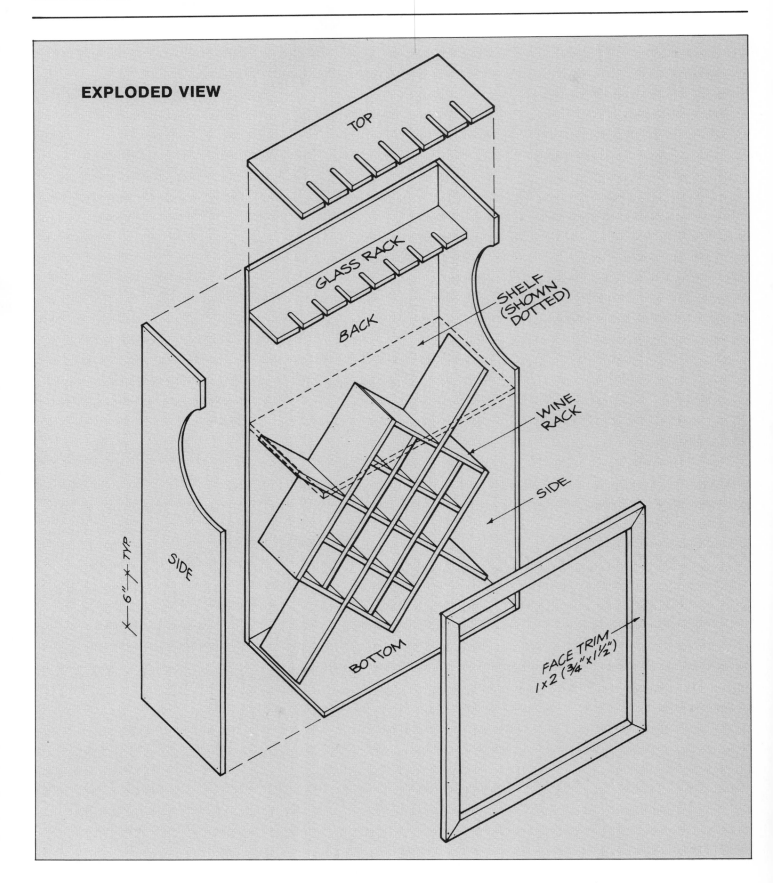

TOP

GLASS RACK

BACK

SHELF (SHOWN DOTTED)

WINE RACK

SIDE

SIDE

6" TYP.

BOTTOM

FACE TRIM 1x2 (3/4"x1 1/2")

Barn Toybox

MATERIALS LIST

Quantity	Description
1	4 ft. x 8 ft. plywood panel of 1/2 in. APA grademarked A-B Interior, A-C Exterior, or Medium Density Overlay (MDO)
8 linear ft.	2 in. x 1/4 in. lattice trim for windows and doors
4	1-1/2 in. door hinges
6	1-1/2 in. roof hinges
4	Furniture glides
1	Bolt, 1-1/4 in. long, for door latch
As required	6d finishing nails
As required	White or urea-resin glue
As required	Wood dough for filling any small voids in plywood edges
As required	Fine sandpaper
As required	Top-quality latex paint

CONSTRUCTION NOTES

Dimensions given on panel layout are finished sizes. Allow for saw kerf width when making layout on plywood.

Cut out parts. Make cut between front and back, and other parts first. Then make long cut between top roof and side.

Assemble sides, front and back with nails and glue.

Drill pilot holes for screws for six hinges on roof pieces, and attach hinges.

Glue-nail roof to barn assembly.

Sand and paint barn before attaching trim.

Saw trim into 1/2 inch wide strips for windows and into 1/2 inch or 1 inch wide strips for doors, as shown for drawings.

Paint trim and attach.

Paint doors.

Make windows out of lattice trim. Paint as desired and attach to sides and ends of assembly with glue as shown.

Attach lattice trim to doors as shown.

Mortise trim for door hinges. Use trim to make latch as shown in details. Attach latch to door with bolt.

Attach doors to front with door hinges.

Attach furniture glides to four corners of bottom.

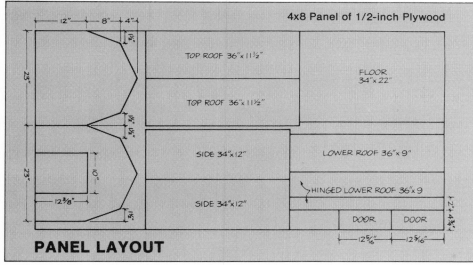

PANEL LAYOUT

4x8 Panel of 1/2-inch Plywood

TOP ROOF 36"x 11½"

TOP ROOF 36"x 11½"

FLOOR 34"x 22"

SIDE 34"x 12"

LOWER ROOF 36"x 9"

HINGED LOWER ROOF 36"x 9

SIDE 34"x 12"

DOOR   DOOR

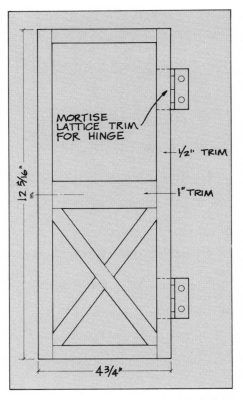

MORTISE LATTICE TRIM FOR HINGE

½" TRIM

1" TRIM

12 5/16"

4 3/4"

DOOR

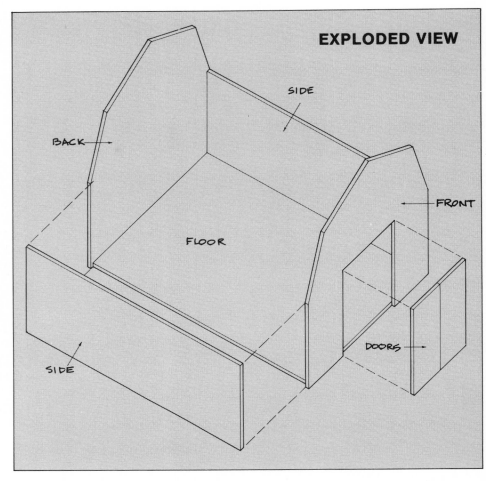

EXPLODED VIEW

SIDE

BACK

FRONT

FLOOR

SIDE

DOORS

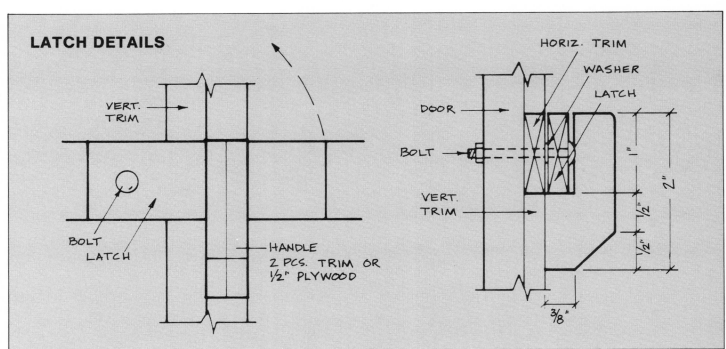

LATCH DETAILS

VERT. TRIM

BOLT LATCH

HANDLE
2 PCS. TRIM OR
½" PLYWOOD

HORIZ. TRIM

WASHER

LATCH

DOOR

BOLT

VERT. TRIM

1"

2"

½"

½"

3/8"

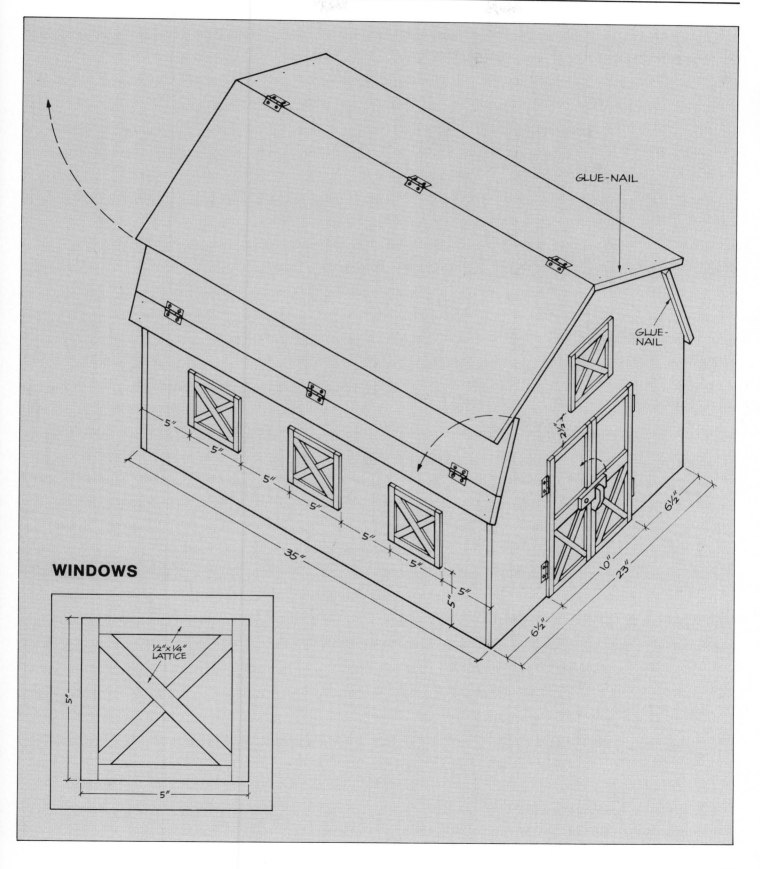

WINDOWS

All-Purpose Table

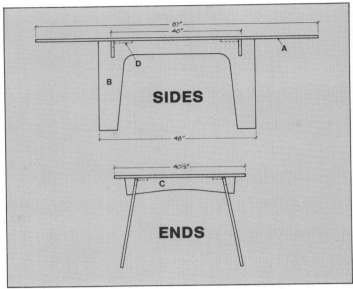

SIDES

ENDS

MATERIALS LIST

Quantity	Description
1	4 ft. x 8 ft. plywood panel of 3/4 in. APA grademarked A-B or A-D Interior, A-B or A-C Exterior, or Medium Density Overlay (MDO)
8	Furniture glides
As required	Wood dough to fill small voids in plywood cut edges
As required	Fine sandpaper to smooth edges and cured wood dough
As required	White glue for mounting spacers and permanently assembling table if desired
As required	Finishing materials.

CONSTRUCTION NOTES

Lay out all parts on plywood as shown in panel layout. To draw the table side radii, tie a string to a sharp pencil. Set end of string 44-1/4 inches from panel edge to pencil point held vertically above the panel surface. Use string and pencil as a large compass. Use a compass or make a cardboard template for the corner radii.

Start cutting at any line between parts D and B, because the curved end on D parts will allow smooth access to cutting lines of the table top. On all parts, center saw cuts on layout lines to equalize saw kerf width.

Lightly sand plywood cut edges smooth. Fill edge voids, if any, with wood dough. Allow to dry and sand smooth.

Assemble legs to check fit of slots. Adjust if necessary.

Cut slots accurately using a saw and chisel or a router. Note that slots are not the same depth. The cross braces, Parts D, extend 1/4 in. above the legs, Parts B, so that no beveling of leg top edges is needed. The table top has been designed to rest only on the cross braces. If desired, top edges of leg assemblies may be beveled to fit and slots lengthened to allow leg support of table.

Lay table top face down. Arrange assembled legs and cross braces in position as shown, and mark locations for spacers. Glue spacers in place and clamp or weight down until dry.

Finish the table as desired. For take-apart construction, disassemble legs before finishing. Parts may be glued in place for permanent use if desired. Wood veneer strip may be applied to edges.

Install furniture glides on legs.

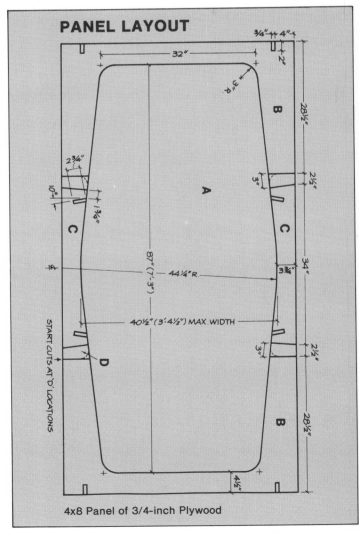

PANEL LAYOUT

4x8 Panel of 3/4-inch Plywood

BOTTOM VIEW

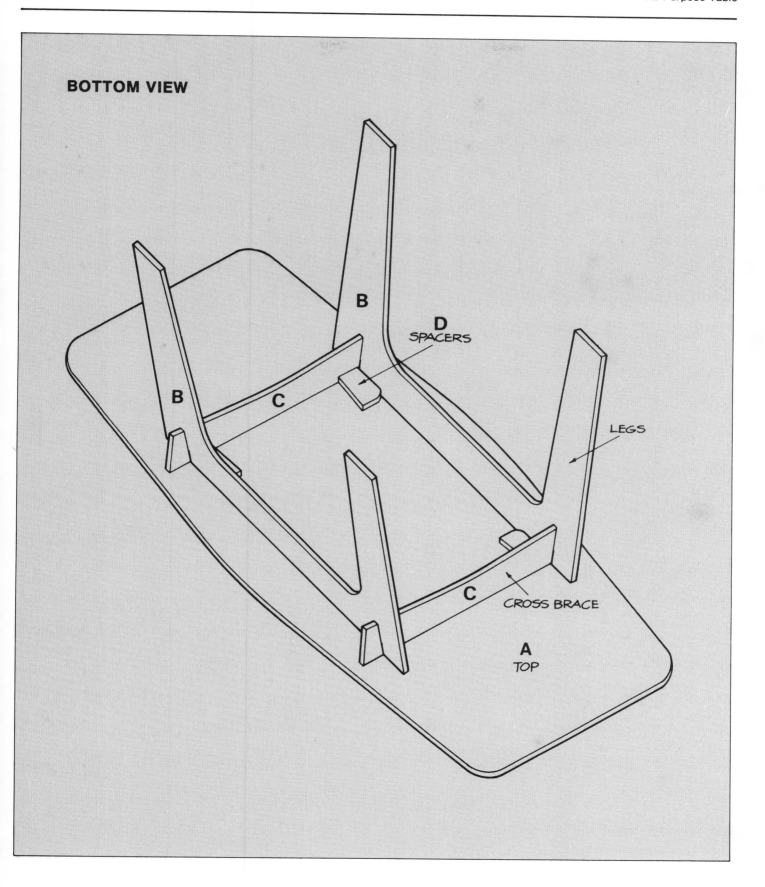

Laminated Coffee Table

MATERIALS LIST

Quantity	Description
1	4 ft. x 8 ft. plywood panel of 3/4 in. APA grademarked A-B or A-D Interior, or A-B or A-C Exterior
1 pt. (powder)	Plastic-resin glue for laminating
1 pt.	Satin-finish clear varnish, preferably a synthetic like Varathane that is compatible with resin glue.
As required	Fine sandpaper
As required	Wood dough or other wood filler

PANEL LAYOUT

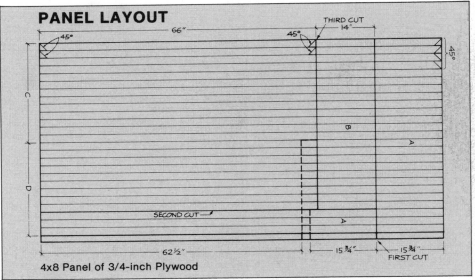

4x8 Panel of 3/4-inch Plywood

CONSTRUCTION NOTES

Make sure you center saw cuts on layout lines so that pieces have a consistent width.

When sawing is completed, you should have the following:

28 pieces 1-3/4 in. by 15-3/4 in. — A
22 pieces 1-3/4 in. by 14 in. — B
13 pieces 1-3/4 in. by 66 in. — C
12 pieces 1-3/4 in. by 62-1/2 in. — D

Miter corners of two C pieces and four A pieces.

Lay all pieces in proper sequence for assembly according to the drawing. Assembly surface should be large enough to accommodate as much of the table as you will laminate at one time. For ease of handling, you may wish to laminate in sections and then join the sections when all are dry.

Apply glue to angle cuts of a mitered C piece and two mitered A pieces. Join them to form a U-shaped piece. Let glue dry.

Apply glue to one side of the U assembly and to one side of two unmitered A pieces and one D piece. Lay these in position on the glued U assembly. Clamp and allow to set.

Stand the U assembly with C and D pieces down. Apply glue to both sides of a C piece and to two B pieces, and to the U assembly (pieces A and D). Join C to D and B to A.

Apply glue to both sides of a D and two A pieces. Set these in place against the adjoining C and B pieces.

Continue gluing and joining C and B pieces and D and A pieces alternately until you complete as much as you can conveniently handle. Bar-clamp and allow to dry. If constructing by section, glue and clamp or weight sections together to complete table.

Complete assembly with two mitered A pieces and one mitered C piece.

Use wood dough or other wood filler to fill edge voids. Sand all edges and top smooth, then finish as desired according to product manufacturer's directions.

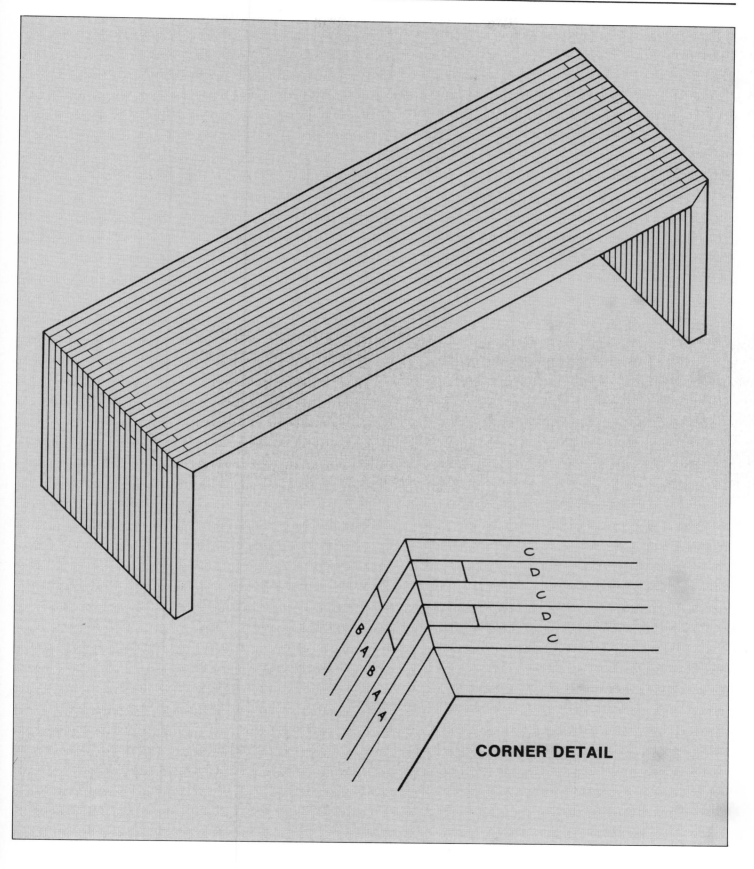

CORNER DETAIL

English Butler's Tray Table

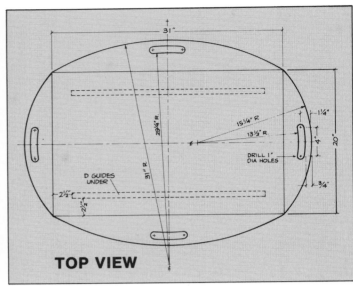

TOP VIEW

MATERIALS LIST

Quantity	Description
1	4 ft. x 8 ft. plywood panel of 1/2 in. APA grademarked A-A, A-B or B-B Interior, or Medium Density Overlay (MDO) for A through G
4	2x2s, 18-1/2 inches long, for legs H
As required	6d finishing nails for glue-nailing sides and end to bottom (optional)
8	Butler tray hinges (Brass Hinges No. 12004, available from Minnesota Woodworkers Supply Co., 925 Winnetka Ave., No., Minneapolis, Minnesota 55427)
1 set	Furniture glides for bottom of legs
As required	Urea-resin glue for attaching legs and gluing sides and ends to bottom and glides to top
As required	Surfacing putty for filling exposed plywood edges and countersunk nail holes
As required	Fine sandpaper for smoothing and rounding edges and surfacing putty
As required	Paint or stain for finishing

CONSTRUCTION NOTES

Lay out pieces as shown on panel layout. Allow for saw kerf width when making layout.

Cut out parts. Bevel corners of bottom by removing 1-1/2 by 1-1/2-inch piece from each corner. Fill and smooth edges.

Draw locations of guides, parts D on underside of top, part A.

Draw locations of sides, E, and ends, F, on upper side of bottom, G, to ensure proper fit.

Glue guides in place on underside of top, E, and clamp until dry. Wipe off excess glue.

Glue sides and ends to upper side of bottom. For a stronger bond, use 6d finishing nails with the glue. Countersink all nails. Wipe off excess glue and fill and sand nail holes.

Cut out 1/2-inch diagonal slot corner-to-corner half-way through legs 3-1/2 inches from top. Fit slots onto beveled corners of bottom and glue in place.

Paint or stain all parts as desired.

Attach tray sides and ends with hinges. Set tray in place on table.

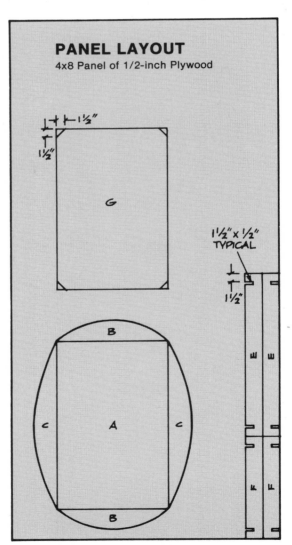

PANEL LAYOUT
4x8 Panel of 1/2-inch Plywood

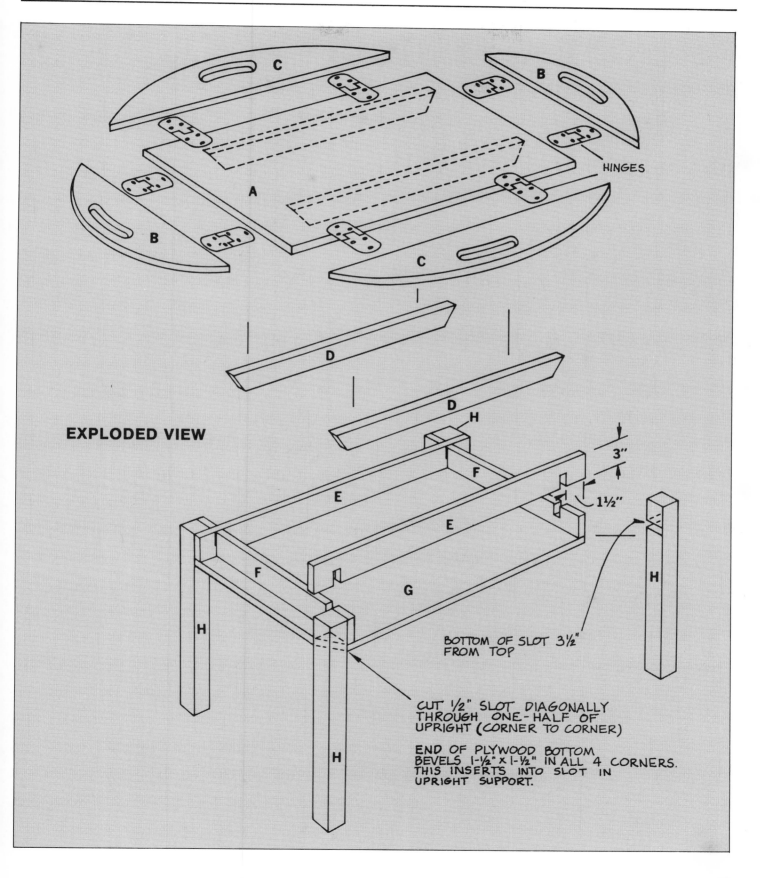

EXPLODED VIEW

HINGES

3"

1½"

H

BOTTOM OF SLOT 3½"
FROM TOP

CUT ½" SLOT DIAGONALLY
THROUGH ONE-HALF OF
UPRIGHT (CORNER TO CORNER)

END OF PLYWOOD BOTTOM
BEVELS 1-½" x 1-½" IN ALL 4 CORNERS.
THIS INSERTS INTO SLOT IN
UPRIGHT SUPPORT.

House Number Lamp Post

MATERIALS LIST

Quantity	Description
1	4 ft. x 8 ft. plywood panel of 5/8 in. APA grademarked A-C Exterior, 303 Exterior siding, or Medium Density Overlay (MDO)
1	4x4. 8 ft. long, for standard post.
1	1 in. diameter dowel, 2 ft. long, for bird perch and name plaque
1	10 in. x 20 in. x 1/8 in. sheet of translucent white Plexiglas, or similar material, for lighted house number
1	11 in. x 14 in. x 1/8 in. sheet of clear or transparent bronze Plexiglas, or similar material, for lantern front
2	14 in. x 11-1/8 in. sheets of clear or transparent bronze Plexiglas, or similar material, for lantern sides
1	4 in. outlet box
1	Ceramic or porcelain light socket and large light globe with mounting screws
1	Depending on local code, #12 or #14 outdoor, underground electrical wire. Length as required
3	Cable clamps to attach light wire to inside back of outlet box
1	Name plaque with hooks and eyes for attachment
1	8 in. diameter flower pot for planter
As required	1 in. #8 flathead wood screws for glue-screw attachment of stiffeners B and C and backing strips D and E
As required	1/2 in #4 or #6 roundhead wood screws for attaching Plexiglas lantern and number plate
As required	Waterproof glue for glue-nailing joints
As required	3d galvanized casing or finishing nails for glue-nailing
As required	Wood dough for filling countersunk nail holes and any small voids in plywood edges
As required	Caulking for sealing around Plexiglas edges
As required	Fine sandpaper for smoothing edges
As required	Paint or stain for finishing

CONSTRUCTION NOTES

Cut 45° miters for all vertical joints.

Attach inside pieces F, H, J and Q to post.

Construct box using drawings as guide. Install back U and associated stiffeners, then sides N and O, pieces A and I, electrical cable, outlet box and light socket, window pieces, and remaining top pieces G, R, S and T. Glue-nail all joints using waterproof glue.

Lay out panel K and cut out house number numerals. Install clear plastic and pieces D and E as shown.

Install front panels K and M and remaining attaching parts.

After glue-nailing top assembly, apply a caulking sealer to the edge joints of piece G to keep moisture out of the lamp area.

Light bulbs may be changed by removing one of the window pieces, or—make a hinged door in U right behind the lamp socket.

Seal edges of Plexiglas with caulking.

Use drill bit recommended for plastic for Plexiglas installation. Make screw holes slightly oversize to allow for material expansion.

Underground portion of post should be treated with preservative. Sink up to 4 ft. in ground depending on soil conditions, if post is not anchored in concrete. Otherwise, 18 to 24 inches is adequate. Shorten post as required.

Finish as desired.

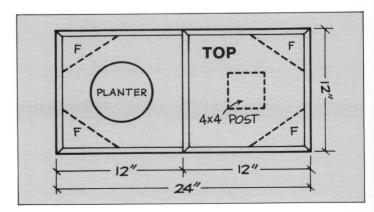

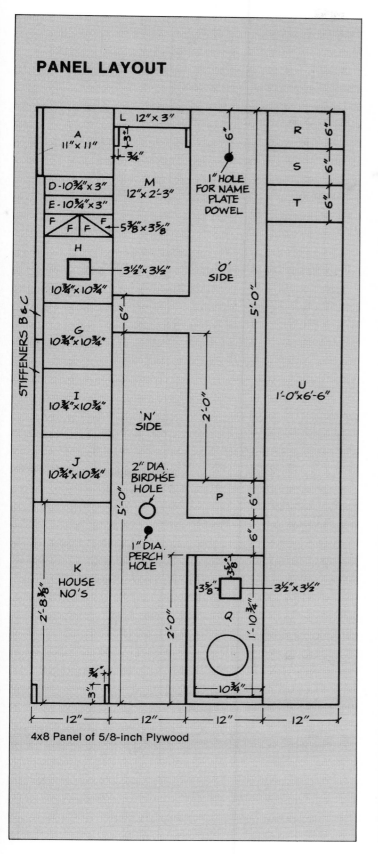

PANEL LAYOUT

L 12" x 3"

3"

3/4"

A
11" x 11"

D - 10¾" x 3"

E - 10¾" x 3"

F   F   F
5⅝" x 3⅝"

H
3½" x 3½"

10¾" x 10¾"

M
12" x 2'-3"

1" HOLE
FOR NAME
PLATE
DOWEL

'O' SIDE

STIFFENERS B & C

G
10¾" x 10¾"

6"

I
10¾" x 10¾"

'N' SIDE

2" DIA.
BIRDHSE
HOLE

J
10¾" x 10¾"

1" DIA.
PERCH
HOLE

5'-0"

2'-0"

K
HOUSE
NO'S

2'-8⅜"

2'-0"

P

Q

3⅝"

3½" x 3½"

10¾"

1'-10¾"

¾"

3"

R   6"

S   6"

T   6"

5'-0"

U
1'-0" x 6'-6"

6"

6"

12"   12"   12"   12"

4x8 Panel of 5/8-inch Plywood

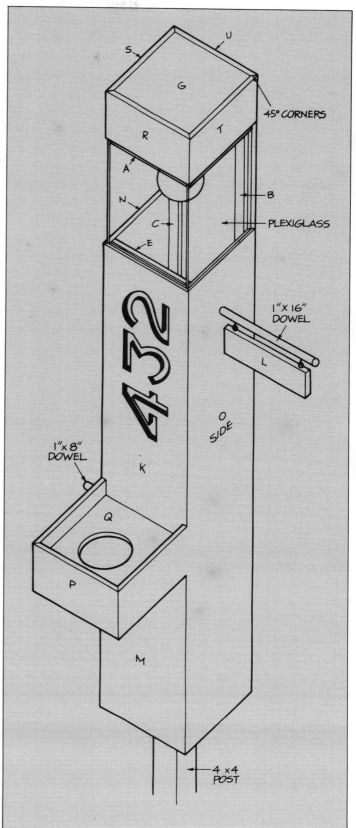

U

S

G

R   T

45° CORNERS

A

N

C

E

B

PLEXIGLASS

432

1" x 16"
DOWEL

L

1" x 8"
DOWEL

O
SIDE

K

Q

P

M

4 x 4
POST

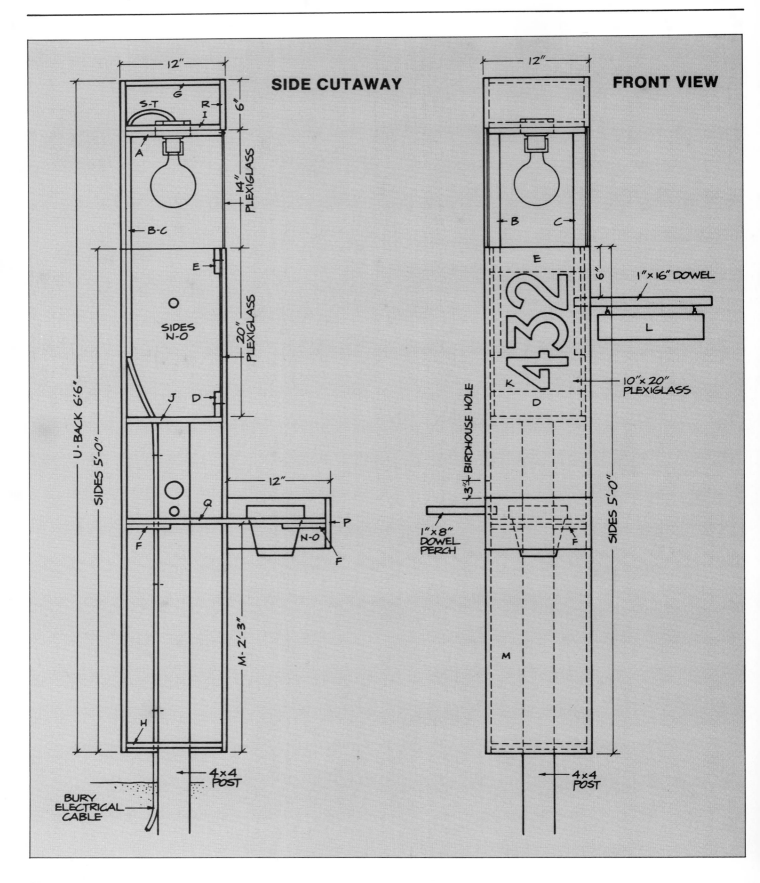

SIDE CUTAWAY

FRONT VIEW

Dollhouse Toy Cart

MATERIALS LIST

Quantity	Description
1	4 ft. x 4 ft. plywood panel of 1/2 in. APA grademarked A-B Interior, A-C Exterior, or Medium Density Overlay (MDO)
2	5/8 in. diameter dowel, 24 in. long
1	1-1/2 in. diameter wood dowel, 18 in. long
4	2 in. washers for wheels
4	3/4 in. door hinges
2 (optional)	Door latches
As required	6d finishing nails
As required	Wood dough
As required	Fine sandpaper
As required	White glue
As required	Interior semi-gloss enamel paint

CONSTRUCTION NOTES

Lay out pieces on plywood. Allow space in cuts for saw kerf width.
Cut out sides.
Cut out a rough square piece for each wheel. Trace each wheel and cut carefully. Glue two circles together to make each wheel. You may wish to cut out at least two circles at a time, to assure uniformity when gluing each pair together.
Glue-nail gussets to bottom of sections A and B as shown.
Assemble remaining pieces of the dollhouse as shown.
Glue-nail gussets to bottom. Check alignment by placing dowels through gussets before final attachment.
Glue wheels in place. Attach doors with hinges. You may wish to paint wheels and doors before you attach them.
Sand as needed and paint.

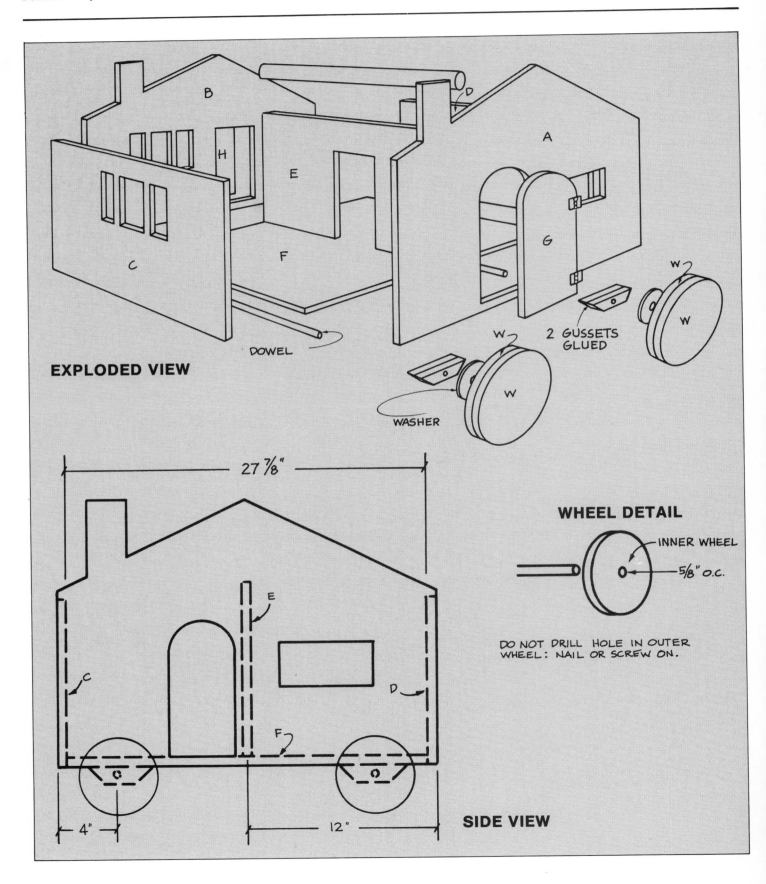

EXPLODED VIEW

B

H

E

C

F

DOWEL

D

A

G

W

2 GUSSETS GLUED

W

W

W

WASHER

27 7/8"

WHEEL DETAIL

INNER WHEEL

5/8" O.C.

DO NOT DRILL HOLE IN OUTER WHEEL: NAIL OR SCREW ON.

E

C

D

F

4"

12"

SIDE VIEW

PANEL LAYOUT

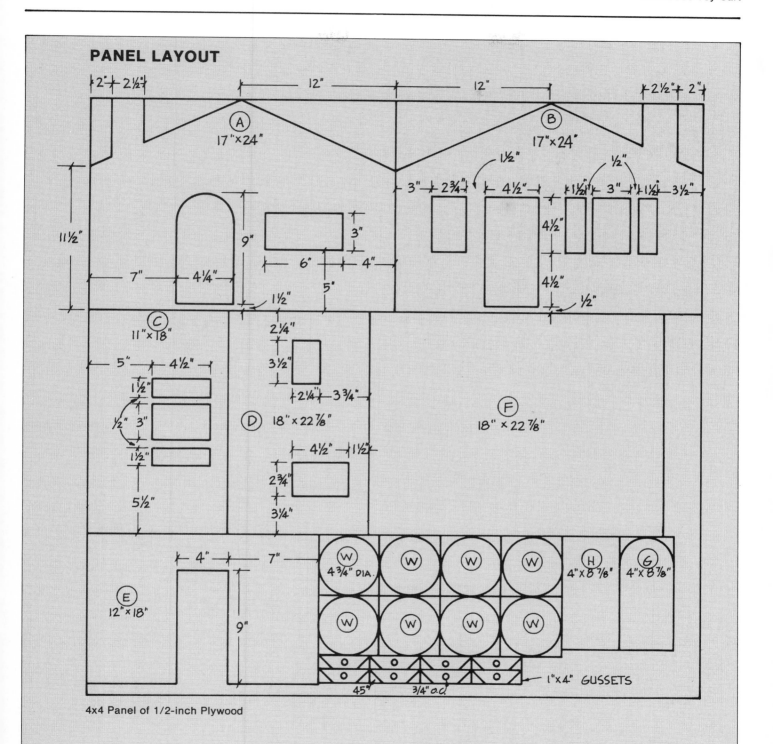

4x4 Panel of 1/2-inch Plywood

Mini-Pram

MATERIALS LIST

Quantity	Description
1	4 ft. x 8 ft. panel 3/8 in. APA grademarked Marine, A-B Exterior, or Medium Density Overlay (MDO)
1	4 ft. x 8 ft. panel 1/2 in. APA grademarked Marine, A-B Exterior, or Medium Density Overlay (MDO)
6	1x2s, 9-3/4 in. long for vertical framing
3	1x2s, 45-1/2 in. long for top cross framing
1	1x2, 44 in. long for transom base framing
2	1x2s, 88-1/4 in. long for side top framing
2	1x2s, 72-3/4 in. long for side bottom framing
3	1x2s, 67-3/4 in. long for bottom panel nailers
5	1x2s, 21-3/8 in. long for front (bow) supports
22	1x2s, 47 in. long for floor cross strips
2	1x2s, 78-3/4 in. long for side top trim
1	1x2, 72-1/4 in. long for keel
1	1x4, 44 in. long for spreader
2	Commercial oarlocks and mounting sockets available from marine supply outlet
4	1/4 in. dia. x 3 in. long carriage bolts with washers and nuts for oarlock mounting block assemblies
2	Wood block approx. 1 in. x 2-3/8 in. x 5 in. for oarlock mounting block assemblies
2	1-1/2 in. diam. x 57 in. long dowel for oar handles
As required	Waterproof glue
As required	2d non-staining, non-corrosive casing or finishing nails for glue-nailing
As required	3d non-staining, non-corrosive casing or finishing nails for glue-nailing
20	1-1/2 corrugated fasteners for glue-fastening
60 to 70	#8 x 1-1/2 in. brass or stainless steel, ovalhead or flathead wood screws
8	#8 x 3/4 in. brass or stainless steel, ovalhead or flathead wood screws
As required	Waterproof wood preservative compatible with finish
As required	Fine sandpaper for smoothing plywood cut edges
As required	Wood-compatible primer and marine paint for finishing

OARLOCK ASSEMBLY

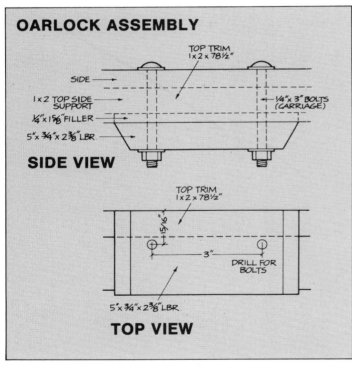

SIDE VIEW

TOP VIEW

OAR

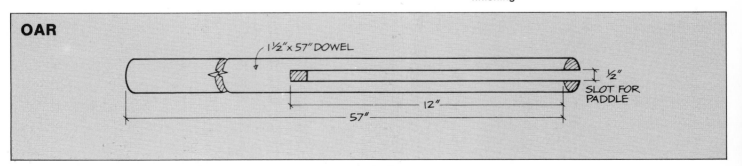

CONSTRUCTION NOTES

Lay out all parts as shown on panel layout. Mark parts for easy identification.

Cut out parts. Center saw cuts on pencil lines to equalize saw kerf on all parts.

Dimensions given in materials list for lumber framing are finished dimensions. For pieces with bevel cuts in the front (bow) area, you may want to cut square a little longer first and then cut or plane the bevel to the finished length.

Fill any voids in cut edges and lightly sand smooth.

Treat all parts with waterproof wood preservative according to manufacturer's instructions.

Construct boat frame from 1x2 lumber as shown in exploded view and side front detail. Use waterproof glue and 3d nails or corrugated fasteners as appropriate to make strong joints. Do not install the floor boards or middle 3 bow supports at this time.

Lay the plywood bottom panel down, bottom surface up, and set the frame, right side up, on top. Arrange the frame 1/2 inch in from each side and 1/2 inch forward of the aft end of the bottom panel, just as it will later be fastened to the reverse side of the panel. Lightly trace in pencil the outlines of the bottom framing pieces.

Remove the frame and set it down bottom side up. Support bottom frame pieces from beneath with bricks or wooden blocks so that you will be able to drive nails into the frame through the bottom panel.

Coat bottom surfaces of the bottom frame pieces with waterproof glue according to manufacturer's instructions and set plywood bottom panel in place over the frame, bottom surface up. Arrange precisely so that boat bottom extends 1/2 inch out from each side of frame and 1/2 inch behind rear of frame. Use scrap 1/2-inch plywood as gauge. Using 2d casing or finishing nails (1-inch maximum length) and penciled guidelines, fasten bottom panel to frame. Place nails roughly every 6 inches along all framing pieces. (Primary function of nails is to firmly clamp bottom panel to frame for good glue bond.)

Carefully turn boat right side up. Install transom using glue and 1-1/2-inch screws placed every 10 to 12 inches. Drill pilot holes first.

Install boat sides using glue and 1-1/2 inch screws. Drill pilot holes first.

Bevel edges of plywood bow piece as necessary, drill pilot holes and install using glue and 1-1/2-inch screws. Front end of bottom panel can be beveled to fit bow plane at this time.

Install 3 remaining bow supports and floor boards (except those for seat base) as shown in exploded view. Use glue and 1-1/2-inch screws for attaching bow supports through bow piece into supports. Use glue and nails for floor boards.

Begin seat assembly outside of the boat. Make seat base by edge-gluing 8 lumber pieces together as a set. Use bar or pipe clamp to hold until dry. Drill pilot holes and, using 1-1/2-inch screws, glue-screw the middle 4 seat supports and seat back to seat base and to each other with approximate spacing shown in finished drawing. Do not install 2 outermost seat supports yet.

Install partially completed seat assembly in boat and glue-nail seat base to bottom 1x2 nailers. Drill pilot holes and using glue and four 3/4 inch screws each side, install outer seat supports against boat sides. Install screws through boat sides into seat supports.

Drill pilot holes. Using 1-1/2-inch screws, glue-screw seat in position over seat supports and seat back.

Drill pilot holes and install front and rear top pieces using glue and 1-1/2-inch screws.

Install top side trim pieces (gunwales) using nails and glue.

Install oarlock mounting block as shown in finished drawing and in detail.

Construct oars using glue and 1-1/2-inch screws, or purchase 6-foot oars.

Attach oarlocks.

Install oarlock sockets to mounting blocks.

Install flotation blocks, such as Styrofoam, in side compartments of seat.

Drill pilot holes and using 1-1/2-inch screws, glue-screw keel board to bottom center of boat and bevel front end to match bow angle.

Finish with primer and two finish coats of marine paint.

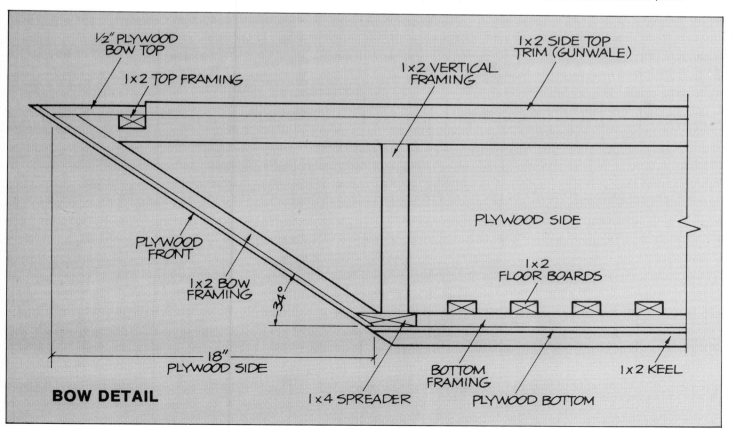

BOW DETAIL

PANEL LAYOUT

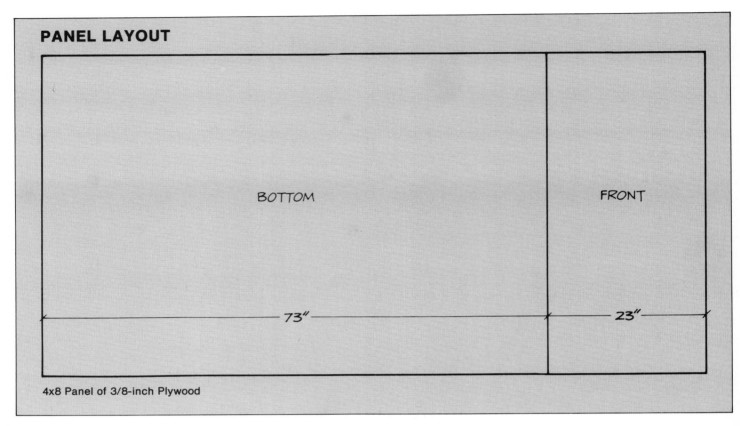

BOTTOM

FRONT

73"

23"

4x8 Panel of 3/8-inch Plywood

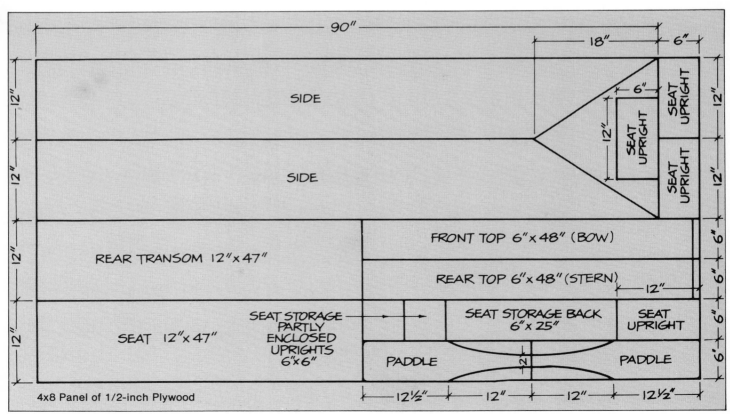

90"

18"

6"

12"

SIDE

6"

SEAT UPRIGHT

12"

SEAT UPRIGHT

12"

SIDE

SEAT UPRIGHT

12"

SEAT UPRIGHT

12"

FRONT TOP 6" x 48" (BOW)

6"

REAR TRANSOM 12" x 47"

REAR TOP 6" x 48" (STERN)

12"

6"

SEAT STORAGE PARTLY ENCLOSED UPRIGHTS 6" x 6"

SEAT STORAGE BACK 6" x 25"

SEAT UPRIGHT

6"

SEAT 12" x 47"

PADDLE

2

PADDLE

6"

4x8 Panel of 1/2-inch Plywood

12½"

12"

12"

12½"

EXPLODED VIEW

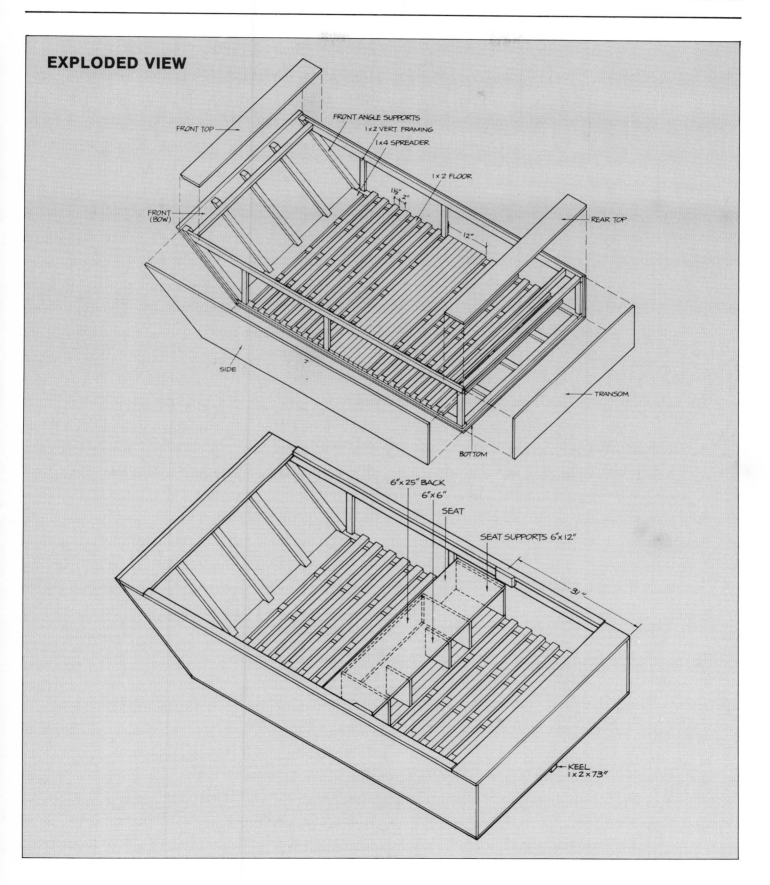

Tool Storage Workbench

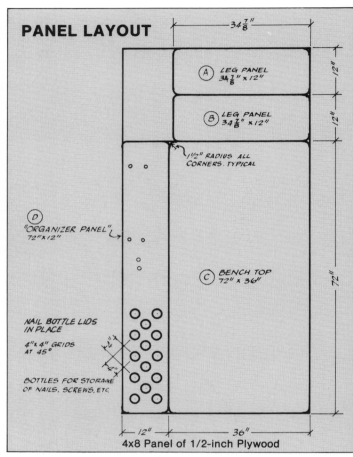

PANEL LAYOUT

(A) LEG PANEL 34⅞" x 12"

(B) LEG PANEL 34⅞" x 12"

1½" RADIUS ALL CORNERS. TYPICAL

(D) "ORGANIZER PANEL" 72" x 12"

(C) BENCH TOP 72" x 36"

NAIL BOTTLE LIDS IN PLACE

4" x 4" GRIDS AT 45°

BOTTLES FOR STORAGE OF NAILS, SCREWS, ETC.

4x8 Panel of 1/2-inch Plywood

MATERIALS LIST

Quantity	Description
1	4 ft. x 8 ft. plywood panel of 3/4 in. APA grademarked A-A, A-B, or B-B Interior or Medium Density Overlay (MDO)
8	4 in. long zinc-plated strap hinges for fastening bench to legs, wall and floor (Sears Cat. No. 9HT59502 or equivalent)
As required	1/2 in. diameter dowel cut to 2-1/2 in. lengths for holding tools. Locate dowel positions to fit your tools, then drill locations into organizer panel. Glue dowels in place
As required	Urea-resin glue for dowels
As required	Small jars with screw lids to hold nails, washers, bolts and other small parts on organizer panel
As required	6d nails to mount bottle lids on organizer panel
As required	1/4 in. diameter cadmium-plated lag screws, 1-1/2 in. long, for mounting organizer panel into wall studs
As required	Fine sandpaper to smooth plywood cut edges
As required	Paint or stain for finishing

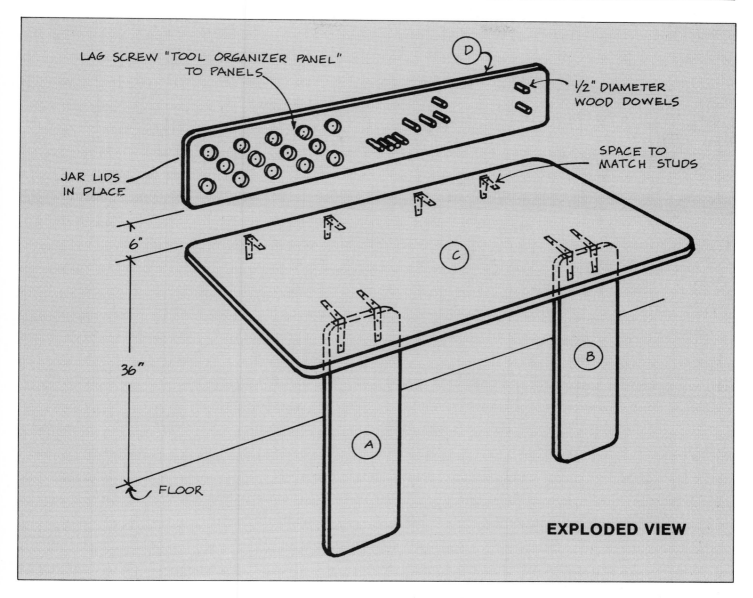

LAG SCREW "TOOL ORGANIZER PANEL" TO PANELS

D

½" DIAMETER WOOD DOWELS

JAR LIDS IN PLACE

SPACE TO MATCH STUDS

6"

C

36"

B

A

FLOOR

EXPLODED VIEW

CONSTRUCTION NOTES

Lay out plywood panel for cutting as shown in cutting diagram. Allow for saw kerf width when plotting dimensions.

Cut out pieces and true edges with a sanding block. Fill and sand any voids in edges. Paint or stain as desired.

Attach hinges to wall studs. You may wish to use lag screws to ensure a firm hold. Leave enough room between table top and wall for top and legs to fold flush against wall.

Attach leg panels to bench top with hinges.

Attach bench top to hinges on wall. Lifting legs will allow bench to fold against wall.

Arrange organizer panel with jar lids and 1/2-inch dowels to suit your needs.

Mount organizer panel with lag screws driven into wall studs.

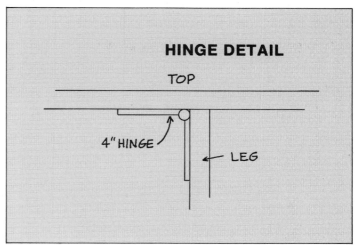

HINGE DETAIL

TOP

4" HINGE

LEG

Recipe File & Cookbook Shelf

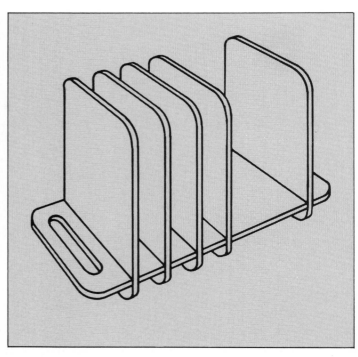

PANEL LAYOUT

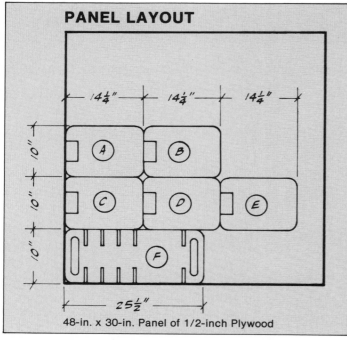

48-in. x 30-in. Panel of 1/2-inch Plywood

MATERIALS LIST

Quantity	Description
1	4 ft. x 4 ft. plywood panel of 1/2 in. APA grademarked A-A, A-B or B-B Interior, or Medium Density Overlay (MDO)
2	1/2 in. diameter dowel, 19-1/2 in. long
10	Felt or cork pads for bottom of shelf sections
As required	Urea-resin type glue for gluing horizontal edge of cutout on Parts A through E
As required	Fine sandpaper for smoothing edges of plywood
As required	Wood filler for exposed plywood edges
As required	Paint or stain for finishing

CONSTRUCTION NOTES

Lay out plywood panel for cutting as shown in cutting diagram. Allow for saw kerf width when plotting dimensions.

Cut out parts. Clamp dividers to cut notches in bottom. Fill and sand edges. For best results, clamp dividers, parts A through E, together and sand together. Drill hole for dowel while still clamped.

Cut out slots and holes in base.

Glue dividers into slots and lock in place with dowels.

Place felt or cork pads on bottom of dividers.

Paint or stain pieces as desired.

EXPLODED VIEW

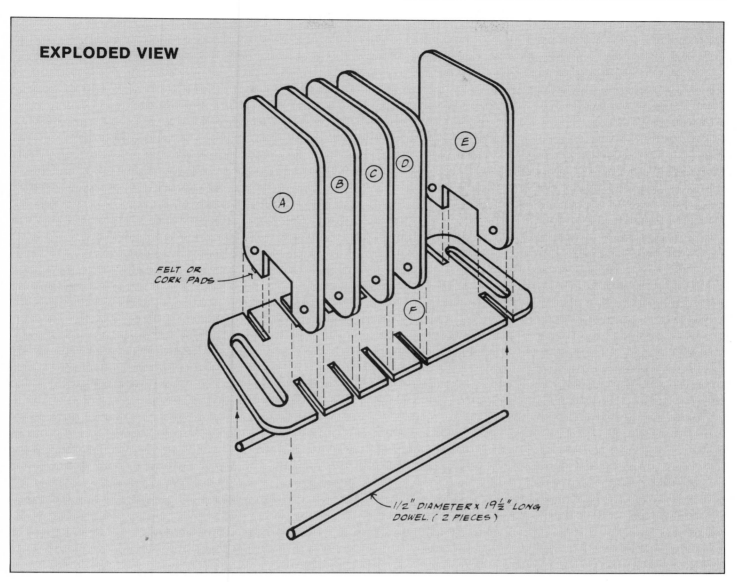

FELT OR
CORK PADS

1/2" DIAMETER x 19 1/2" LONG
DOWEL (2 PIECES)

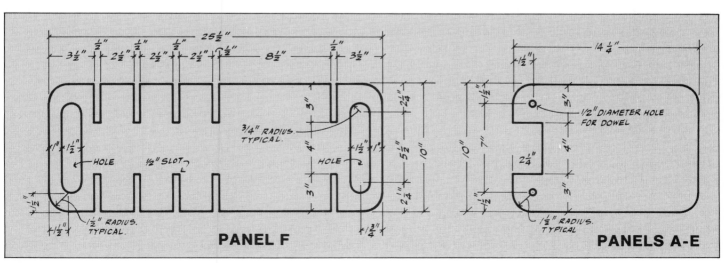

PANEL F

25 1/2"
3 1/2"   1/2"   2 1/2"   1/2"   2 1/2"   1/2"   2 1/2"   1/2"   8 1/2"   1/2"   3 1/2"

3"
3/4" RADIUS.
TYPICAL.
2 1/4"
5 1/2"
10"
4"
3"
2 1/4"

1" x 1 1/2"
HOLE
1/2" SLOT
1 1/2" x 1"
HOLE

1/2"
1/2" RADIUS.
TYPICAL.
1 1/2"
1 3/4"

PANELS A-E

14 1/4"
1/2"
1/2"
10"
7"
3"
4"
2 1/4"
3"
1/2"

1/2" DIAMETER HOLE
FOR DOWEL

1 1/2" RADIUS.
TYPICAL

Toy Storage Bench

MATERIALS LIST

Quantity	Description
2	4 ft. x 8 ft. plywood panels of 3/4 in. APA grademarked A-A, A-B or B-B Exterior, or Medium Density Overlay (MDO)
16	1-1/2 in. diameter dowels, 3 in. long, for slot and tab assembly
12	Casters for drawers
8	Furniture glides for tab separators
As required	8d finishing nails for glue-nailing drawers
As required	Urea-resin glue for glue-nailing drawers
As required	Filler for countersunk nail holes and, if necessary, for filling small gaps in cut plywood edges
As required	Fine sandpaper for smoothing plywood edges and filler material
As required	Top-quality nontoxic paint for finishing. A primer coat is recommended

CONSTRUCTION NOTES

Lay out parts on panels according to plans. Allow for saw kerf width when measuring.

Make parts for easy identification.

Cut out parts.

Construct three drawers as shown on page 116. Glue-nail all joints for added strength. Nails can be countersunk.

Drill holes in bench supports for dowels.

Assemble bench as shown. Bench supports are held in place by 1-1/2-inch dowels as shown in detail. Dowels can be glued or left free.

Fill voids in plywood edges and nail holes with wood dough. Sand smooth.

Paint as desired with non-toxic paint.

TAB DETAIL

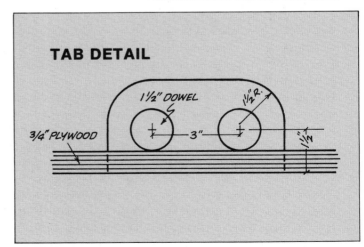

PANEL LAYOUT

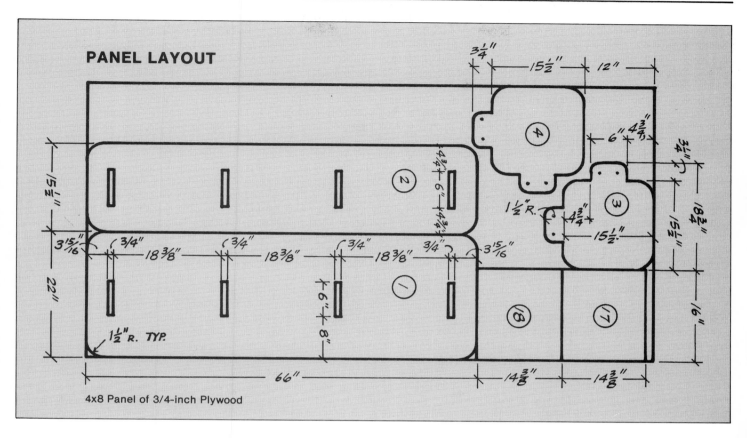

4x8 Panel of 3/4-inch Plywood

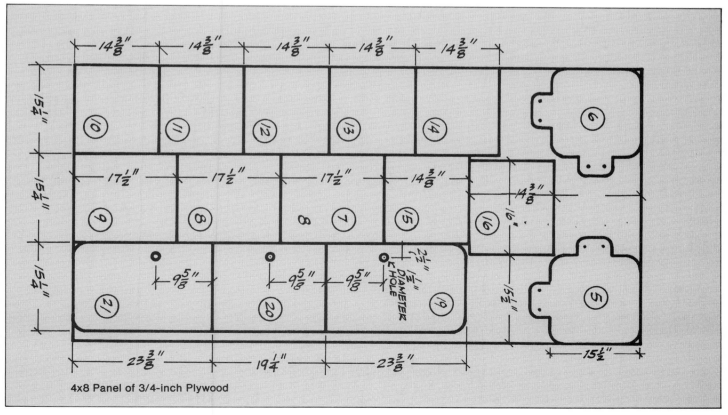

4x8 Panel of 3/4-inch Plywood

EXPLODED VIEW

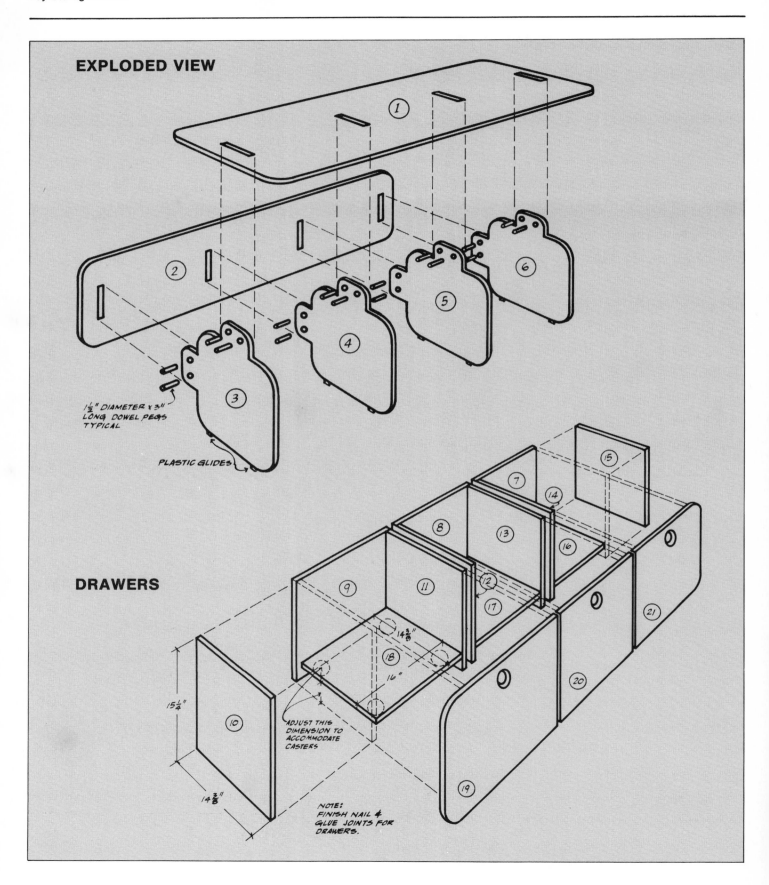

1½" DIAMETER x 3"
LONG DOWEL PEGS
TYPICAL

PLASTIC GLIDES

DRAWERS

15¼"

14⅜"

14⅜"

16"

ADJUST THIS
DIMENSION TO
ACCOMMODATE
CASTERS

NOTE:
FINISH NAIL &
GLUE JOINTS FOR
DRAWERS.

Early American Wall Shelf

MATERIALS LIST

Quantity	Description
1	4 ft. x 4 ft. plywood panel of 1/2 in. APA grademarked A-A, A-B, B-B Interior or Medium Density Overlay (MDO) for A through D
4	1/2 in. x 1/2 in. pieces of facing, 24 inches long
4	1-1/8 in. diameter wooden balls
24	4d finishing nails for attaching sides and shelves to back
12	1 in. brads for attaching facing strips to shelves
As required	Urea-resin glue for glue-nailing
As required	Surfacing putty for filling countersunk nail holes and exposed plywood edges
As required	Fine sandpaper for smoothing

CONSTRUCTION NOTES

Lay out plywood for cutting as shown in the cutting diagram. Allow for saw kerf width when plotting dimensions.

Cut out pieces and fill and sand edges. Cut 1/2-inch by 1/4-inch deep notches in sides as shown. Use the layout grid detail for back design.

Glue shelves to sides as shown.

Glue-nail back to sides and shelves.

Glue-nail wooden balls to bottom. If shelf will be hung, only two balls are required on front corners.

Glue-nail bottom to back and sides.

Attach facing with brads and glue.

Fill nail holes and sand.

Paint or stain as desired.

PANEL LAYOUT
4x4 Panel of 1/2-inch Plywood

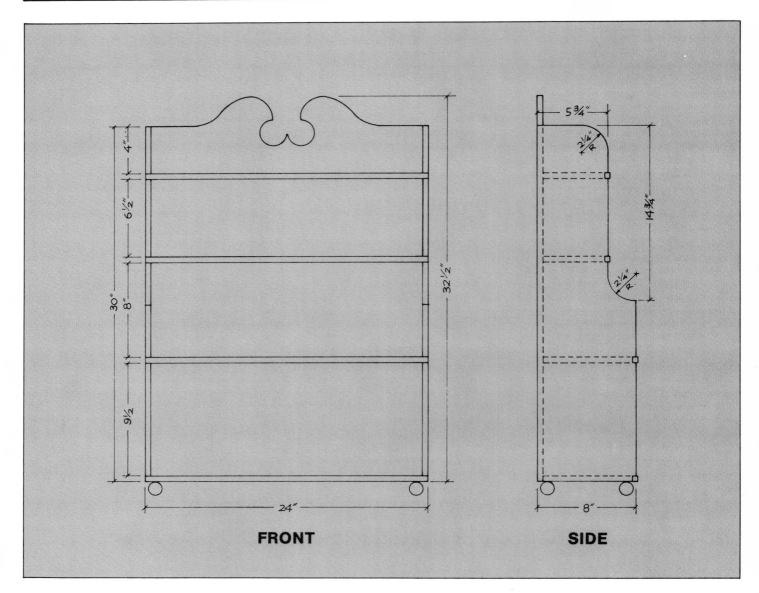

FRONT

SIDE

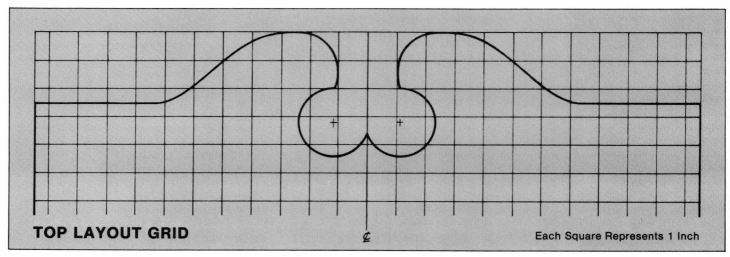

TOP LAYOUT GRID

Each Square Represents 1 Inch

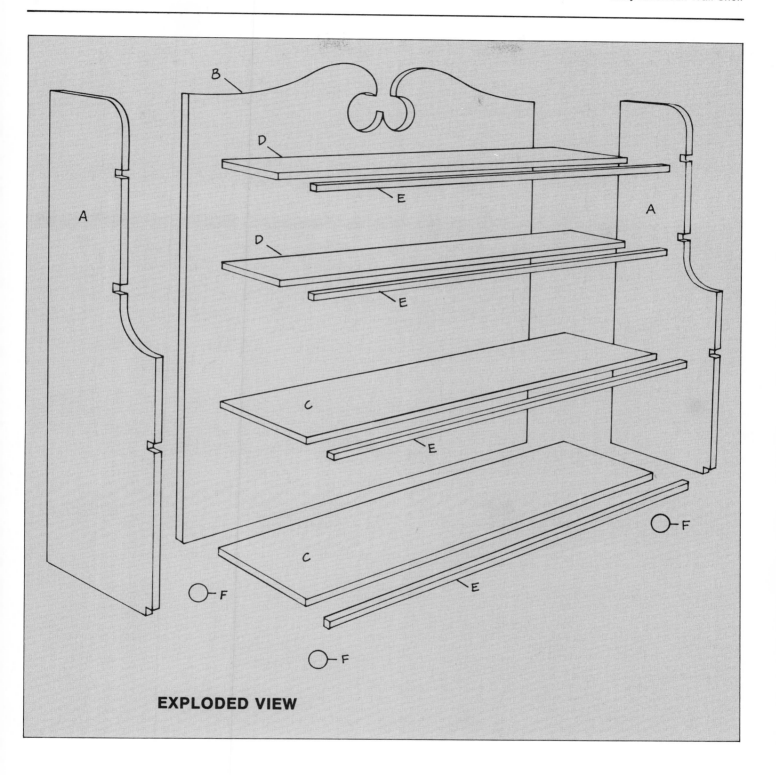

EXPLODED VIEW

Compact Desk

MATERIALS LIST

Quantity	Description
1	4 ft. x 8 ft. plywood panel of 3/4 in. APA grademarked A-B Interior, A-C Exterior, or Medium Density Overlaid (MDO)
16 linear ft.	1-1/2 in. diameter wooden half-round
14 linear ft.	3/4 in. diameter wooden half-round
1 yd.	Vinyl material
As required	8d finishing nails
As required	Wood dough
As required	Fine sandpaper
As required	White glue
As required	Interior semi-gloss enamel paint

CONSTRUCTION NOTES

Lay out pieces on plywood. Allow space for saw kerf width on cuts.

Cut out parts.

Glue-nail each pair of A sections together to form the double-thickness desk sides.

Cut the 1-1/2-inch half-rounds to fit A section dimensions. Allow enough length to cut the 45° mitered half-round corners, as shown.

Glue-nail 3/4 inch half-round to section B, as shown. Cover the entire piece with vinyl.

Glue-nail 3/4-inch half-rounds to sections C and D as shown.

Assemble the desk. Fill joints with wood dough as needed and let dry.

Sand as needed and paint as desired.

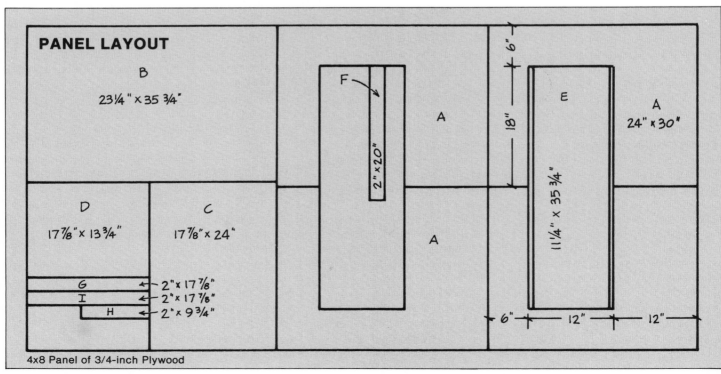

PANEL LAYOUT

B
23¼" x 35 ¾"

D
17⅞" x 13¾"

C
17⅞" x 24"

G — 2" x 17⅞"
I — 2" x 17⅞"
H — 2" x 9¾"

F
2" x 20"

A

A

6"

18"

E
11¼" x 35 ¾"

A
24" x 30"

6"   12"   12"

4x8 Panel of 3/4-inch Plywood

SIDE

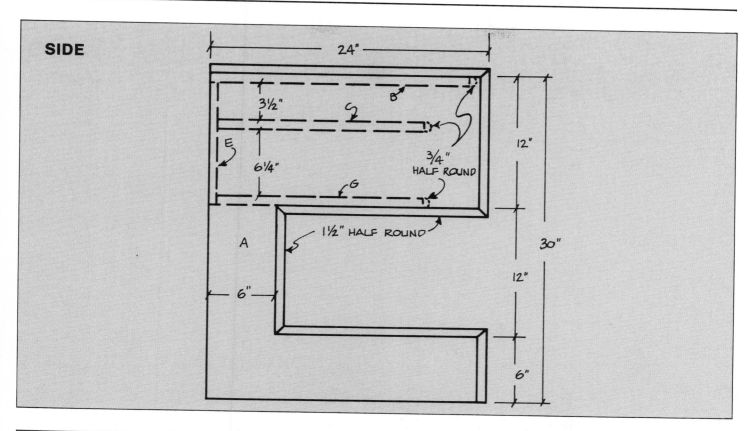

FRONT

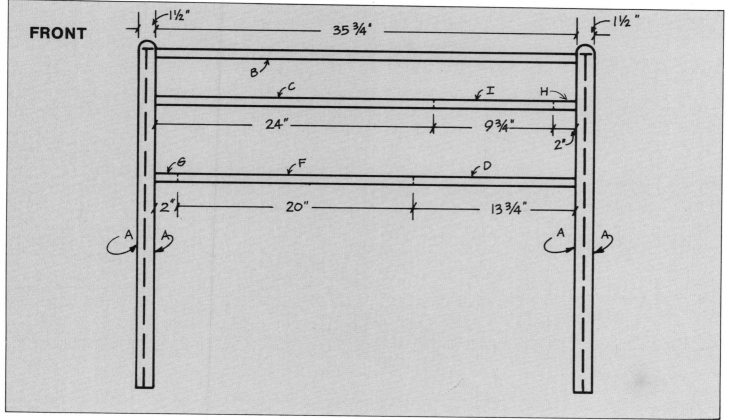

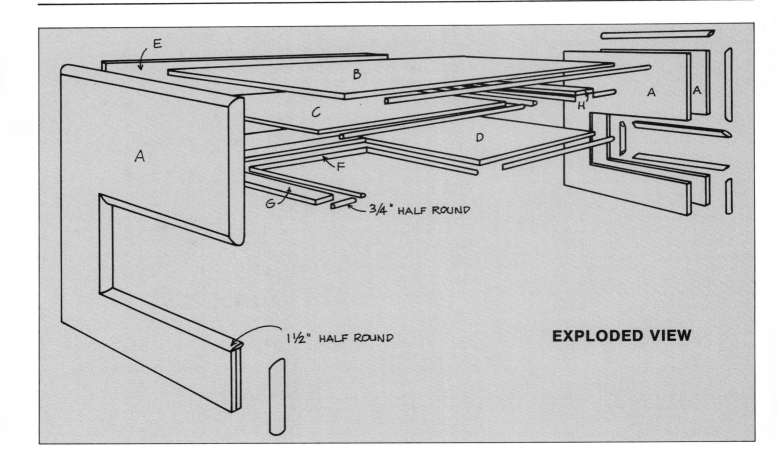

E

B

C

A

D

F

G

3/4" HALF ROUND

H

A

A

1½" HALF ROUND

EXPLODED VIEW

Planter Benches

MATERIALS LIST

Quantity	Description
1	4 ft. x 8 ft. plywood panel of 3/8 in. APA grademarked 303 Exterior siding of any texture for straight bench
1	4 ft. x 8 ft. plywood panel of 3/8 in. of the same grade for L-shape bench
52 linear ft.	2x4s for straight bench. Recommended lumber: No. 2 and better WWP grade-stamped 2x4s for straight bench.
53 linear ft.	2x2s for straight bench
6 linear ft.	1x3s for straight bench
2 linear ft.	1 in.diameter dowel
107 linear ft.	2x4s for L-shape bench
96 linear ft.	2x2s for L-shape bench
12 linear ft.	1x3s for L-shape bench
4 linear ft.	1 in. diameter dowel
As required	2 in. #8 flathead wood screws
As required	4d nonstaining finishing nails
As required	Wood preservative for inside planter boxes
As required	Waterproof glue for glue-nail and glue-screw assembly
As required	Stain for finishing

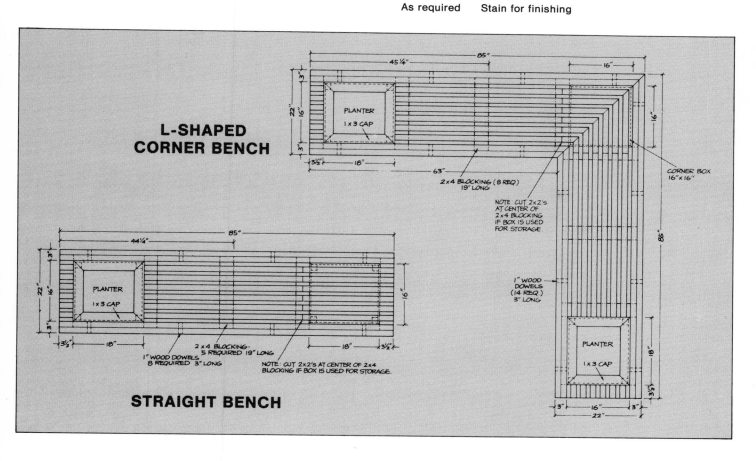

L-SHAPED CORNER BENCH

STRAIGHT BENCH

CONSTRUCTION NOTES

Lay out parts according to plans. Be sure to allow for saw kerf width.

Cut out parts.

Screws are used to attach 2x4 lumber to 2x2 bench slats. You'll need 1 screw for every intersection of the pieces. Drill through the 2x4 into the 2x2. Spread glue between pieces and drive screw through the 2x4 into 2x2. Wipe away any excess glue when bench top assembly is complete.

Assemble 2x4 base, using glue and four nails per corner. Line up mitered corner of a box side along one edge of a 2x2 corner brace. Spread glue along 2x2 and nail the plywood to the glued piece. Use nonstaining nails spaced about every 3 inches. Repeat gluing and nailing to complete the corner, then repeat with other

corners. When box shell is complete, slide plywood planter bottom into end and nail to 2x2 corner pieces. Set the box onto the 2x4 base. Nail through box sides into 2x4 base.

To attach planter box to bench top, nail along edges of box into 2x4 blocking of bench. Space nails about 3 inches apart.

To attach 1x3 cap, nail it to the 2x2 corner braces of the box and, if desired, toenail it into the 2x4 blocking at 3-inch intervals. Countersink nails.

One version is a straight bench, 85 inches long, with a planter box in one end and storage box at the other. The other, for round-the-corner seating, is 85 inches on a side and has a planter at each end.

PANEL LAYOUT

STRAIGHT BENCH

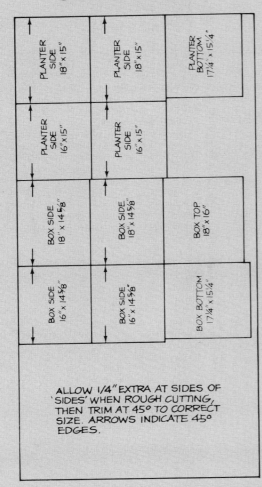

ALLOW 1/4" EXTRA AT SIDES OF 'SIDES' WHEN ROUGH CUTTING, THEN TRIM AT 45° TO CORRECT SIZE. ARROWS INDICATE 45° EDGES.

4x8 Panel of 3/8-inch Plywood

L-SHAPED CORNER BENCH

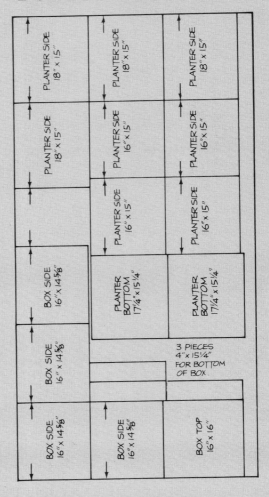

4x8 Panel of 3/8-inch Plywood

CORNER BENCH

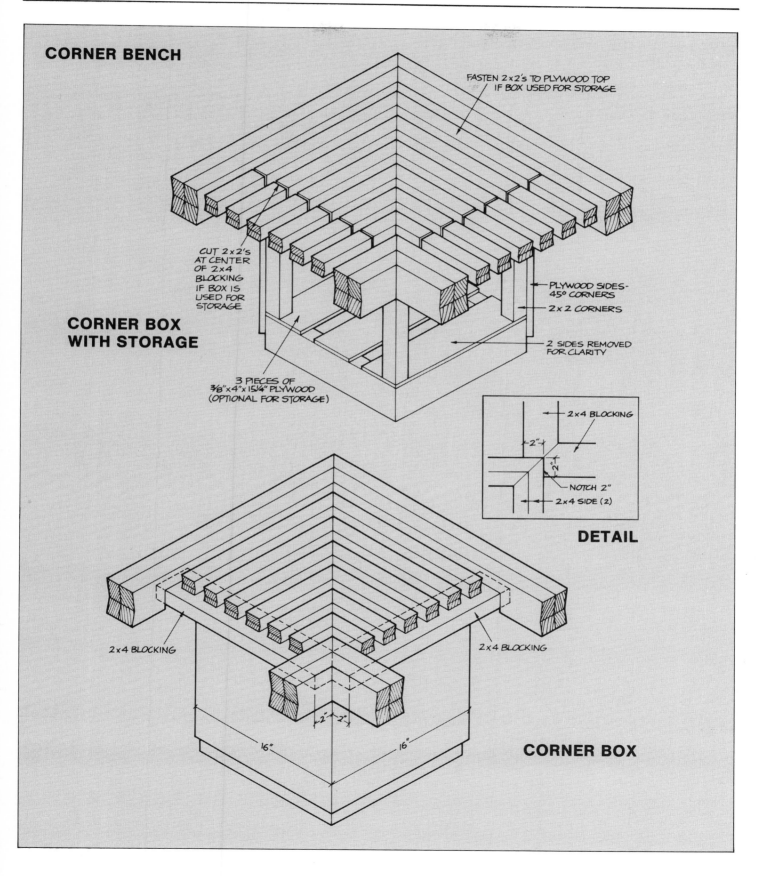

FASTEN 2 x 2's TO PLYWOOD TOP IF BOX USED FOR STORAGE

CUT 2 x 2's AT CENTER OF 2 x 4 BLOCKING IF BOX IS USED FOR STORAGE

PLYWOOD SIDES - 45° CORNERS

2 x 2 CORNERS

CORNER BOX WITH STORAGE

2 SIDES REMOVED FOR CLARITY

3 PIECES OF 3/8" x 4" x 15¼" PLYWOOD (OPTIONAL FOR STORAGE)

2 x 4 BLOCKING

NOTCH 2"

2 x 4 SIDE (2)

DETAIL

2 x 4 BLOCKING

2 x 4 BLOCKING

16"

16"

CORNER BOX

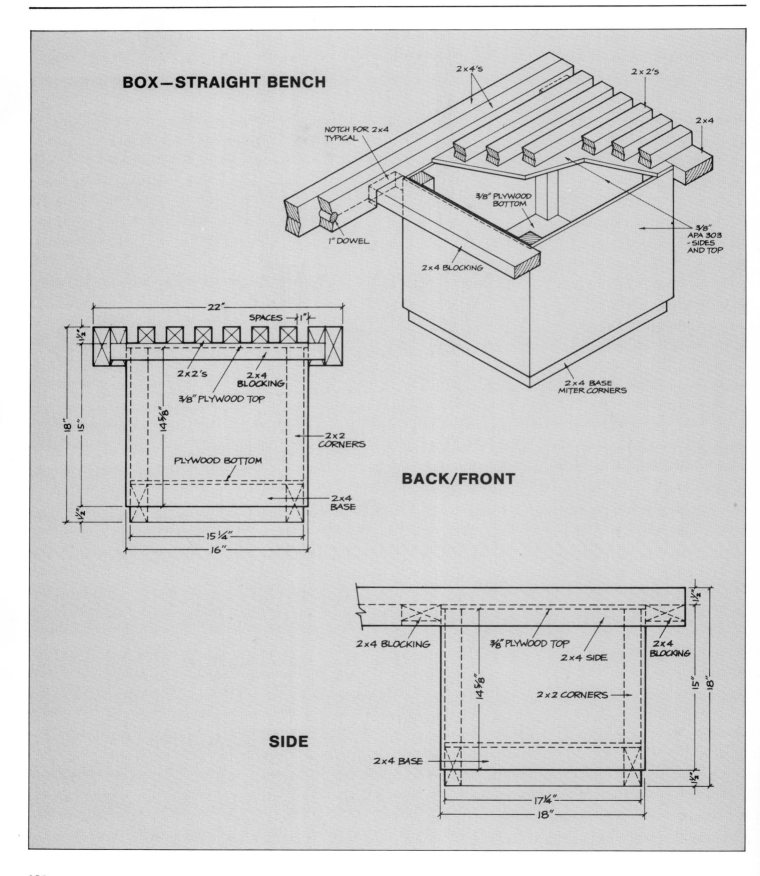

BOX—STRAIGHT BENCH

2x4's

2x2's

2x4

NOTCH FOR 2x4 TYPICAL

3/8" PLYWOOD BOTTOM

3/8" APA 303 -SIDES AND TOP

1" DOWEL

2x4 BLOCKING

2x4 BASE MITER CORNERS

22"

SPACES 1"

1/2"

2x2's

2x4 BLOCKING

3/8" PLYWOOD TOP

14 5/8"

18"

15"

2x2 CORNERS

PLYWOOD BOTTOM

BACK/FRONT

1/2"

2x4 BASE

15 1/4"

16"

2x4 BLOCKING

3/8" PLYWOOD TOP

2x4 SIDE

2x4 BLOCKING

1 1/2"

14 5/8"

2x2 CORNERS

15"

18"

SIDE

2x4 BASE

1/2"

17 1/4"

18"

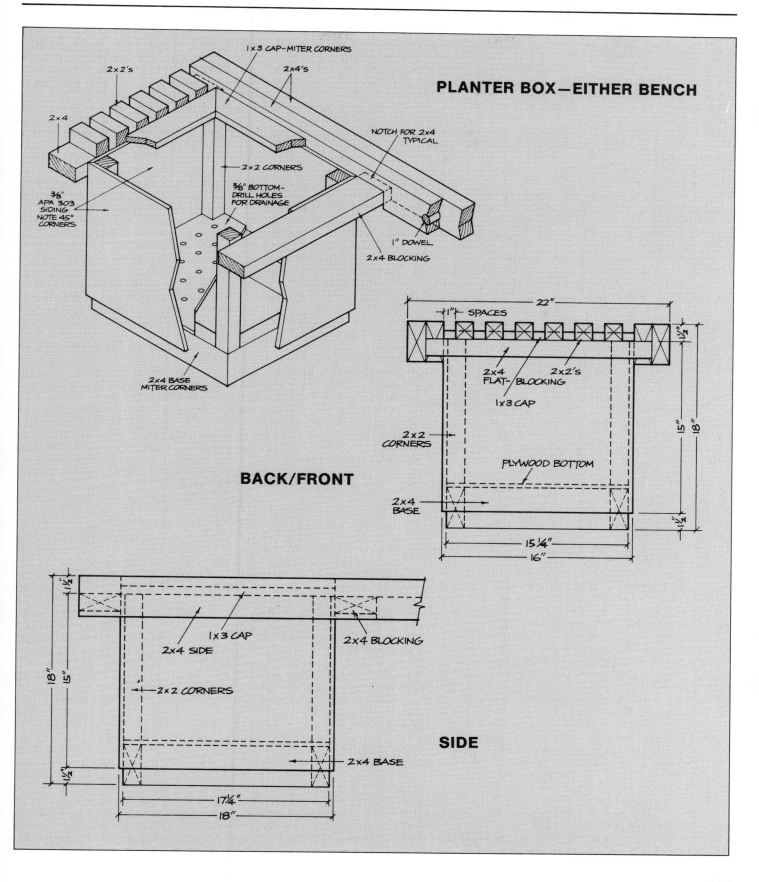

PLANTER BOX—EITHER BENCH

1x3 CAP-MITER CORNERS

2x2's

2x4's

2x4

NOTCH FOR 2x4 TYPICAL

2x2 CORNERS

3/8" APA 303 SIDING NOTE 45° CORNERS

3/8" BOTTOM-DRILL HOLES FOR DRAINAGE

1" DOWEL

2x4 BLOCKING

2x4 BASE MITER CORNERS

BACK/FRONT

1" SPACES

22"

1/2"

2x4 FLAT-BLOCKING

2x2's

1x3 CAP

2x2 CORNERS

PLYWOOD BOTTOM

15"

18"

2x4 BASE

1 1/2"

15 1/4"

16"

1 1/2"

1x3 CAP

2x4 SIDE

2x4 BLOCKING

2x2 CORNERS

18"

15"

1/2"

2x4 BASE

17 1/4"

18"

SIDE

Slot Together Coffee Table

MATERIALS LIST

Quantity	Description
1	4 ft. x 4 ft. plywood panel of 3/4 in. APA grademarked A-B or A-D Interior, A-B or A-C Exterior, or Medium Density Overlay (MDO)
12	3d finishing or 1-1/4 in. flathead nails for installing blocks
As required	White glue for holding blocks in place and for permanent assembly, if desired
As required	Fine sandpaper
As required	Wood dough for filling any small voids in plywood edges
As required	Primer and enamel or plastic laminate and edge stripping

CONSTRUCTION NOTES

Draw all parts on panel except for slots.

Use a compass or make a 1-inch radius template of cardboard or construction paper for marking corner curves.

Cut out parts except for slots.

Clamp legs together. Draw slots on one panel face and cut both panels simultaneously. Cut slot sides. Unclamp, and mark slot depth accurately on each piece. Remove slot piece with a chisel and hammer. Repeat for slots in cross members.

Assemble legs.

Lay table top face down and center leg assembly in place. Mark locations for blocks.

Remove leg assembly and take apart. Glue blocks in place and clamp until dry.

Smooth plywood cut edges with fine sandpaper. Fill any edge voids with wood dough, allow to dry, and sand.

Finish each piece separately, using primer and paint. Assemble when dry. Table is designed for quick take-apart and storage when not in use. Parts may be glued in place for permanent use, if desired.

PANEL LAYOUT

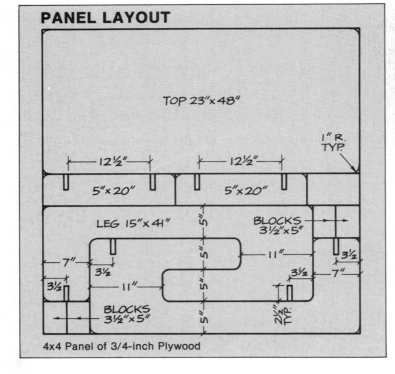

TOP 23" x 48"

1" R. TYP.

12½"   12½"

5" x 20"   5" x 20"

LEG 15" x 41"

BLOCKS 3½" x 5"

5"   5"   5"   5"   5"

11"   3½"

7"   3½"

3½"   11"   3½"   7"

BLOCKS 3½" x 5"

2½" TYP.

4x4 Panel of 3/4-inch Plywood

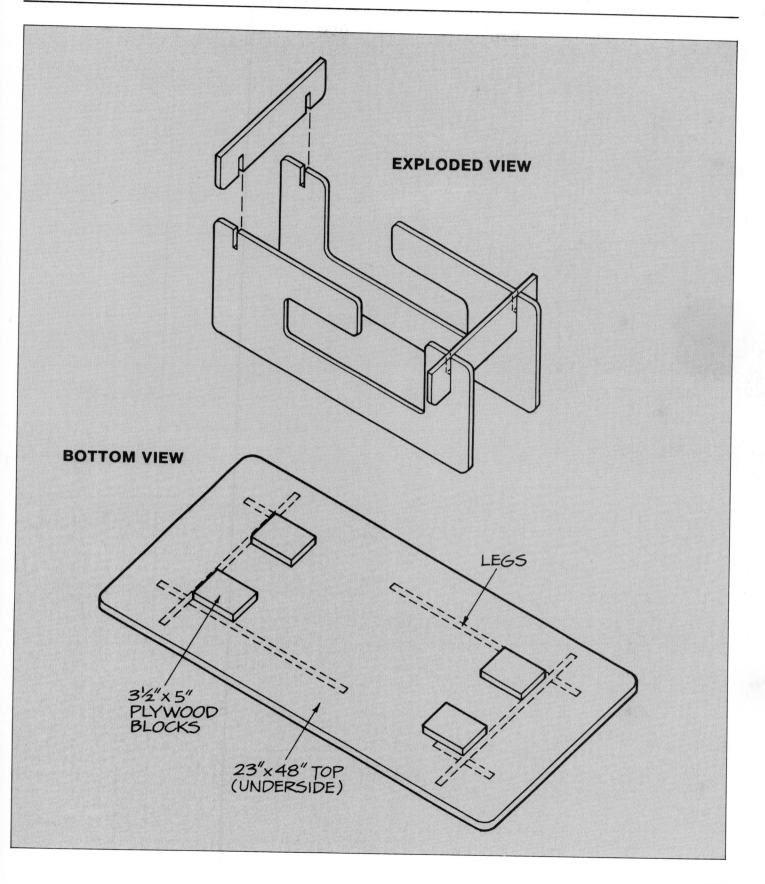

EXPLODED VIEW

BOTTOM VIEW

LEGS

3½″ x 5″
PLYWOOD
BLOCKS

23″ x 48″ TOP
(UNDERSIDE)

Kitchen Storage Cart

MATERIALS LIST

Quantity	Description
2	4 ft. x 8 ft. plywood panels of 3/4 in. APA grademarked A-A or A-B Interior or Medium Density Overlay (MDO)
1 set	1-1/2 in. heavy-duty globe casters (Sears Cat. No. 9H74444 with antique English finish or 9H74043 with brass finish, or equivalent)
1	23-7/8 in. x 36 in. plastic laminate for top
2	3 in. x 36 in. plastic laminate for sides
2	3 in. x 23-7/8 in. plastic laminate for ends
10 linear ft.	1x1s for shelf support cleats, cut to lengths
1	1 in. diameter pull bar, approximately 18 in. long
As required	4d finishing nails for glue-nail assembly of shelf-support cleats
As required	6d finishing nails for glue-nail assembly of plywood unit
As required	White or urea-resin glue for glue-nail assembly
As required	Wood dough to fill any small gaps in plywood cut edges
As required	Fine sandpaper for smoothing edges and cured wood dough
As required	Paint, stain, or antiquing for finishing

CONSTRUCTION NOTES

Lay out plywood for cutting as shown in cutting diagram. Allow for saw kerf width when plotting dimensions. Mark parts for easy identification.

Cut out plywood parts and fill and sand edges.

Cut six 14-3/4-inch pieces from 1x1 stock. Bevel one end of each so they will be less visible. Glue-nail three of these pieces to vertical divider K and three to side J with 4d finishing nails. Space as shown in end view. Beveled ends should be on end side of cart.

Glue-nail shelves F, G and H to shelf supports on vertical divider K and side J.

Glue-nail shelf assembly to bottom B.

Glue-nail I to bottom B, vertical divider C and end M.

Cut three 23-7/8-inch shelf supports from remaining 1x1 stock. Bevel both ends of each so they will be less visible.

Glue-nail shelf supports into position on vertical divider C, end D and bottom B as shown in side view. Use 4d finishing nails.

Glue-nail end D to sides I and J and bottom B.

Glue-nail shelf E and support L into place.

Glue-nail top A to assembly.

Fill and sand all nail holes.

Paint, stain or antique as desired.

Cover top and edges of top with plastic laminate.

Attach pull bar to end M.

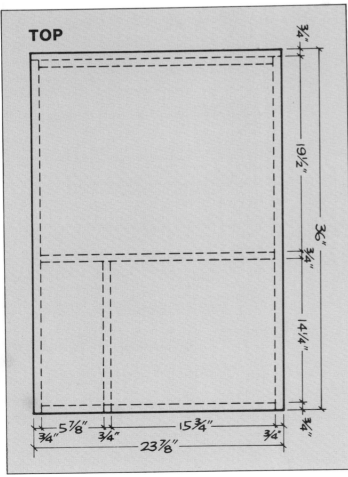

TOP

PANEL LAYOUT

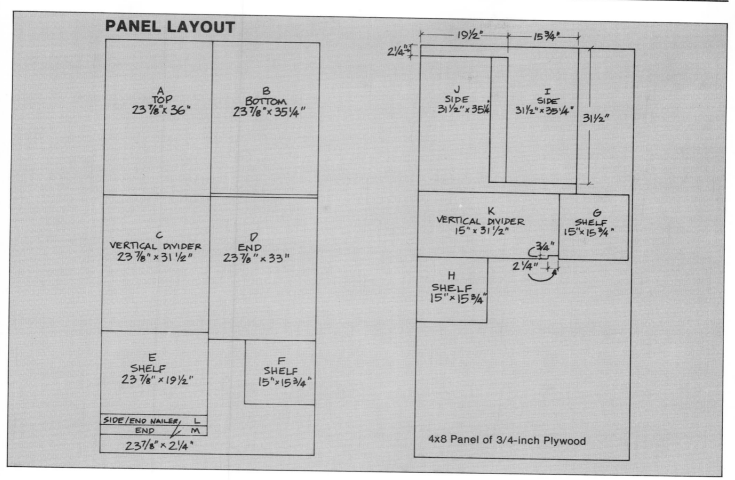

A
TOP
23 7/8" x 36"

B
BOTTOM
23 7/8" x 35 1/4"

C
VERTICAL DIVIDER
23 7/8" x 31 1/2"

D
END
23 7/8" x 33"

E
SHELF
23 7/8" x 19 1/2"

F
SHELF
15" x 15 3/4"

SIDE/END NAILER, L
END / M
23 7/8" x 2 1/4"

19 1/2"   15 3/4"
2 1/4"

J
SIDE
31 1/2" x 35 1/4"

I
SIDE
31 1/2" x 35 1/4"

31 1/2"

K
VERTICAL DIVIDER
15" x 31 1/2"

G
SHELF
15" x 15 3/4"

3/4"
2 1/4"

H
SHELF
15" x 15 3/4"

4x8 Panel of 3/4-inch Plywood

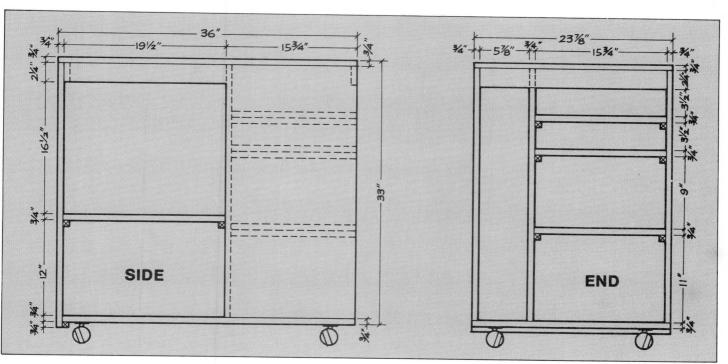

SIDE

END

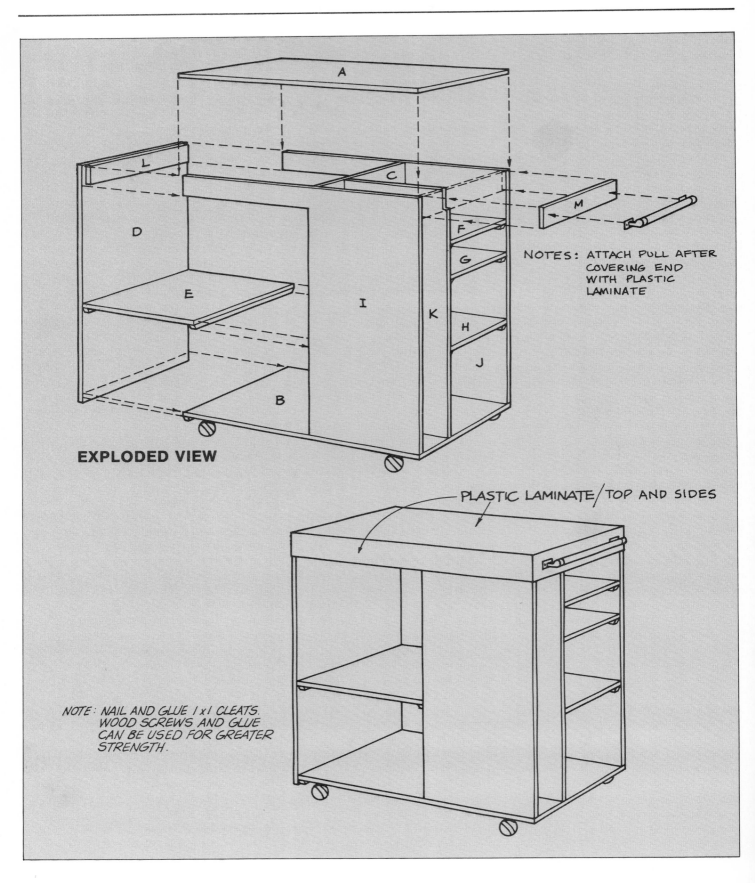

EXPLODED VIEW

NOTES: ATTACH PULL AFTER COVERING END WITH PLASTIC LAMINATE

PLASTIC LAMINATE/TOP AND SIDES

NOTE: NAIL AND GLUE 1 x 1 CLEATS. WOOD SCREWS AND GLUE CAN BE USED FOR GREATER STRENGTH.

Umbrella Table

MATERIALS LIST

Quantity	Description
1	4 ft. x 8 ft. plywood panel of 3/4 in. APA grademarked A-B Exterior
4	4x4s, 10 in. long
4	3/8 in. diameter galvanized lag bolts, 2-1/2 in. long, with washers
8	3/8 in. diameter galvanized roundhead bolts, 8 in. long, with washers and nuts
4	Table leg buttons
As required	Finishing sandpaper
As required	Paint or stain for finishing

CONSTRUCTION NOTES

Using the table leg layout as a guide, draw the outline of one table leg on plywood as shown in the cutting diagram.

Cut out this leg and use it as a pattern to draw the outline of the remaining legs in place on the plywood.

Mark the table top by drilling two 1/8-inch diameter holes 24 inches apart through a yardstick or similar slat. Position one of the holes over a finishing nail driven into the center point of remaining plywood. Insert the point of a pencil into the other hole to draw the 48-inch diameter circle of the table top and cut out. Cut a 2-inch hole through the center of the circle for the umbrella pole.

Round off all corner edges of 4x4s.

Draw a line down the center on one side of each 4x4. Place marks across these lines 2 inches in from each end. On the adjacent side of each 4x4 draw another center line and place marks across these, 3 inches in from each end.

With a 1-inch spade wood drill bit, drill into these marks to a depth of about 1/4 inch. Then with a 3/8-inch bit, drill on through the centers of these shallow holes and through the 4x4 as squarely as possible to form countersunk holes.

Place one of the legs on a flat surface and position one 4x4 so that one end is flush with the top end of the table leg and the side edge of the block overlaps the inside edge of the leg by 5/8 inch. The countersunk holes should be up. With the block held firmly in position, drill through the holes in the block and the table leg.

Repeat this step on all four legs, making certain that two of the legs are drilled using the holes 2 inches from the ends of the blocks as guides and two are drilled using the holes drilled 3 inches from the ends.

Sandwich one of the table legs between two blocks and insert two roundhead bolts through the holes to hold the assembly together. Sandwich the other leg with matching holes between the remaining two blocks and bolt together.

Stand the leg assemblies facing each other, and sandwich the remaining legs in between them. Bolt the assembly firmly together with roundhead screws.

Place the table top in position on top of the legs. Drill through the top of the table with a 3/8-inch bit, into the center of the top end of each block to a total depth of about 1-1/2 inches. Place a lag bolt with washer down into each hole and tap with a hammer. Then drive each bolt firmly into place with a wrench.

Sand as needed, and paint or stain as desired.

Drive a table leg button into the bottom of each leg, when dry.

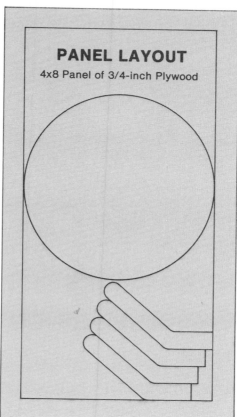

PANEL LAYOUT

4x8 Panel of 3/4-inch Plywood

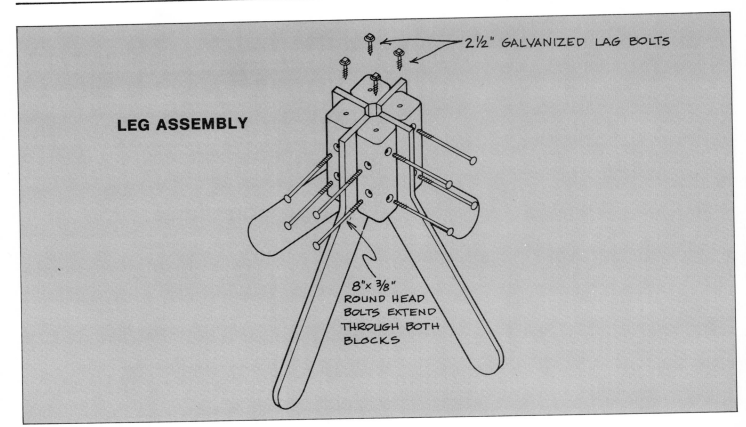

LEG ASSEMBLY

2½" GALVANIZED LAG BOLTS

8" x ⅜" ROUND HEAD BOLTS EXTEND THROUGH BOTH BLOCKS

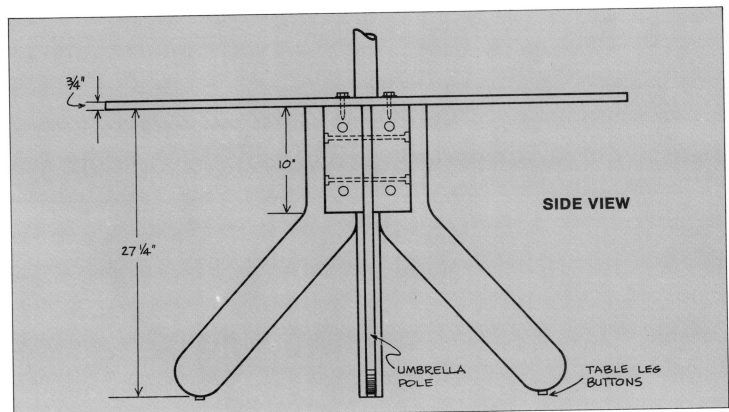

SIDE VIEW

¾"

10"

27 ¼"

UMBRELLA POLE

TABLE LEG BUTTONS

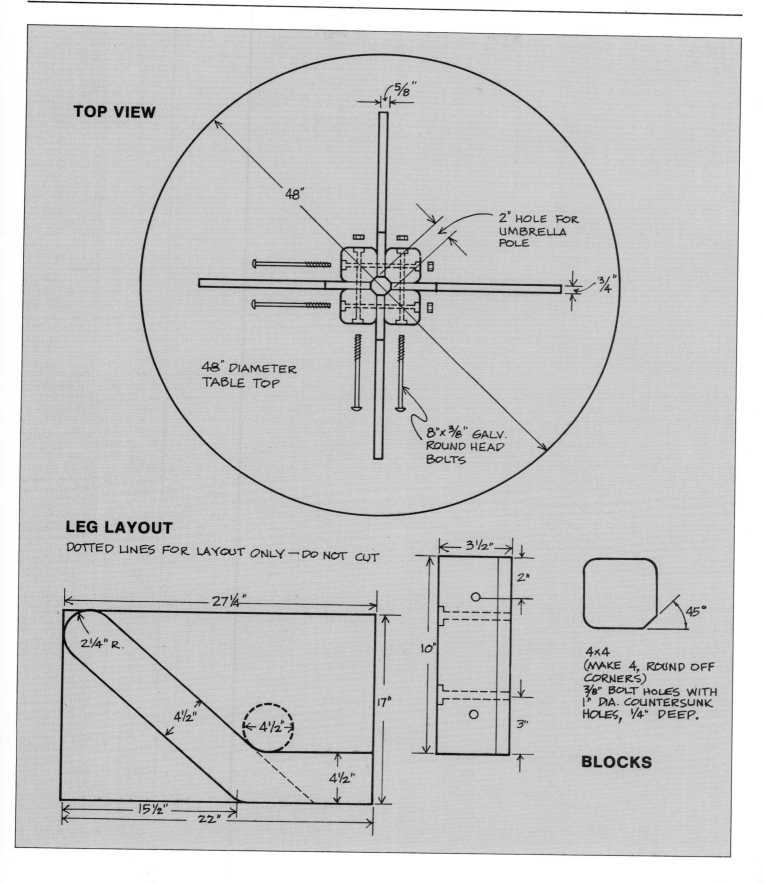

TOP VIEW

5/8"

48"

2" HOLE FOR UMBRELLA POLE

3/4"

48" DIAMETER TABLE TOP

8"x 3/8" GALV. ROUND HEAD BOLTS

LEG LAYOUT

DOTTED LINES FOR LAYOUT ONLY — DO NOT CUT

27 1/4"

2 1/4" R.

4 1/2"

4 1/2"

17"

4 1/2"

15 1/2"

22"

3 1/2"

2"

10"

3"

45°

4x4
(MAKE 4, ROUND OFF CORNERS)
3/8" BOLT HOLES WITH 1" DIA. COUNTERSUNK HOLES, 1/4" DEEP.

BLOCKS

Privacy Screens

MATERIALS LIST

Quantity	Description
2	4 ft. x 8 ft. plywood panels of 1/4-inch or 3/8 in. APA grademarked textured T-11 exterior grade
6	2x4s, 4 feet long for center and ends
2	2x4s, 5 feet 10-1/2 inches long for sides
30 linear feet	1x2s for interior blocking
27 linear feet	3/8-inch trim
2	4x4s, 18 inches long for posts. Use pressure-treated wood or treat wood to protect from rotting due to contact with soil.
4	Angle irons
As required	Bolts for angle irons
As required	4d nails
As required	Resorcinol-type waterproof glue

CONSTRUCTION NOTES

Glue-nail 2x4 sides to center and ends to form frame.

Cut two 48-inch pieces of 1x2 and glue-nail to either side of center 2x4.

Cut two 31-inch pieces of 1x2 and glue-nail between center and ends to divide frame into quarters.

Cut four 23-inch pieces of 1x2 and glue-nail two on inside of each end.

Cut panels according to panel layout. Arrange cut pieces as shown in plan and mark new cut lines. Cut pieces along lines, or choose your own pattern and cut accordingly.

Before completing framing, place panel pieces in position in frame. The diagonals where the plywood panels join will give you the positions of the diagonal 1x2 supports.

Measure and cut 1x2s for diagonal support. Glue-nail in place.

Lay frame on a flat surface and brace 1x2s from underneath with scrap wood to make a solid nailing surface.

Glue-nail plywood to frame.

Glue-nail 3/8-inch trim to inside of frame. Countersink nails and fill holes with compound designed for exterior exposure.

Attach angle irons to frame.

Turn screen over and glue-nail plywood into place.

Glue-nail trim to frame. Countersink and fill holes.

Finish as desired with weather-resistant finish.

Bolt posts to angle-irons.

To set up, place posts in holes and fill with cement. For stability, attach screen to your house, garage or other securely anchored structure, or bolt two or more screens at right angles with lag bolts. Drill holes for bolts to prevent splitting wood.

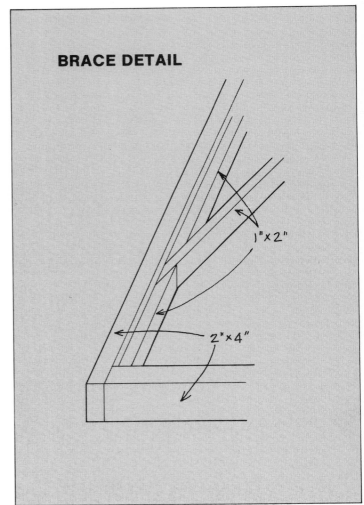

BRACE DETAIL

1" x 2"

2" x 4"

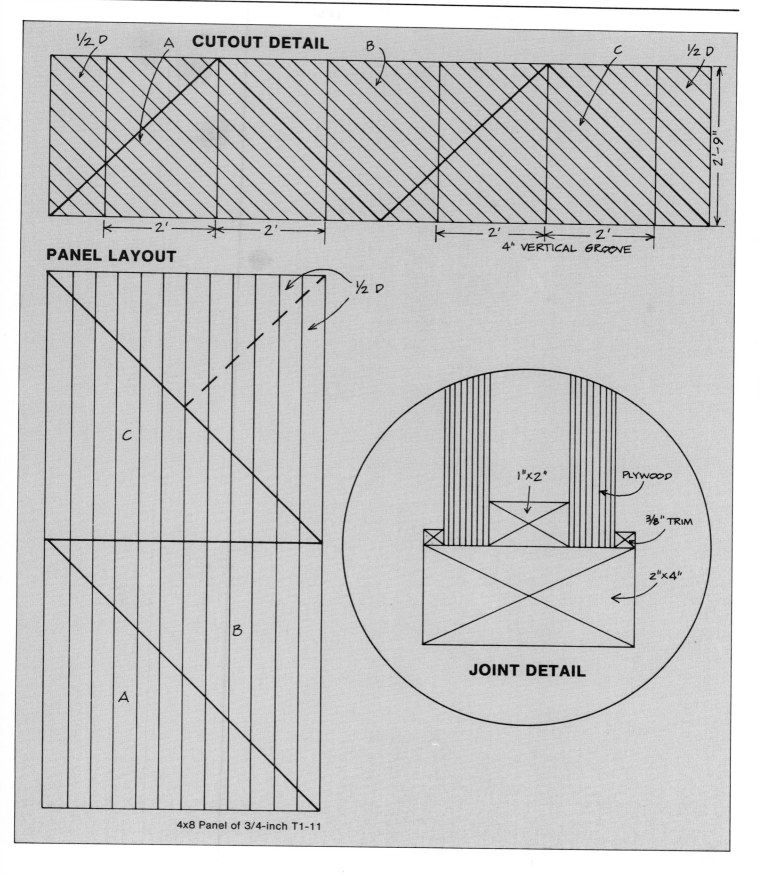

CUTOUT DETAIL

½ D   A   B   C   ½ D

2'-9"

2'   2'   2'   2'

4" VERTICAL GROOVE

PANEL LAYOUT

½ D

C

B

A

4x8 Panel of 3/4-inch T1-11

1"x2"

PLYWOOD

3/8" TRIM

2"x4"

JOINT DETAIL

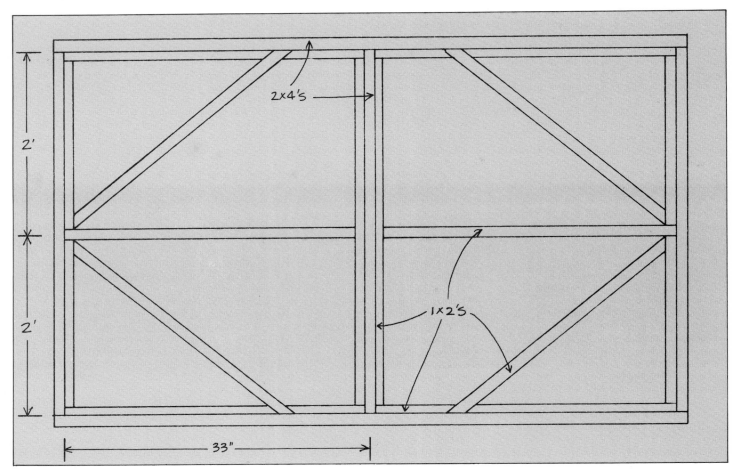

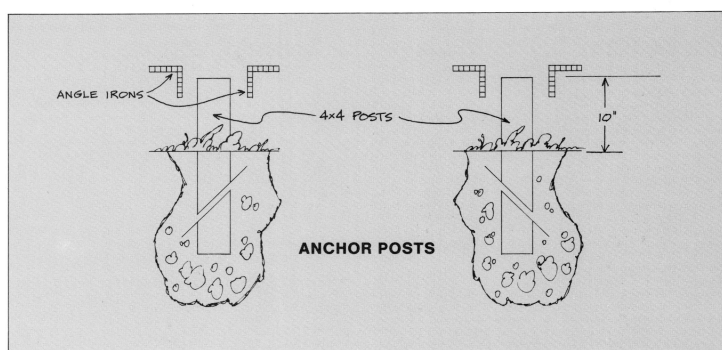

Shaker Trestle Table

MATERIALS LIST

Quantity	Description
1	4 ft. x 8 ft. plywood panels of 3/4 in. APA grademarked A-A, A-B, or B-B Interior, or Medium Density Overlay (MDO) for tops (A), uprights (B), stretchers (C), and wings (D)
4	1-1/2 in. x 3-1/2 in. wood. 16-1/2 in. long, for base (E). Cut to L shape and miter one end as shown in plan
2	1x3s, 72 in. long, for center top edges (F)
2	1/2 in. x 3/4 in. wood, 72 in. long, for outer top edges (G)
4	1/2 in x 3/4 in. wood, 18-3/8 in. long, for end top edges (H)
4	3/4 in. x 3/4 in. wood, 3 in. long, for pegs (I)
1	Continuous hinge, 16 in. long, cut into four 4-in. pieces
4	1-1/2 in. #10 flathead wood screws
4	Plugs for screw holes in base
As required	Fine sandpaper for removing any small blemishes or smoothing rough edges
As required	Urea-resin glue for gluing base
As required	Paint of stain for finishing

CONSTRUCTION NOTES

Lay out plywood as shown in cutting diagram. Use the layout grid for uprights and wings. Allow for saw kerf when plotting dimensions.

Cut out plywood pieces. Cut square hole in stretchers to fit pegs. Fill and sand edges that will be visible.

Attach wings to uprights with hinges as shown.

Attach bases to uprights with glue and #10 flathead screws as shown in plan. Countersink screws and fill holes with plugs.

Fit stretchers into uprights as shown in plan. Pin with removable pegs.

Glue edges to both tops as shown.

Place tops on table as shown, with wings extended, or lay one top on the other with edges (F) on opposite sides and folded wings.

Table can be taken apart for finishing by removing pegs.

PANEL LAYOUT

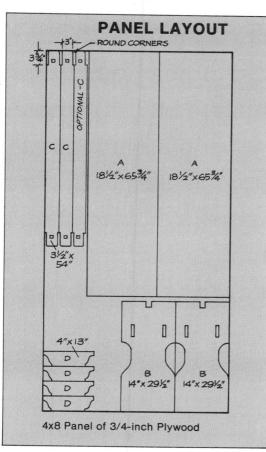

3"
3¾"
ROUND CORNERS
OPTIONAL-C
C C
A
18½"x65¾"
A
18½"x65¾"
3½"x 54"
4"x13"
D
D
D
D
B
14"x29½"
B
14"x29½"

4x8 Panel of 3/4-inch Plywood

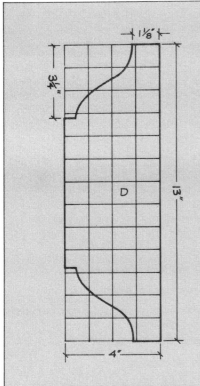

WING LAYOUT GRID
Each Square Represents 1 Inch

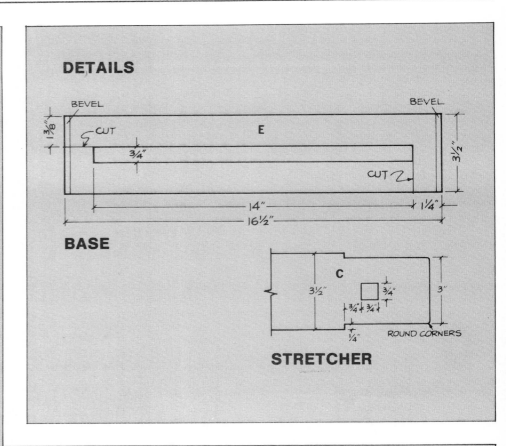

DETAILS

BASE

STRETCHER

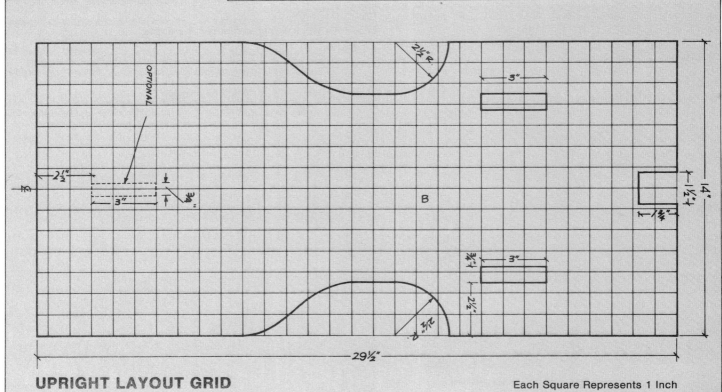

UPRIGHT LAYOUT GRID

Each Square Represents 1 Inch

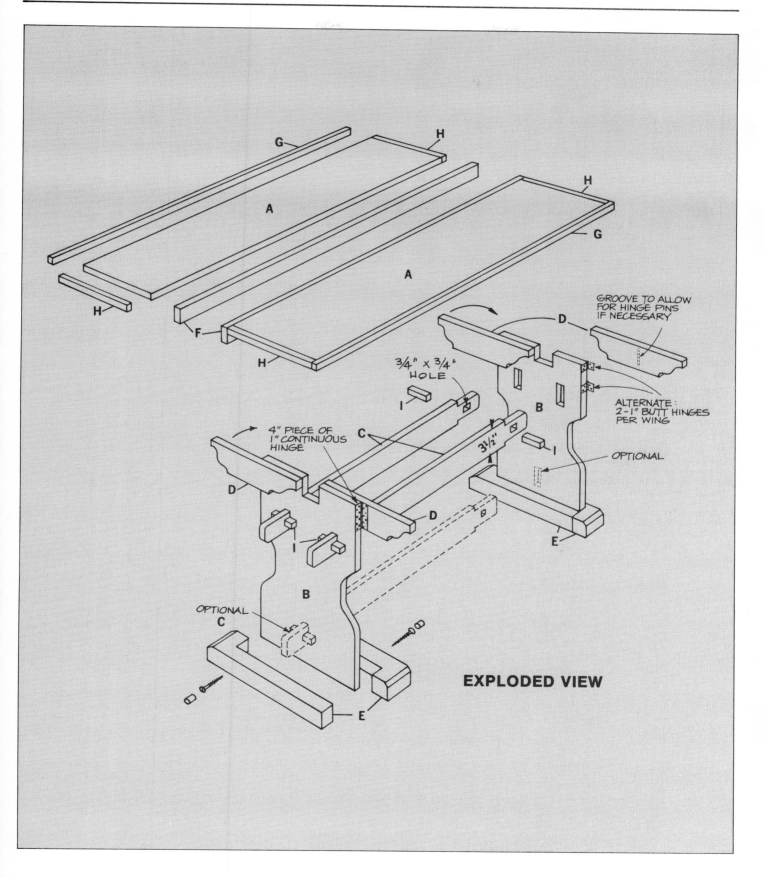

G

H

A

H

G

A

F

H

GROOVE TO ALLOW
FOR HINGE PINS
IF NECESSARY

D

3/4" X 3/4"
HOLE

I

ALTERNATE:
2-1" BUTT HINGES
PER WING

B

4" PIECE OF
1" CONTINUOUS
HINGE

C

3½"

I

OPTIONAL

D

I

D

B

E

OPTIONAL
C

I

B

E

EXPLODED VIEW

E

Cookware Rack

MATERIALS LIST

Quantity	Description
1	1 ft. x 4 ft. plywood panel of 1/2 in. APA grademarked A-B Interior, A-C Exterior, or Medium Density Overlay (MDO)
6	5/8 in. dia. dowels 3-1/2 in. long
4	5/8 in. dia. dowels 5-1/4 in. long
As required	Fine sandpaper
As required	Interior semi-gloss enamel paint
As required	Molly bolts for fastening the rack to the wall, or wood screws for screwing it into wall studs.

CONSTRUCTION NOTES

Cut out two rack pieces from plywood.

Lay out your pots, pans and their lids on a rack piece before drilling dowel holes. Dowel spacing may differ from the placement shown here, depending on the size of your pans and lids.

To assure alignment of the assembled rack pieces, clamp pieces together and drill the dowel holes for both pieces at once.

Notch one end of the pot hanger dowels with a knife or saw to fit the rings on your pot handles so the pots can't be knocked easily off the rack.

Adjust the diameter of the half-circles shown on the plan to the size of your lid knobs.

If you want the dowels painted, do it before assembling the rack. When all painted pieces are thoroughly dry, gently pound the dowels in place on back piece.

Mount back piece on wall with Molly bolts or wood screws.

Position front piece and gently pound it into place over dowels.

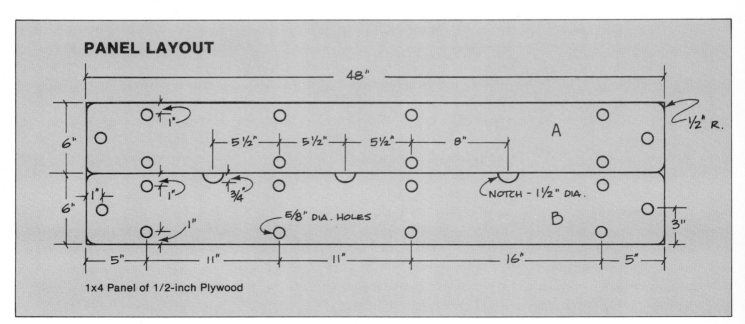

PANEL LAYOUT

48"

6"

5 1/2"   5 1/2"   5 1/2"   8"

A

1/2" R.

1"

3/4"

NOTCH - 1 1/2" DIA.

6"

1"

B

3"

1"

5/8" DIA. HOLES

5"   11"   11"   16"   5"

1x4 Panel of 1/2-inch Plywood

EXPLODED VIEW

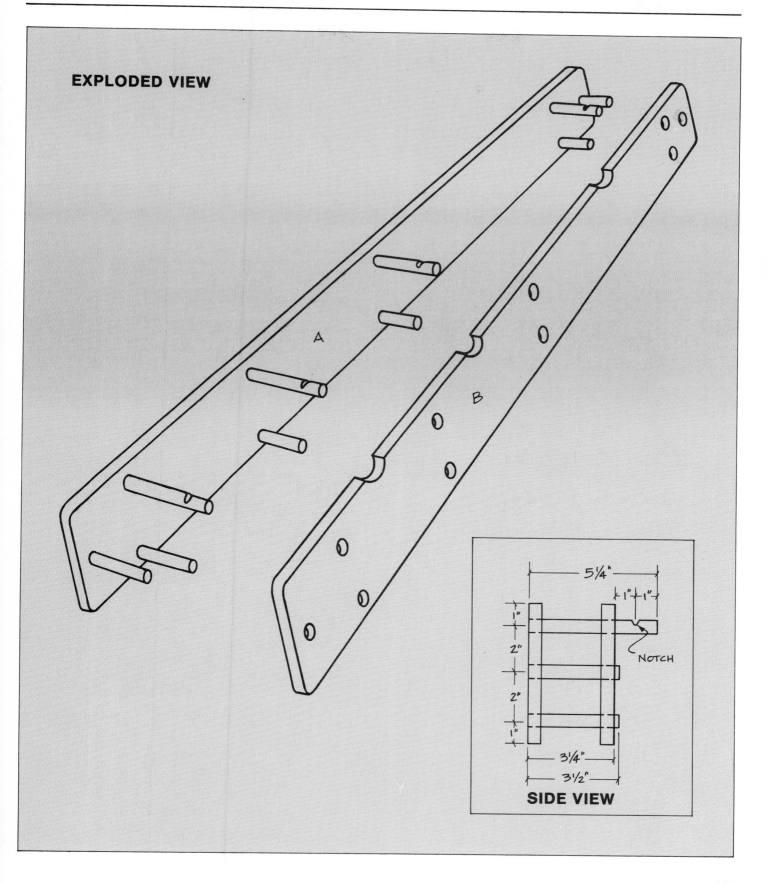

5¼"

1" 1"

1"

2"

2"

1"

NOTCH

3¼"

3½"

SIDE VIEW

Study Center

MATERIALS LIST

Quantity	Description
1	4 ft. x 8 ft. plywood panel of 3/4 in. APA grademarked A-B or A-D Interior, A-B or A-C Exterior, or Medium Density Overlay (MDO)
2	24 in. long 1x2s for desk supports
40	#10 x 2 in. oval or flathead wood screws
8 to 10	3d casing or finishing nails for glue-nailing ledger strips
As required	Wood dough for filling countersunk screw holes and any small gaps in plywood edges
As required	Fine sandpaper for smoothing cut edges and cured wood dough
As required	Finishing materials; primer and paint, antiquing kit, or synthetic satin-finish varnish, such as Varathane, with or without stain

CONSTRUCTION NOTES

Draw parts on plywood. Use a compass or make a cardboard template to draw corner radii.

Cut out parts. Center saw cut on layout lines to equalize saw kerf on all parts. Cutouts from desk sides form bench ends, so make cuts carefully. Drill several small holes on cutline for saw access if necessary.

Fill and sand smooth plywood cut edges.

Drill pilot holes and fasten backstops to shelves using screws and glue according to manufacturer's instructions. Repeat process with desk top and its facing.

Mark locations for shelves, desk top and cross-braces on inside surfaces of desk sides. Drill pilot holes and glue and end-screw parts in position through desk sides. Glue-nail 1x2 ledger strips in place under desk sides.

Lay bench seat slats face down. Glue-screw seat supports in place using pilot holes.

Mark locations for seat and cross-braces on inside surfaces of bench ends and drill pilot holes. Glue and screw cross-braces in place. Glue and screw seat in position, screwing through bench ends into seat supports.

Fill screw holes and any small voids in plywood edges. When filler is dry, sand smooth. Finish as desired.

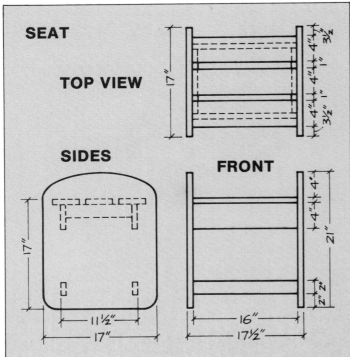

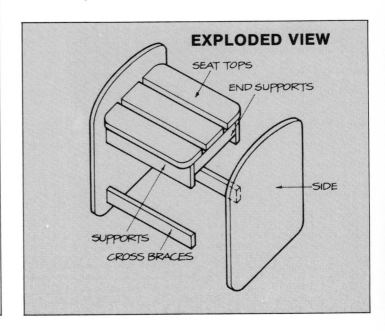

EXPLODED VIEW

DESK

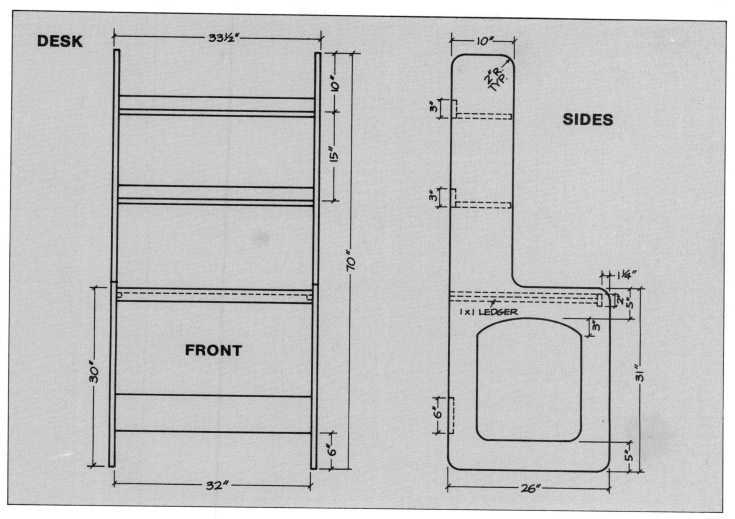

FRONT

SIDES

1 x 1 LEDGER

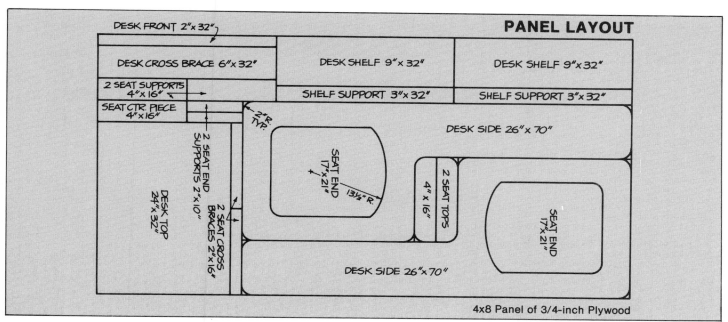

PANEL LAYOUT

DESK FRONT 2" x 32"

DESK CROSS BRACE 6" x 32"

DESK SHELF 9" x 32"

DESK SHELF 9" x 32"

2 SEAT SUPPORTS 4" x 16"

SHELF SUPPORT 3" x 32"

SHELF SUPPORT 3" x 32"

SEAT CTR. PIECE 4" x 16"

DESK SIDE 26" x 70"

2 SEAT END SUPPORTS 2" x 10"

DESK TOP 24" x 32"

2 SEAT CROSS BRACES 2" x 16"

SEAT END 17" x 21"

13½" R.

2 SEAT TOPS 4" x 16"

SEAT END 17" x 21"

DESK SIDE 26" x 70"

4x8 Panel of 3/4-inch Plywood

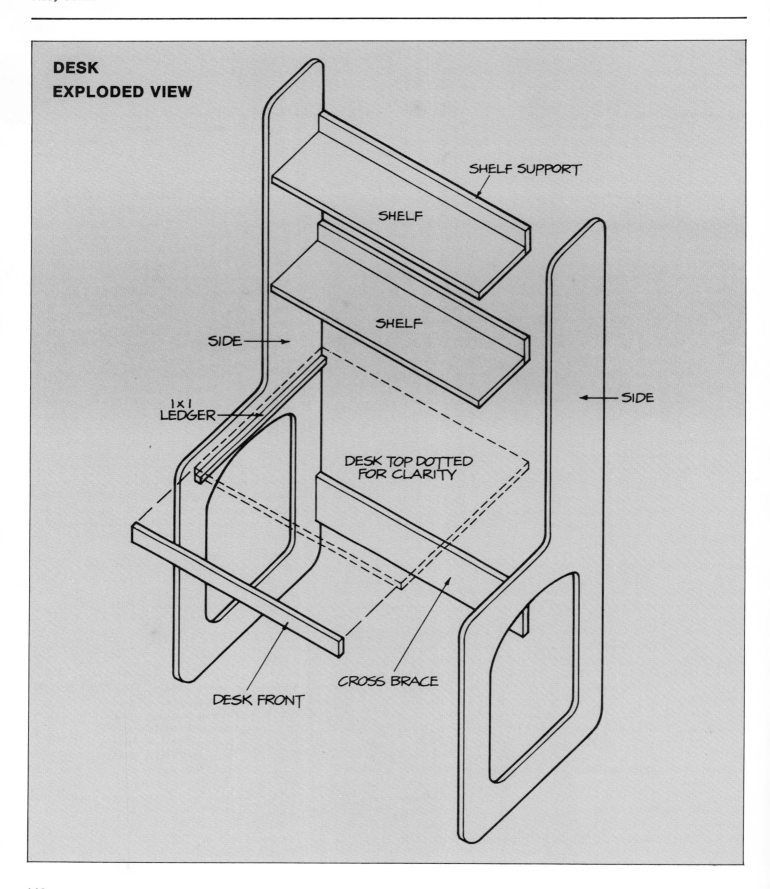

**DESK
EXPLODED VIEW**

SHELF SUPPORT

SHELF

SHELF

SIDE

SIDE

1x1
LEDGER

DESK TOP DOTTED
FOR CLARITY

CROSS BRACE

DESK FRONT

Store-It-All Barn

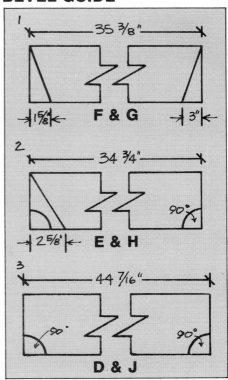

MATERIALS LIST

Quantity	Description
4	4 ft. x 8 ft. plywood panels of 1/2 in. APA grademarked A-C Exterior or C-D Interior sheathing with exterior glue
6	4 ft. x 8 ft. plywood panels of 5/8 in. APA grademarked 303 Exterior siding, any surface texture
27 linear ft.	2x4s pressure-treated with preservative for framing
224 linear ft.	2x4s for framing
8 linear ft.	2x6s for framing
176 linear ft.	1x4s for trim
12	1/4 in. diameter galvanized bolts, 3-1/2 in. long
8	1/4 in. diameter galvanized bolts, 4 in. long
5-1/2 linear ft.	3/4 in diameter steel pipe cut into 16 in. long pieces
4	3 in. strap hinges for doors
1	3 in. lock hasp
8 linear ft.	Flashing for roof cap
As required	Roofing material to cover 96 square ft.
As required	Nonstaining 10d common nails
As required	Nonstaining 8d finishing nails
As required	Paint or stain

CONSTRUCTION NOTES

Lay out pieces on plywood panels. Be sure front and rear panels (B and K) match properly. Allow for saw kerf on layout lines. Mark each panel for easy identification.

Cut panels.

Join the two panels to form the front by nailing 2x4s with 10d nails shown in plans. Note that the side 2x4s are inset 5/8 inch from the plywood edge to leave room for the side panels.

Join back with framing 2x4s with 10d nails. Note that sides are recessed as on front.

Join side panel with 2x4 framing with 10d nails. Make sure the direction of the grooves in the plywood runs across the panels.

Place 2x4 framing on roof panels as shown in plans with 8d nails. Note that the ends of 2x4s on panels E, F, G and H are beveled so they will fit properly to form the roof.

Attach 1x4 trim to sides and ends of barn.

To erect barn, attach sides to ends. Attach 2x6 ridge beam for roof. Then nail roof in place.

Bolt doors to front with strap hinges. Bolt lock hasp to doors.

Cover roof with waterproof roofing material.

Paint or stain barn as desired.

Barn requires no foundation, but can be anchored in place with 3/4-inch steel pipe as shown in detail. Be sure to anchor both sides of the door opening as well as the sides and back of the barn.

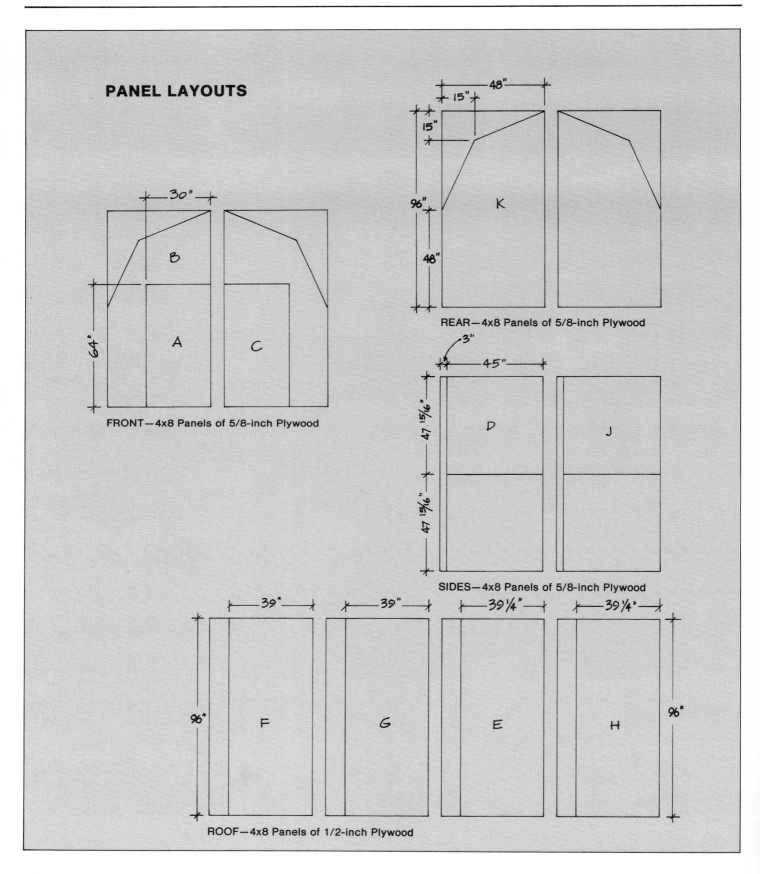

PANEL LAYOUTS

FRONT—4x8 Panels of 5/8-inch Plywood

REAR—4x8 Panels of 5/8-inch Plywood

SIDES—4x8 Panels of 5/8-inch Plywood

ROOF—4x8 Panels of 1/2-inch Plywood

DETAILS

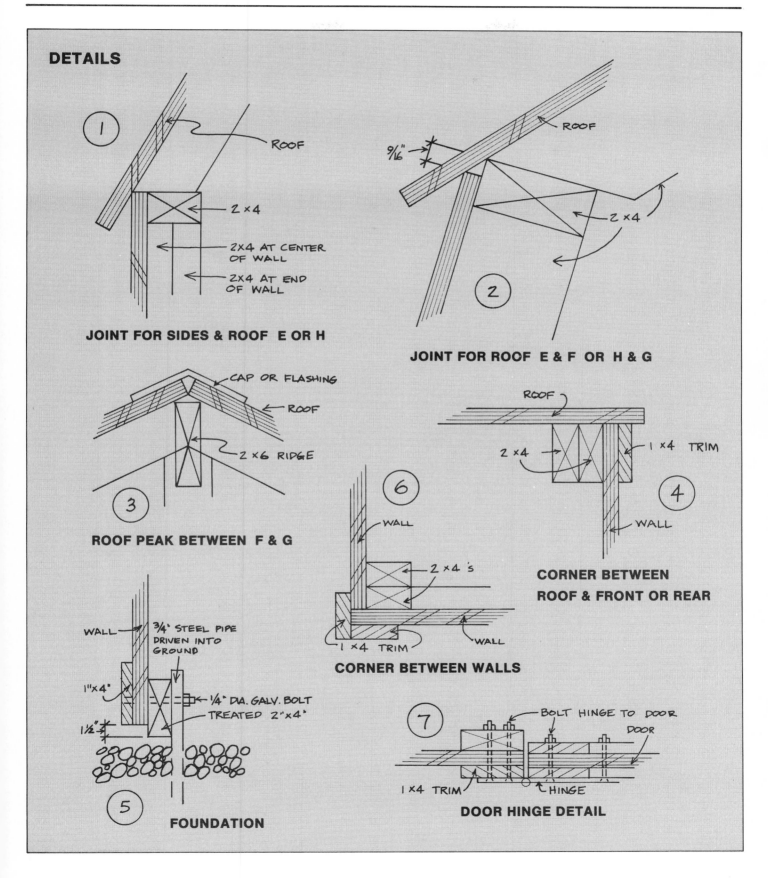

JOINT FOR SIDES & ROOF E OR H

ROOF

2 × 4

2X4 AT CENTER OF WALL

2X4 AT END OF WALL

JOINT FOR ROOF E & F OR H & G

ROOF

9/16"

2 × 4

ROOF PEAK BETWEEN F & G

CAP OR FLASHING

ROOF

2 × 6 RIDGE

CORNER BETWEEN ROOF & FRONT OR REAR

ROOF

2 × 4

1 × 4 TRIM

WALL

CORNER BETWEEN WALLS

WALL

2 × 4's

1 × 4 TRIM

WALL

FOUNDATION

WALL

3/4" STEEL PIPE DRIVEN INTO GROUND

1"×4"

1½"

¼" DIA. GALV. BOLT

TREATED 2"×4"

DOOR HINGE DETAIL

BOLT HINGE TO DOOR

DOOR

1 × 4 TRIM

HINGE

BASIC FRAMING

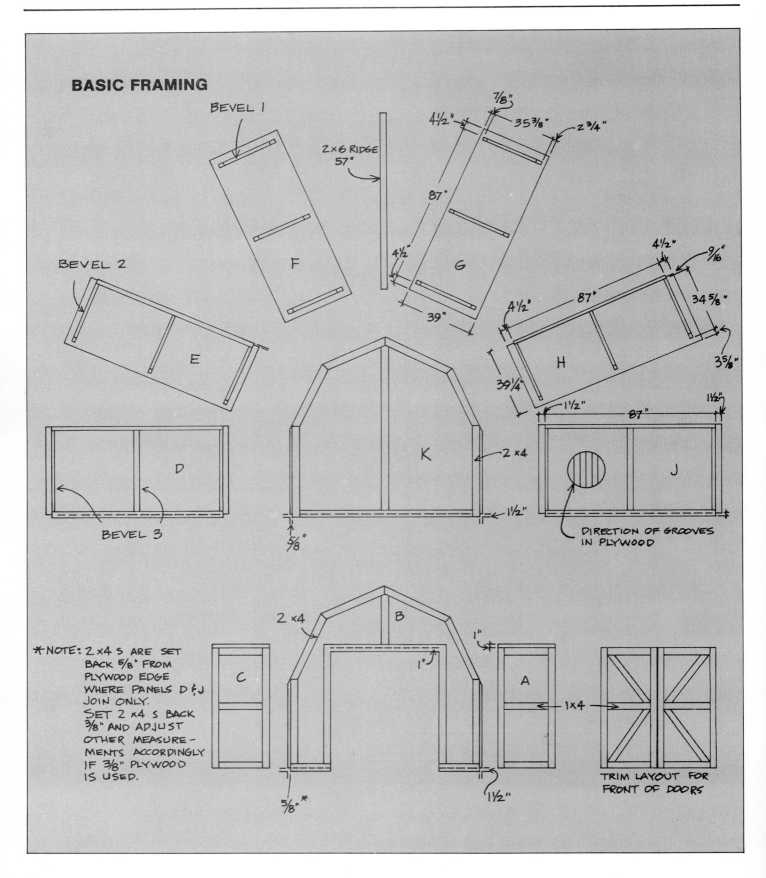

BEVEL 1

2×6 RIDGE
57"

7/8"

4½"   35⅜"   2¾"

87"

4½"

G

4½"

39"

BEVEL 2

F

4½"   9/16"

87"   34⅝"

4½"

H   3⅝"

E

1½"   87"   1½"

D

39¼"

K   2×4

J

BEVEL 3   5/8"   1½"

DIRECTION OF GROOVES
IN PLYWOOD

*NOTE: 2×4 S ARE SET
BACK 5/8" FROM
PLYWOOD EDGE
WHERE PANELS D & J
JOIN ONLY.
SET 2×4 S BACK
3/8" AND ADJUST
OTHER MEASURE-
MENTS ACCORDINGLY
IF 3/8" PLYWOOD
IS USED.

2×4   B

C   1"

1"

A

1×4

5/8" *   1½"

TRIM LAYOUT FOR
FRONT OF DOORS

EXPLODED VIEW

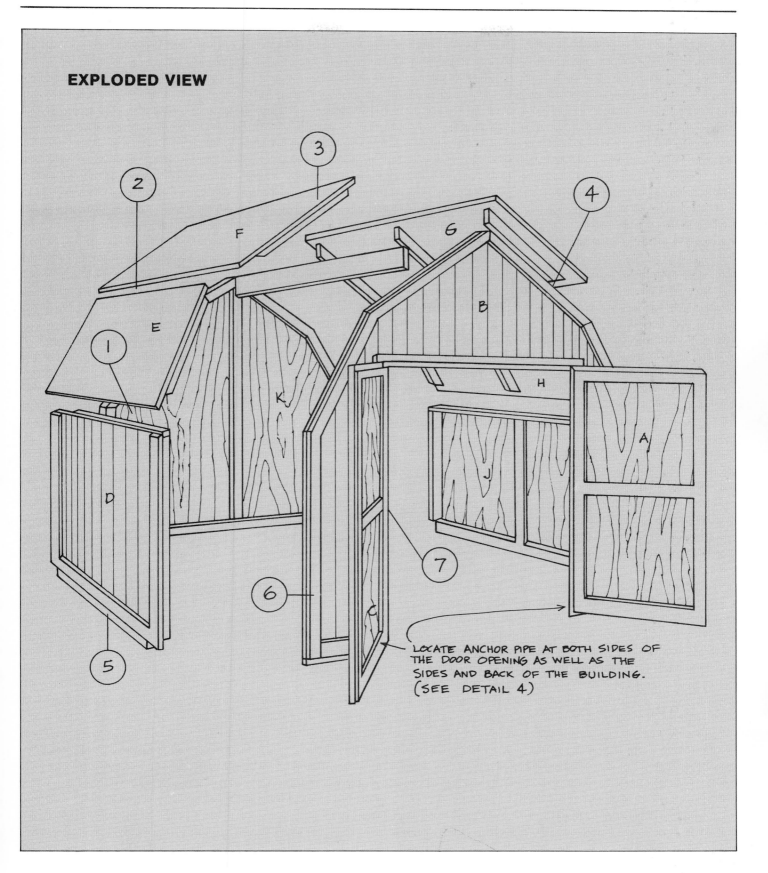

LOCATE ANCHOR PIPE AT BOTH SIDES OF
THE DOOR OPENING AS WELL AS THE
SIDES AND BACK OF THE BUILDING.
(SEE DETAIL 4)

Modular Plant Boxes

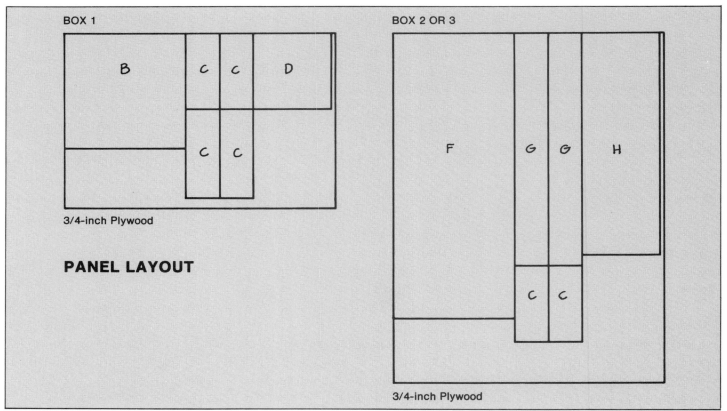

BOX 1

B   C   C   D

C   C

3/4-inch Plywood

PANEL LAYOUT

BOX 2 OR 3

F   G   G   H

C   C

3/4-inch Plywood

MATERIALS LIST

Plant Box No. 1

Part Code	Quantity	Size	Part Identification
A	4	12" x 22" pieces 2" Texture 1-11	Sides
B	1	16" x 16" piece 3/4" exterior A-C	Bottom
C	2	4-1/2" x 10-1/2" pieces 3/4" exterior A-C	Sides of Base
C	2	4-1/2" x 12" pieces 3/4" exterior A-C	Sides of Base
D	1	10-1/2" x 12" piece 3/4" exterior A-C	Bottom of Base
	8 Lin. ft.	1x2	Top Framing
	5 Lin. ft.	2x2	Bottom Framing
	4	1" x 3" Angle Braces	For Corners

Plant Box No. 2

Part Code	Quantity	Size	Part Identification
A	2	12" x 22" pieces 2" Texture 1-11	Ends
E	2	12" x 46" pieces 2" Texture 1-11	Sides
F	1	16" x 39-1/4" piece 3/4" exterior A-C	Bottom
G	2	4-1/2" x 32" pieces 3/4" exterior A-C	Sides of Base
G	2	4-1/2" x 10-1/2" pieces 3/4" exterior A-C	Ends of Base
H	1	10-1/2" x 30-1/2" piece 3/4" exterior A-C	Bottom of Base
	12 Lin. ft.	1x2	Top Framing
	2 Lin. ft.	2x4	Bottom Framing
	7 Lin. ft.	2x2	Bottom Framing
	4	1" x 3" Angle Braces	For Corners

Plant Box No. 3

Part Code	Quantity	Size	Part Identification
I	2	12" x 40" pieces 4" Texture 1-11	Sides
J	2	12" x 16-3/4" pieces 4" Texture 1-11	Ends
F	1	15-1/4" x 38-1/2" piece 3/4" exterior A-C	Bottom
G	2	4-1/2" x 32" pieces 3/4" exterior A-C	Sides of Base
C	2	4-1/2" x 10"-1/2 piece 3/4" exterior A-C	Ends of Base
H	1	1-1/2" x 30-1/2" piece 3/4" exterior A-C	Bottom of Base
	10 Lin. ft.	1x2	Top Framing
	2 Lin. ft.	2x4	Bottom Framing
	7 Lin. ft.	2x2	Bottom Framing
	4	1" x 3" Angle Braces	For Corners

For All Plant Boxes

As required 6d finish nails, ring shank or cement coated
As required waterproof glue
As required asphalt emulsion or corprus lingnum

CONSTRUCTION NOTES

Check the part schedule for sizes and lay out the parts on plywood as shown in the cutting diagrams. Be sure to allow for saw kerf width between each part. Grooves on Texture 1-11 should match on all sides of finished boxes.

First cut bottom panels to size for the boxes you are going to build. Drill drain holes as shown.

Cut T 1-11 plywood sides and ends to size and miter corners. Check for perfect fit before assembly to prevent leaks.

Cut 2x2 and 2x4 bottom framing to size. If you are building designs 1 or 2, bevel sides, framing and edges of bottom panel to conform to slope.

Glue-nail framing to bottom and then the sides to the frame. Glue-nail the mitered corners and then reinforce the joints on the inside near the top with galvanized angle braces and short screws. Miter 1x2 top frames and nail into place as shown.

Cut and drill parts for drainage boxes and then assemble with waterproof glue and nails. Drill 3/4-inch holes 4 inches apart on all sides for evaporation. Paint the inside of both drainage and plant boxes with two coats of asphalt emulsion or coprus lignum as indicated.

Smooth edges of top frames with a block plane or 1-0 sandpaper. Then apply two coats of stain in your favorite color or finish with a coat of primer and two coats of good quality house paint.

BOX 1

BOX 2

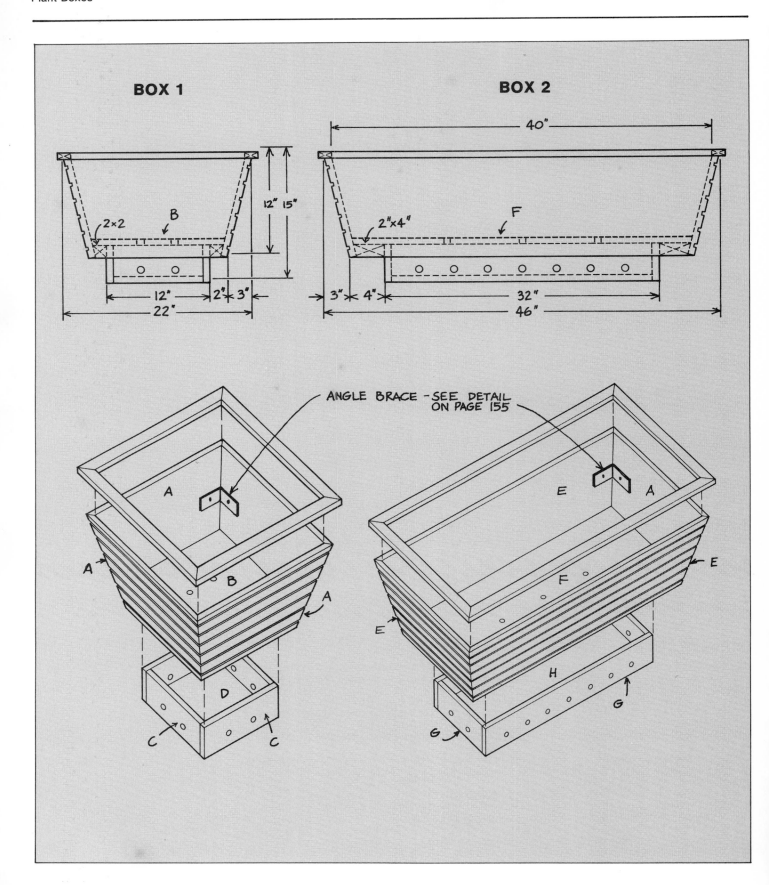

ANGLE BRACE – SEE DETAIL ON PAGE 155

BOX 3

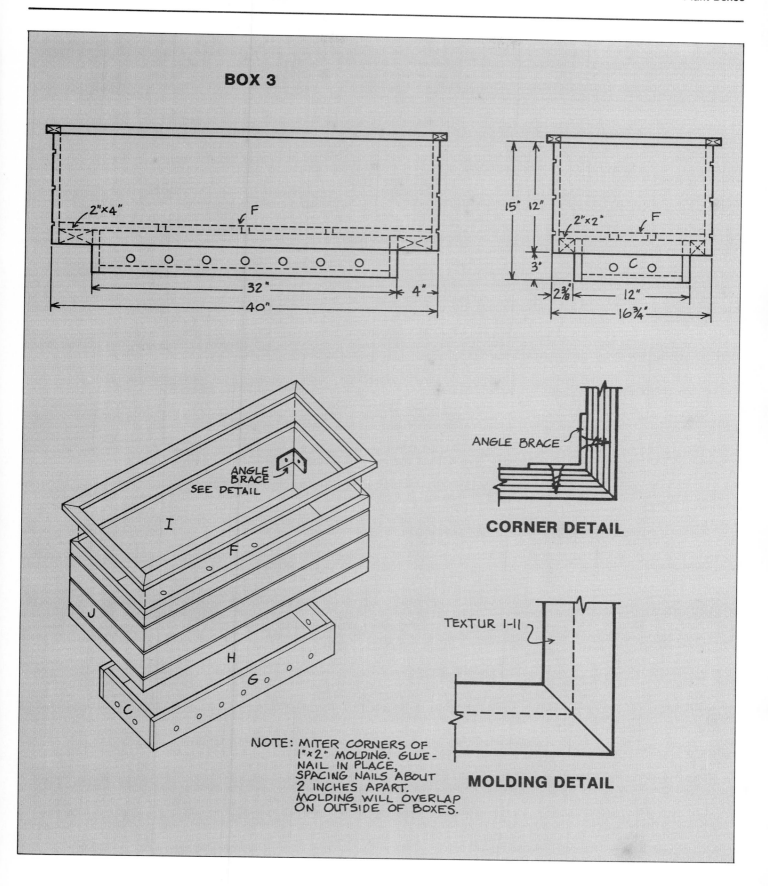

2"×4"

F

32"

4"

40"

15" 12"

2"×2"

F

C

3"

2⅜"

12"

16¾"

ANGLE
BRACE
SEE DETAIL

I

F

J

H

G

C

ANGLE BRACE

CORNER DETAIL

TEXTUR 1-11

MOLDING DETAIL

NOTE: MITER CORNERS OF
1"×2" MOLDING. GLUE-
NAIL IN PLACE,
SPACING NAILS ABOUT
2 INCHES APART.
MOLDING WILL OVERLAP
ON OUTSIDE OF BOXES.

PANEL LAYOUT

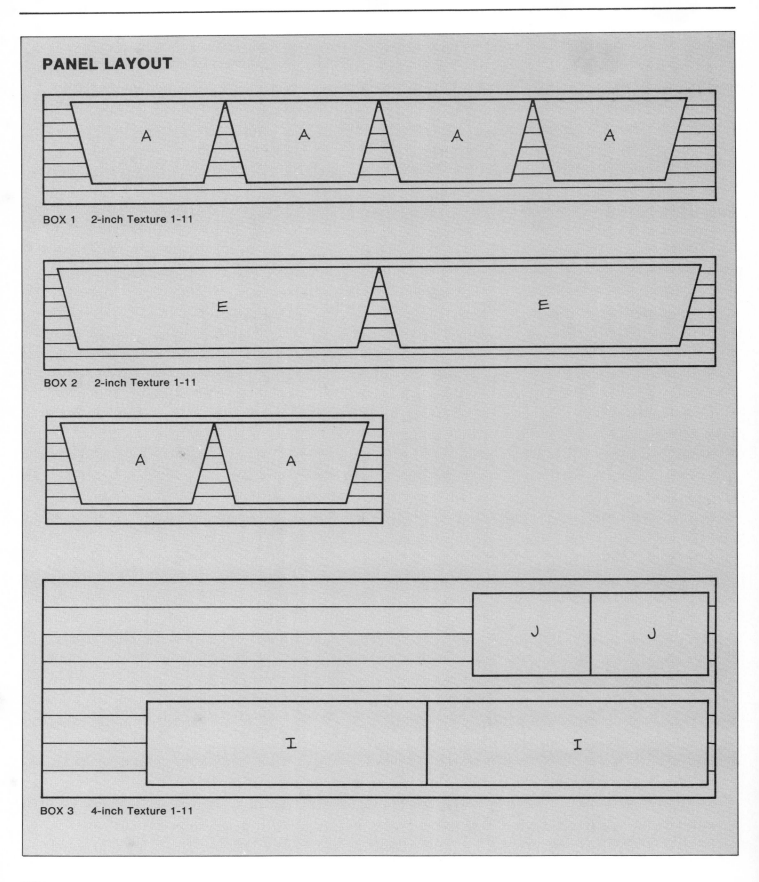

BOX 1   2-inch Texture 1-11

BOX 2   2-inch Texture 1-11

BOX 3   4-inch Texture 1-11

THE DECIMAL EQUIVALENTS OF MOST COMMON FRACTIONS

Fractions	Decimal
1/64	.015625
2/64—1/32	.03125
3/64	.046875
4/64—2/32—1/16	.0625
5/64	.078125
6/64—3/32	.09375
7/64	.109375
8/64—4/32—2/16—1/8	.125
9/64	.140625
10/64—5/32	.15625
11/64	.171875
12/64—6/32—3/16	.1875
13/64	.203125
14/64—7/32	.21875
15/64	.234375
16/64—8/32—4/16—1/4	.250
17/64	.265625
18/64—9/32	.28125
19/64	.296875
20/64—10/32—5/16	.3125
21/64	.328125
22/64—11/32	.34375
23/64	.359375
24/64—12/32—6/16—3/8	.3750
25/64	.390625
26/64—13/32	.40625
27/64	.421875
28/64—14/32—7/16	.4375
29/64	.453125
30/64—15/32	.46875
31/64	.484375
32/64—16/32—8/16—4/8—2/4—1/2	.5
33/64	.515625
34/64—17/32	.53125
35/64	.546875
36/64—18/32—9/16	.5625
37/64	.578125
38/64—19/32	.59375
39/64	.609375
40/64—20/32—10/16—5/8	.625
41/64	.640625
42/64—21/32	.65625
43/64	.671875
44/64—22/32—11/16	.6875
45/64	.703125
46/64—23/32	.71875
47/64	.734375
48/64—24/32—12/16—6/8—3/4	.750
49/64	.765625
50/64—25/32	.78125
51/64	.796875
52//64—26/32—13/16	.8125
53/64	.828125
54/64—27/32	.84375
55/64	.859375
56/64—28/32—14/16—7/8	.8750
57/64	.890625
58/64—29/32	.90625
59/64	.921875
60/64—30/32—15/16	.9375
61/64	.953125
62/64—31/32	.96875
63/64	.984375
64/64—32/32—16/16—8/8—4/4—2/2—1	1.000

QUICK FACTS ABOUT METRICS

THE MOST COMMON PREFIXES
milli — .001 (one thousandth)
centi — .01 (one hundredth)
kilo — 1000 (one thousand)

RELATIONSHIPS
10 millimeters (mm) = 1 centimeter (cm)
10 centimeters (cm) = 1 decimeter (dm)
10 decimeters (dm) = 1 meter (m)
10 meters (m) = 1 decameter (Dm)
10 decameters (Dm) = 1 hectometer (Hm)
10 hectometer (Hm) = 1 kilometer (Km)

EQUIVALENTS
1 mm = .03937 inches
1 cm = .3937 inches
1 dm = 3.937 inches
1 m = 39.37 inches or 3.281 feet or 1.094 yards
1 Km = .62137 miles

ENGLISH EQUIVALENTS
1 inch = 2.54 cm
1 foot = 30.48 cm or .3048 m
1 yard = 91.44 cm or .9144 m
1 mile = 1.6093

CONVERSIONS
mm X .03937 = inches
mm divided by 25.4 = inches
cm X .3937 = inches
cm divided by 2.54 = inches
m X 39.37 = inches
m X 3.2809 = feet
m X 1.094 = yards
Km X .621377 = miles

TO CHANGE A FRACTION TO A DECIMAL:
• Divide the numerator by the denominator.
• Example: To change 3/16 to its decimal equivalent, divide 3.0000 by 16 which equals .1875.

INDEX

Also see Guide To Plywood Plans, page 160.

GUIDE TO PLYWOOD PLANS

Project	4x8 Sheets	Difficulty	Page	Project	4x8 Sheets	Difficulty	Page
Sewing & Hobby Center	7	Hard	30	Laminated Coffee Table	1	Medium	96
Dining Table	1-1/2	Medium	37	English Butler's Tray Table	1	Easy	98
A Desk to Grow with	2	Medium	40	House Number Lamp Post	1	Hard	100
Convex Cubbyhole Shelf	1	Medium	44	Dollhouse Toy Cart	1/2	Easy	103
Butcher Block Table	1	Medium	47	Mini-Pram	2	Hard	106
Dihedral Table	1	Easy	50	Tool Storage Workbench	1	Easy	110
Bird House		Easy	53	Recipe File & Cookbook Shelf	1/2	Easy	112
Slot Together Patio Chairs	1	Easy	56	Toy Storage Bench	2	Medium	114
Patio Side Cart	1	Medium	58	Early American Wall Shelf	1/2	Easy	117
Whale Rocker & Desk	1	Medium	60	Compact Desk	1	Medium	120
Truck Toybox	1	Medium	63	Planter Benches	2	Hard	123
Potter's Kick Wheel	1	Hard	68	Slot Together Coffee Table	1/2	Easy	128
Sketch Bench	2	Medium	71	Kitchen Storage Cart	2	Medium	130
Fire Engine Bunkbed	5	Hard	75	Umbrella Table	1	Easy	133
Wine Storage Rack	1/4	Easy	81	Privacy Screens	2	Medium	136
Foldaway Vise Table & Sawhorse	1	Medium	84	Shaker Trestle Table	1	Medium	139
				Cookware Rack	1/8	Easy	142
Wine & Glass Rack	1	Easy	88	Study Center	1	Medium	144
Barn Toybox	1	Easy	91	Store-It-All-Barn	12	Medium	147
All-Purpose Table	1	Easy	94	Plant Boxes	2	Medium	152

ACKNOWLEDGEMENTS

Projects on pages 37, 40, 44, 47, 50, 56, 58, 60, 63, 68, 84, 88, 94, 96, 100, 106, 128 and 144 first appeared in Popular Science Magazine. Projects on pages 81, 98, 110, 112, 114, 117, 120, 139 and 142 first appeared in Family Circle. Projects on pages 30, 75, 91, 103, 123 and 130 first appeared in Good Housekeeping Magazine.

Photo on page 2 courtesy of the American Forest Institute.

8.35485985322